Y0-CCU-391

GEOFFREY CHAUCER

LITERATURE AND LIFE: BRITISH WRITERS

Select list of titles in the series:

W. H. Auden	Wendell Stacy Johnson
Jane Austen	June Dwyer
The Brontës	Bettina L. Knapp
Joseph Conrad	Carl D. Bennett
Noel Coward	Robert F. Kiernan
Arthur Conan Doyle	Don Richard Cox
Ford Madox Ford	Sondra J. Stang
E. M. Forster	Claude J. Summers
Frivolity Unbound: Six Masters of the Camp Novel	Robert F. Kiernan
Graham Greene	Richard Kelly
Aldous Huxley	Guinevera A. Nance
Christopher Isherwood	Claude J. Summers
James Joyce	Bernard Benstock
Christopher Marlowe	Gerald Pinciss
Katherine Mansfield	Rhoda B. Nathan
John Masefield	June Dwyer
W. Somerset Maugham	Archie K. Loss
John Milton	Gerald J. Schiffhorst
V. S. Naipaul	Richard Kelly
Barbara Pym	Robert Emmet Long
Jean Rhys	Arnold E. Davidson
Sir Walter Scott	Edward Wagenknecht
Shakespeare's Comedies	Jack A. Vaughn
Shakespeare's Histories	George J. Becker
Shakespeare's Tragedies	Phyllis Rackin
Muriel Spark	Velma Bourgeois Richmond
Tom Stoppard	Felicia Londré
J. R. R. Tolkien	Katharyn W. Crabbe
Evelyn Waugh	Katharyn W. Crabbe
H. G. Wells	Brian Murray

Complete list of titles in the series available from the publisher on request

GEOFFREY CHAUCER

Velma Bourgeois Richmond

A Frederick Ungar Book
CONTINUUM · NEW YORK

1992

The Continuum Publishing Company
370 Lexington Avenue, New York, NY 10017

Printed in the United States of America

Library of Congress Cataloging-in-Publication Data

Richmond. Velma Bourgeois.
Geoffrey Chaucer / Velma Bourgeois Richmond.
p. cm.—(Literature and life. British writers)
"A Frederick Ungar book."
Includes bibliographical references (p.) and index.
ISBN 0-8264-0545-2 (cloth)
1. Chaucer, Geoffrey, d. 1400. 2. Poets, English—Middle English, 1100–1500—Biography. I. Title. II. Series.
PR1905.R5 1992
821′.1—dc20
[B] 91-15955
CIP

For my students at Holy Names College,

fellow pilgrims and

readers of Chauccer

Contents

Chronology

1340?	Geoffrey Chaucer was born in London.
1357	The first record of Chaucer is as a member of the household of Prince Lionel, King Edward III's son, and Elizabeth, countess of Ulster. "Philippa Pan."(Paon?) is also listed in the household.
1359–60	Chaucer, in France with the English army, was taken prisoner near Reims. He was ransomed by the king, went home, and then returned to France as a courtier in peace negotiations.
136?	Chaucer married; Philippa Chaucer is first so designated in 1366, when given a royal annuity of twenty marks.
1366	Chaucer traveled to Spain, probably on a diplomatic mission.
1367	Chaucer was enrolled among the Esquires of the Royal Household. In the king's service, he received an annuity of twenty marks.
1368–69	Chaucer was again in France. Blanche, duchess of Lancaster, wife of John of Gaunt, died. Chaucer, who was with John of Gaunt on a raid in Picardy, began his elegy *The Book of the Duchess*. Philippa joined Gaunt's household.
1370	Chaucer was again abroad in the service of the king. He probably translated *Roman de la Rose* and wrote "An ABC."
1372	Chaucer made his first trip to Italy, on a mission to Genoa; he also visited Florence and almost certainly bought Italian books, including Dante's *Divine Comedy*.

1373	Chaucer returned to London, wrote some tragedies that became part of the *Monk's Tale,* and St. Cecilia's legend, which became the *Second Nun's Tale.* A son Thomas was probably born about this time.
1374	Chaucer was made controller of customs, leased a house at Aldgate, and was financially prosperous. Both Geoffrey and Philippa Chaucer received annuities (ten pounds) from Gaunt.
1376–77	Chaucer was on a mission to Calais, and another to Flanders, about peace and the marriage of Richard II, who succeeded his grandfather King Edward III.
1378	A return to Italy took Chaucer to Lombardy to negotiate for war support with Bernabò Visconti, whose splendid library may have introduced him to Boccaccio and Petrarch.
1380	A charge of *raptus* against Chaucer was dropped by Cecily Champain. A son Lewis was probably born about this time. 1378–80 was a period of poetic development: *The House of Fame* and *Anelida and Arcite* were written, and *The Parliament of Fowls* begun, as well as the *Knight's Tale.*
1381	The Peasants' Revolt occurred. Chaucer was working on *Boece* and *balades* and also began *Troilus and Criseyde*, which was finished 1386.
1382	Chaucer was appointed controller of petty customs. King Richard II married Anne of Bohemia.
1385	Chaucer was made justice of the peace in Kent, probably lived at Greenwich. He began work on *The Legend of Good Women* and was writing "Complaint of Mars" and "Complaint of Venus" about this time.
1386	Chaucer, no longer at customs, was appointed knight of the shire and sat in Parliament from Kent.
1387	Philippa's last receipt of an annuity suggests that she died. Chaucer began to get into debt. He was on a mission to Calais.
1388	Chaucer was working on *General Prologue* and early *Canterbury Tales.*

1389	Richard II came of age; he appointed Chaucer clerk of king's works, which brought an income of thirty pounds a year, large administrative responsibilities, and some danger (Chaucer was robbed three times).
1390	Chaucer oversaw repairs to St. George's Chapel, Windsor, the building of jousts at Smithfield, and Thames sewer repairs.
1391–92	Chaucer wrote *The Treatise on the Astrolabe.*
1392–95	Most of *The Canterbury Tales,* including the Marriage Group, were written. Chaucer was granted a new annuity (twenty pounds), received a gift of ten pounds from King Richard, who married Isabella of France.
1399	King Richard II was deposed and killed; John of Gaunt died. King Henry IV doubled Chaucer's annuity on his coronation day. Chaucer signed a fifty-three-year lease on a house in the garden of Westminster Abbey and was in the king's service.
1400	Chaucer died, on October 25, according to the inscription of his tomb (erected 1556) in "Poet's Corner" of Westminster Abbey.

1

A Man of the Fourteenth Century

Many details are known about the life of Geoffrey Chaucer because he had a distinguished career as a civil servant, diplomat, and courtier. Nearly five hundred items, some for almost every year from 1360 to Chaucer's death on October 25, 1400, are included in the *Chaucer Life Records,* but they detail his public career rather than his private life or work as a writer. So much information is remarkable to find about a fourteenth-century Englishman who was neither a noble nor an important political figure. Chaucer was, however, a soldier, a member of the king's household and of diplomatic missions abroad, a controller of customs, justice of the peace, a knight of the shire who sat in Parliament, clerk of the king's works and thus in charge of extensive building, and finally forester. In short, his career was richly diversified, showing that his administrative work was highly respected and in constant demand. Its steadiness through several periods of political upheaval shows Chaucer as a competent and prudent man; indeed he received benefits from both King Richard II and Henry IV, who had deposed Richard. The items in *Life Records,* some of which suggest correspondences with details in the poetry, outline his life and indicate contexts helpful for understanding Chaucer as a man of the fourteenth century.

Although the exact date and place of Chaucer's birth are unknown, the family, which came from Ipswich, can be traced back to the thirteenth century and had business interests in London, where the poet's grandfather Robert Chaucer had settled with his wife Mary late in the century. Geoffrey, son of John Chaucer and Agnes de Compton, was born in the early 1340s, probably in the family house in Thames Street in an area largely occupied by vintners. The cosmopolitan quality of the situation is indicated by those living nearby—Gascon wine merchants, Flemings, and Italians. The name (Fr. *chaussier*) suggests shoemaker, and the merchant family's trade interests were leather and wine. Chaucer identified his father's profession as vintner in a legal deposition of 1381, when he gave his own age as forty years "and more."

There are no records of Chaucer's schooling, but as the son of a wealthy vintner he very likely attended a good school, possibly the Almonry of St. Paul's Cathedral. Here he would have read English and then Latin (he knew French as well), and he would have learned arithmetic, crucial to his later work as an accountant. A surviving inventory of books, made by the schoolmaster William de Ravenstone, indicates that this school had an unusually fine library, and many titles are ones that Chaucer refers to or uses in his poetry: Virgil's *Georgics,* ten books of Lucan, Claudian's *Rape of Proserpine,* Statius's *Thebaid,* as well as Chaucer's favorite classical source, Ovid's *Metamorphoses.* This was in addition to the usual Latin grammars and textbooks of theology and music. Chaucer's most appealing self-portrait is of a private and solitary reader: the hardworking public man, who as controller of wool customs in London had to keep accounts in his own hand, returns from a long day and instead of resting or seeking public entertainment, "dombe as any stoon, / Thou sittest at another book / Tyl fully dawsed ys thy look," charges the eagle in *The House of Fame.* This suggests a long habit of devotion to books, and indeed Chaucer is perhaps more explicit about his reading than any other poet.

While a boy in London Chaucer survived the Black Death, the most devastating outbreak of bubonic plague. It began in Asia Minor in 1346 and closely followed the trade routes to Sicily, Genoa, Venice, across to Spain, France, and Germany, and to England in 1348. Estimates vary, but a loss of a third of the population is conservative for the severe losses of 1348–49. Almost every village was affected, as well as the cities. Later occurrences of the plague took the lives of those whom Chaucer knew at court, in 1369 both Queen Philippa and Blanche, duchess of Lancaster. These calamities touched everyone. They contributed to the vividness of the opening tavern scene and the seeking of Death in the *Pardoner's Tale,* but stoic resignation and deep reliance upon an afterlife were more frequent responses.

Many biographical details suggest a very public life. The earliest naming of Chaucer is as a member of the household of Elizabeth, countess of Ulster, wife of Lionel, duke of Clarence, the second son of King Edward III. Costs are recorded for the purchase of clothing, a short jacket and red and black hose (?), and a modest gift of two shillings and sixpence, for the Christmas season of 1357. This suggests his role as young page, and he would have gone to a number of royal estates. Two years later Chaucer went to France with Prince Lionel in the army of Edward III, was taken prisoner at Reims, and ransomed in 1360. He also first served as a messenger, a role that was to develop into his frequent travels for diplomatic negotiations.

The court of King Edward III (1327–77) was brilliant, and its chivalric glories in the 1360s were extolled by the French chronicler Jean Froissart, who probably knew Chaucer but only includes his name in a list. Edward's fifty-year reign brought great renown to his line. Early idealism was inspired by victories like the battle of Crécy in 1346 and the Order of the Garter was instituted in 1347, after the capture of Calais, on the model of Arthur's Knights of the Round Table. Edward's acceptance and furthering of contemporary chivalric and military practices brought renown and praise; his relations with the Church and his subjects were loyal. But the colorful pageantry and decorativeness, courtesy, and wealth have an underside. Edward's reign and all of Chaucer's lifetime saw the Hundred Years' War with France, a dismal and endless series of raids and pillaging as England gradually retreated from its French positions. Much of Chaucer's diplomatic work was a seeking of peace. Edward's private lack of austerity led to an early senility; his vanity and ostentation seem improper to many but were expected in his time. Courtly amusements find a reflection in Chaucer's poetry that has awareness of both glamour and overindulgence. His own career was not simply that of a courtier. There is a six-year gap in the records, when Chaucer probably continued his education at the Inns of Court and Inns of Chancery, where he would have acquired skills for keeping records in Chancery hand and using legal formulas in Latin and French. These were crucial to his later work as controller of customs and keeper of the king's works.

By 1366 many changes had occurred; his father John Chaucer died, his mother remarried, and Chaucer himself married. His wife was Philippa, daughter of Sir Paon de Roet, one of Queen Philippa's countrymen from Hainault. The couple were often separated, by Chaucer's travels abroad and by Philippa's attendance upon several women of the royal family: Elizabeth, daughter-in-law of King Edward III; Queen Philippa herself; and then Constanze of Castile, the second wife of John of Gaunt. Philippa was also the sister of Katherine Swynford, who in 1396 became the third wife of John of Gaunt, after having been his mistress for many years and governess to his children by Blanche of Lancaster. With John of Gaunt, the wealthiest baron in Britain and the man who essentially controlled the country when Richard became king as a boy of ten, there were other family connections. He granted Philippa several annuities, and in 1374 also gave Chaucer a life annuity of ten pounds; this was for "services rendered" to himself by Chaucer and by Chaucer's wife to Gaunt's mother and consort, Blanche, about whom Chaucer wrote in *The Book of the Duchess*. Philippa, who was living in Lincolnshire, but not Chaucer, was admitted to the fraternity of Lincoln Cathedral in 1386, along with Gaunt's eldest son, who was to become King Henry IV, and two sons of Katherine Swynford. No records mention Philippa after 1387, when she is presumed to have died, after being married to Chaucer for at least twenty-one years. There has been some speculation about Philippa's association with John of Gaunt, but the biographical information upon which this is built is inconclusive.

A son Thomas Chaucer was born, perhaps in 1373, and after using his father's coat of arms he shifted to his mother's de Roet arms. Thomas also advanced very rapidly in favor, but at least part of the family's wealth came from his wife Matilda, through whom he became a large landowner. Their only child Alice married twice, the earl of Salisbury and the earl of Suffolk, William de la Pole, with whom she built the almshouses at Ewelme, near Oxford, where Thomas and Matilda are also buried. The only other child is "lyte Lowys," for whom Chaucer wrote *The Treatise on the Astrolabe*, an elementary textbook about astronomy that was, like other of Chaucer's works, unfinished.[1] The date of Lewis's birth is, like many other details, not certain, but 1380 is suggested. In this year's records occurs the most provocative detail of Chaucer's biography. In May 1380 Cecilia Chaumpaigne, daughter of a London baker, exonerated Chaucer of charges of *raptus*, and there has been much speculation about what this means, physical rape or abduction. Chaucer's legal innocence is a matter of record, and those who gave witness were of high standing: John Philipot, a collector of customs and Richard Morel, a member of Parliament and merchant, who lived near Chaucer in London; and three who were called "Lollard Knights"—Sir William Beauchamp, younger son of Thomas, the powerful earl of Warwick, and chamberlain to the king's household, also somewhat older; Sir William Neville, another younger brother who was admiral of the king's fleet; and his friend Sir John Clanvowe, author of a secular poem *The Book of Cupide* and of a serious religious treatise, perhaps the first by a layperson in English. Cecilia Chaumpaigne appears again in the records a month later, issuing a similar release from all actions of law to two London citizens, Goodchild and Grove, who on the same day had granted

Chaucer a general release. These two men a month later paid Cecilia a sum of ten pounds, which was what Chaucer earned annually at the customs. From these facts have come several speculations, more arguing Chaucer's guilt, even though his legal innocence is the only established fact. Other records in Chaucer's life are more straightforward, or at least are less dependent upon readers' interpretations.

By 1366 Chaucer's career was clearly well under way. He is listed as a member of the king's household as *vallectus* (yeoman) and later as *arminger* (esquire). Young men so designated performed a variety of tasks. An early fifteenth-century account of the duties of esquires emphasizes their entertaining the court by "talking of Chronicles of Kings [cf. *Book of the Duchess,* 57–58] and of otheres pollicies" and by providing instrumental and vocal music. This suggests a likelihood of Chaucer's youthful experience of performance and story telling. One of his earliest poetic attempts was a translation, in the 1360s, of the *Roman de la Rose,* the most influential and popular secular poem of the late Middle Ages, which has survived only in fragments. The other important French literary influence was Guillaume de Machaut, and it has been suggested that Chaucer first wrote French lyrics. Certainly the style at court favored French.

Chaucer made a number of diplomatic missions abroad, at least four in four years. He went to France, Picardy and Aquitaine, for peace negotiations. He also went at least once to Spain, in 1366, perhaps with the Black Prince against Don Pedro of Castile, who is included in the *Monk's Tale* (VII.2375–90), or perhaps, like the Wife of Bath (I.466) as a pilgrim to Compostela, where Saint James was honored.[2] The Black Prince was Edward III's eldest son and had set a chivalric ideal; however, he died young, leaving his son Richard to become a boy king and be manipulated by uncles. John, Duke of Lancaster (John of Gaunt), who was the most powerful, orchestrated the pageantry of Richard II's coronation and during his minority exerted great influence, often irritating the fashionable young man, who had inherited a setting of extravagant courtly life. Chaucer rendered service early in Richard's reign; he returned to France between 1376 and 1378, on "the king's secret business" and, according to Froissart, the French chronicler, as part of a mission trying to negotiate a marriage between Richard and a French princess, one attempt to secure peace. Under papal influence the proposals were rejected, and an alliance was sought with the emperor of Wenceslas. Thus Richard married Anne of Bohemia in 1382.

Although Chaucer's earliest travels abroad were inevitably to France, his journeys to Italy were most crucial to his development as a poet. In 1372–73 Chaucer made his first recorded visit to Italy; he accompanied two Italian merchants, who were London residents, to Genoa to arrange a special commercial port in England for Genoese; one of the Italians was also hiring mercenaries for the king. Chaucer was probably chosen for this mission because he already knew Italian from his situation in London. During the six months that Chaucer was in Italy he also visited Florence, a magnificent city of about sixty-thousand, vastly different from his native London. Beautifully situated between mountains and on the Arno, with Giotto's tower recently completed and the baptistery with its glorious mosaics, Florence was perhaps most startling because of its civic solidity. Stone, not wooden, shops and houses created a massive identity that today remains distinctive. Fine churches like Santa Croce, with the frescoes of Giotto showing scriptural episodes and depicting the inspiring and reforming St. Francis, and Santa Maria Novella, with numerous quattrocento masters like Andrea Orcagna and Andrea da Firenze, provided an alternative to Northern Gothic. Italy also provided a powerful articulation of citizens and cities.

Although it is unlikely that Chaucer went to Sienna, the frescoes of Ambrogio Lorenzetti in the town hall suggest current Italian interests. Evil and Good Government are allegorically represented, and one sees the harmonious relationship between city and field, workers of many kinds, and those that have leisure for amusing entertainments. Sienna was also the city of Saint Catherine, whose pious life showed a way for laypersons who wanted to be free of ecclesiastical rule and fostered inner-directed religion that might have attracted Chaucer. At the very least, in Italy Chaucer encountered the distinctive combination of the secular and the religious that did not flourish in northern Europe and that heralded the lay individualism and piety that were growing in the fourteenth century.

However exhilarating the experiences of being in Italian cities, the most potent learning was of Italy's three great poets—Dante, Boccaccio, and Petrarch—who richly influence Chaucer's poetry. There is no evidence that Chaucer met either Boccaccio (1313–75), who was lecturing about Dante in Florence, or Petrarch (1304–74), who was living in Padua, where Chaucer's Clerk says he learned his tale of Griselda (IV.27). But Chaucer almost certainly acquired manuscripts of Dante and Boccaccio's more secular work, without which he could not have written *Troilus and Criseyde* and the *Knight's Tale,* though he never mentions Boccaccio's name. Another occasion for Chaucer's acquiring knowledge of Italian literature was a mission to Lombardy in 1378, when he went to negotiate with Bernabò Visconti, lord of Milan, about the king's war. The English mercenary, Sir John Hawkwood, whose statue is today in the Duomo at Florence, was Bernabò's son-in-law. King Richard sent rich gifts to both men, but there is no record of the outcome of the negotiations. Chaucer no doubt gained because the Visconti had been patrons of Petrarch and their libraries were renowned. At least, Chaucer notes Bernabò's significance by including him in the *Monk's Tale* (VII.2399–2406), after his fall from power in 1385 and subsequent death. Without the encounters with Italy, already dazzling in what is now esteemed the Italian Renaissance, Chaucer's development as a poet would have been very different.

Chaucer's return from his first travels to Italy was also marked by a significant enriching of his circumstances in England. In 1374 he became financially independent through an unusual grant from King Edward III of a daily gallon pitcher of wine for life, an especially apt gift for the son of a vintner. This provided Chaucer with a respectable income that was strengthened by other gifts, the ten-pound annuity from John of Gaunt already noted and a rent-free house in Aldgate, one of the six points of entry to London. The location of this house made a convenient walk to the customs house, where Chaucer worked for a dozen years as controller of customs, the post to which he was appointed in 1374 and for which he was given another ten pounds a year. The job was to oversee the export taxes and a heavier subsidy in the port of London on wool, sheepskins, and leather. These efforts placed him in the company of the collectors, rich merchants whose records were checked against Chaucer's independent accounts to assure that the revenue was properly received. Evidence of Chaucer's hard work comes not only from his self-portrait but also from the facts that he held the post an unusually long time and that he usually received an additional annual payment for "unremitting labor and diligence." Since the sums received from customs were great—an average of nearly twenty-five-thousand pounds annually—the responsibilities were serious. The evidence suggests that such strenuous demands rather than detracting from his literary efforts perhaps enhanced them by his need to provide a respite from administration. While controller of customs Chaucer wrote *The Parliament of Fowls, The House of Fame, Troilus and Criseyde, The Legend of Good Women,* as well as lesser pieces, and translated Boethius's *Consolation of Philosophy* from the Latin. In addition, Chaucer continued his role as esquire to the king, serving as diplomatic envoy, making further trips to France and Italy, as noted above. In his absences a deputy served as controller, and similar assistance was received at other times in the 1380s, until a permanent deputy was appointed in 1385.

In the mid 1380s there were many notable changes in Chaucer's circumstances. His reputation as an author was noted both in France and England. Eustace Deschamps in a *balade* (c.1385) praised "Great translateur, noble Geoffrey Chaucer" (refrain 10, 20, 30, 36), who enlightened those English that were "ignorant of French" with his translation of the *Roman de la Rose*. Deschamps extols Chaucer through comparisons with classical authors: "O Socrates, full of philosophy, Seneca for morality, for practical life an Aulus Gellius, a great Ovid in your poetry" and praises him as "brief in speech, wise in rhetoric (the art of writing), and knowledgeable." A fellow Londoner, Thomas Usk, who wrote the *Testament of Love* (c. 1387), an imitation of Chaucer's *Boece,* identifies Chaucer as "the noble philosophical poete in Englissh" and praises "his noble sayenges, goodnes of gentyl manlyche speche, ymagynacion in wytte, and good reason of sentence" (meaning) [in which] "he passyth al other makers" (poets). The specific work recommended is *Troilus and Criseyde* that answers the question of reconciling God's foreknowledge with free will. These earliest comments about Chaucer's poetry indicate contemporary reception; notable is the emphasis upon moral seriousness, principles of human conduct, as well as technical skill.

Indeed Chaucer's intention is evident when he "directs this book" (*Troilus and Criseyde,* V.1856) to "moral Gower" and "philosophical Strode," and then prays for mercy "to that sothfast Crist, that starf* on rode†" (*died, †cross, V.1860). John Gower (1330?–1408), Chaucer's friend and fellow poet, was an "Esquire of Kent," who wrote major works in English, French, and Latin. In a first version of Gower's English poem the *Confessio Amantis* (c.1390) Venus sends greetings to Chaucer, "mi disciple and mi poete," who in his youth wrote "ditees" and "glade songes" for which she is most beholden (VIII.2941–57). Ralph Strode (fl. 1350–1400) was a fellow of Merton College, Oxford, a famous teacher of logic and philosophy who engaged in friendly discussion with John Wycliffe and perhaps wrote poetry.[3] These references provide a useful suggestion about the kinds of people that Chaucer counted as friends.[4] Another was Henry Scogan (1361?–1407), a courtier who became tutor to the sons of King Henry IV and addressed a poem to the princes urging "vertuous noblesse." Scogan's poem begins "My mayster Chaucer, god his soule have!" and presents his view, quoting Chaucer's lyric "Gentilesse" in its entirety. This tribute to Chaucer's influence provides a sympathetic response to the anxieties of the older poet who wrote "Chaucer's Lenvoy to Scogan."

Concomitant with the increasing recognition of Chaucer as a poet there were many alterations in his professional and personal circumstances. After withdrawing from his work at the customs, Chaucer apparently lived in Kent, where he served on a peace commission—of practical importance since there was a real threat from France, as the building of Bodiam Castle illustrates—and was appointed a justice of the peace. And in 1386 he was elected to Parliament as a "knight of the shire" (House of Commons). This was a crucial session for King Richard II, who lacked the resources to supply the troops called to London as a defense against the French. John of Gaunt's younger brother Thomas of Woodstock seized the occasion to gain influence, and Gaunt's powerful position was lost. Chaucer, like others associated with Gaunt, was in threatening circumstances, but he had ties outside the Gaunt circle and is not recorded as having taken a strong stance. King Richard's ineffectualness was an issue, and Chaucer's "Lak of Stedfastnesse" and "Truth / Balade de Bon Conseyl" are usually read as his reflections on the situation. The "Merciless Parliament" of 1388 investigated all royal grants, and Chaucer surrendered his annuities to John Scalby in Lincolnshire. The uneasy political situation and consequent greater leisure may have influenced at this time Chaucer's plan for a large and complex poetic work. The *General Prologue* and several early *Canterbury Tales* were written, but Chaucer soon returned to active administrative service.

King Richard II assumed authority in May of 1389, and Thomas of Woodstock was dismissed. On July 12, 1389, Richard appointed Chaucer clerk of the king's works, arguably the most arduous and responsible position of his career, since it required overseeing construction and repair of ten royal residences—Tower of London, Westminster Palace—as well as other castles, manors (Eltham and Sheen are mentioned in the *Prologue to the Legend of Good Women*, F. 497), parks, mills, gardens, fences, mews at Charing Cross, and the wool quay at the Tower, which was the most extensive and expensive project and one for which Chaucer was unusually well prepared. As clerk Chaucer supervised very large staffs and purchasing of materials, though the actual sums of money were less than he dealt with at the customs. Nevertheless, he was robbed by highwaymen while traveling on the king's service in 1390; the court records show that the robbers were convicted and Chaucer was not required to repay the loss. The importance of his office is indicated by some on the payroll, most notably Henry Yevele, a master mason who planned the naves for Canterbury Cathedral (there is a boss of his head in the Cloister) and Westminster Abbey, and the great Westminster Hall, with its hammerbeam ceiling, as well as the tombs of King Richard II and Queen Anne. Chaucer's own pay also acknowledged the significance of his position, two shillings a day, which was three and a half times what he received as controller of customs. Of all his overseeing of building most interesting to readers of Chaucer was that at Smithfield in 1390, when the king had a splendid tournament to which many knights, including those from abroad, were invited. Chaucer was responsible for the construction of scaffolds, seating for royal and noble spectators, and for the lists for combat. This experience is echoed in the *Knight's Tale* (I.1882–84, 1908, 2087–88). Another activity associated with chivalry was a refurbishing of the Chapel of St. George at Windsor Castle for installation of Knights of the Garter, founded by King Edward III (c.1344). Chaucer concluded his clerkship after just less than two years, and for the remainder of his life held only one other appointment, deputy forester of Petherton Park, Somersetshire, to which he had earlier been appointed. Again his responsibilities were handling money, since royal forests were a major source of income.

During the 1390s Chaucer received several additional grants from Richard and also from Henry of Derby, who was born at Bolingbroke. The last years of Chaucer's life saw many changes and much in decline. Richard's zeal to have his own way, particularly from 1397 onwards, made him attempt to impose his rule and take away rights long established by Parliament. He also took merciless revenge on those who opposed him, notably the Appellants, many of whom were Chaucer's friends. One act was the banishment of John of Gaunt's eldest son. Readers of Shakespeare's *Richard II* are familiar with the King's seizure of John of Gaunt's lands upon his death and Henry's return to claim his inheritance and ultimately the throne. Richard's absence from the kingdom, on an ill-fated expedition to Ireland to quell a revolt, exacerbated the situation, placing him in the weak position of returning to the uncertain loyalties of his nobles and Henry's strength. Chaucer seems not to have suffered personally in the transition. He had lamented Henry's mother in his first poem *The Book of the Duchess,* and there are records of other exchanges. The new king, noted for his dedication to learning, doubled Chaucer's annuity from Richard II when he became King Henry IV in October 1399. This was especially welcome, since Chaucer seems to have had difficulty collecting annuities; he had to take advance loans on his annuities and was sued for debt in 1398. The "Complaint of Chaucer to His Purse," perhaps Chaucer's last poem, describes its "lightness" and hopes for better; the "Lenvoy" praises the new king and concludes with a "supplicacion" that suggests he was still awaiting payment. On Christmas Eve of 1399 Chaucer had leased—for fifty-three years—a house near the Lady Chapel at Westminster Abbey. Thus as a member of the parish and a resident in the abbey close, and perhaps also as a royal servant, he was buried in the Abbey, within a few yards of Richard II's tomb. The date of his death on the tomb inscription is October 25, 1400, but this may have been built as late as 1555. There was no "Poets Corner" in Westminster Abbey in 1400, but through the centuries no one has questioned that Chaucer's memorial rightly initiates a long tradition of honoring great British authors. The providential circumstances of his tomb seem fitting for a poet and man of the fourteenth century who wrote so forcefully of "fortune, gentillesse, and pacience" and who concluded *Troilus and Criseyde* with a laugh from the eighth sphere and *The Canterbury Tales* with a Retraction. His two greatest poems, celebrations of the joys of the world, both offer a final view of their smallness and relative insignificance.

The first praises of Chaucer the poet came in his lifetime, and hard upon these followed many more; early in the fifteenth century Chaucer became widely perceived as the most important English poet. John Lydgate (1370?–1451?), prolific versifier and favorite of many patrons, frequently refers to "My maistir Chaucer," "Floure of Poetes." He is most praised for style, as a "noble Rhetor" and one who writes with extraordinary metrical ease, "off Inglissh in makyng was the beste," and thus can teach the craft of poetry, rather than as a poet with the didactic substance that was Lydgate's achievement. Nevertheless, Lydgate, a monk of Bury St. Edmund's monastery, views Chaucer as "wise" and "prudent." At the beginning of *The Siege of Thebes* (1420–22), an imitation of *The Canterbury Tales,* Lydgate enumerates Chaucer's great variety, including some of "desport, moralité, kyghthode, loue, gentillesse, parfit holinesse, and Ribaudye," thus early establishing a claim for attention that persists through the centuries. Similarly, Thomas Hoccleve (c.1368–c.1430) in *The Regement of Princes* (1412) also addresses "Mi maister Chaucer flour of eloquence" and emphasizes Chaucer's position as "fadir reuerent . . . first fyndere of oure faire langage," comparing his rhetoric to Cicero and poetry to Virgil but also near in philosophy to Aristotle as no other English author.

In addition to this picture of the poet's works, Hoccleve included a "lyknesse," and the "peynture" of Chaucer in British Library MS Harley 4866 (f. 87), which is the one nearest to life. It shows the poet as an old man, for his hair and beard are gray. Dressed in black, he holds a rosary in his left hand, while his right index finger points to the text of the manuscript, and a pen is attached to his garment. The miniature in the Ellesmere Manuscript of *The Canterbury Tales* imitates this figure for its equestrian portrait. Also indebted to the Hoccleve miniature is a full-length figure, visibly plump and dressed in dark brown, shown on the wooden panel in the National Portrait Gallery, London. Chaucer again holds his rosary, and here fingers the pen.[5] Sharply contrasted to these pictures of the poet alone is the frontispiece of *Troilus and Criseyde,* MS 61 Corpus Christi College, Cambridge. This fifteenth-century idealization is no longer specifically identified as Chaucer, but it shows a youthful poet (with a general resemblance to a male Gothic figure) standing at a pulpit, reading to an elite courtly audience of men and women, fashionably attired. Attempts at specific identifications (Richard II, for example) have been made, but an idealized scene seems more likely; there are, for example, many stylistically similar representations of preaching that resemble the poet reading, and the procession toward a castle in an upper portion of the picture is also traditional in form. The essential impression is of an important situation for the poet.

Language

Chaucer's place as "maister" is rightly a result both of his thought and his language. Modern Standard English developed from the language that Chaucer's works did so much to initiate, though it was not until the fifteenth century that English was fully ascendant. In fourteenth-century England three languages were commonly used—English, French, and Latin. The tomb effigy of Chaucer's friend John Gower in Southwark Cathedral amusingly illustrates this; Gower's head rests on his three major books, one in each of the three languages. Latin and French were still written by Chaucer in his work as a civil servant, as was true of writing for the church and the court, but English was spoken in these circles and was the language of business and the common people. Many were, of course, bilingual. French remained the language of sophistication; Richard II's court cultivated the Gothic International Style, which reflected France's domination of the Middle Ages. Chaucer's early literary influences are thus French. Old English had, of course, been developed in the early Middle Ages; there is a rich and sophisticated literature, most notably *Beowulf* but also several splendid elegies, as well as powerful Christian poems of Caedmon and Cynewulf, not to mention riddles and charms. Anglo-Saxon prose was highly developed in chronicles and the works of Alfred and Aelfric. One regional variation, West Saxon, was fairly standard by the tenth century. This splendid tradition was, of course, destroyed after the Norman Conquest of 1066, when French became the language of politics and culture. Not until the twelfth century was there a revival of English, and indeed King Henry IV was the first after the conquest to take the oath of office in English. Chaucer's vocabulary is half French, and many of his words are accented, and pronounced, as they would be in French.

The variety of Middle English dialects indicates regional developments. Because London attracted people from so many places there was a blend, but still many variations. A glance at *Sir Gawain and the Green Knight* , written in a Northwest Midland dialect in the last quarter of the fourteenth century, shows a language very different from Chaucer's. By comparison Chaucer's Middle English seems close to Modern English—once differences of spelling (there was no uniform system) and pronunciation (especially of long vowels because of the "great vowel shift" of the next century, the weakening or loss of inflectional endings, sounding of final -e and many consonants that are now silent) are acknowledged.[6] Grammar and vocabulary are not so different, and the idiom of the poetry is remarkably close. There is delight, for example, in finding a phrase like "have good day" (I.2740), heard as a parting every day in America. Chaucer's prose seems less sure than his verse, which comes in the earliest stages of a literary tradition, while prose develops more slowly.

Indeed Chaucer's achievement is remarkable because he wrote in such an elegant and accomplished way, single-handedly proving that English was a great literary language. His affinities with French are shown by his choice consistently to write with rhyme in preference to the alternative general pattern of stress and alliteration of the Germanic tradition that appears in Old English and the poetry of the fourteenth-century Alliterative Revival that included the Gawain Poet, Langland, and the author of the alliterative *Morte Arthure*. Chaucer employed the popular four-stress line that was widely current, for example in "tail-rhyme" romances; it is very effective even in an early poem like *The Book of the Duchess*. However, he favored a longer line, one with five stresses or beats, that permitted greater complexity. This verse appears in different stanza patterns, notably in "rime royal" in *Troilus and Criseyde*, but more typically in couplets as in *The Canterbury Tales*. Iambic pentameter has come to seem the most "natural" verse movement in English. Chaucer's verse has a fluidity and flexibility because it used a greater variety of light syllables to secure the rhythm. Middle English has a verve, energy, and color that are appealing to the modern ear and amply repay the conscientious effort necessary to read Chaucer's original language—at least as it has survived, since all of the manuscripts that preserve his works date from the fifteenth century. Scholarly study re-creates the effects of the language, and is also needed to gain a sense of Chaucer's London, very little of which can be seen today.

Chaucer's London

London in the mid-fourteenth century had a population of about forty-thousand, and filled but one square mile, so that it was only a quarter of the size of Paris and open country was within a half hour's walk. As the only city in England comparable to those on the Continent, London was markedly different from other cities in England; York and Bristol were nearest in size with populations of only about ten-thousand. London's mixed population pursued many interests of trade and industry, government, law, and the Church. The permanent residents made the city a rich center of trade, and there was also a seasonal flow and large population of foreigners. London Bridge was in itself a village with nearly one-hundred-fifty shops. The shrine to St. Thomas à Becket in the middle of the bridge was not unusual in a city with the greatest number of parish churches (at least one-hundred-twenty in all, ninety-nine within the walls) and numerous splendid abbeys, priories, and hospitals in the city or nearby. St. Paul's Cathedral with its magnificent Gothic spire (489 feet, as compared with the present cross on the dome at 365 feet), brightly colored interior, and splendid monuments, like the alabaster one to Blanche and John of Gaunt, dominated the riverside and was a chief meeting place. Its churchyard and the cathedral itself were noisy with the bustle of tradesmen, scriveners, litigants, preachers to gathered crowds, and the sounds of games and wrestling matches; there was even a right-of-way through the transepts. However, these worldly activities coexisted with piety; many came to pray, making offerings at the shrine of St. Erkenwald (estimated at nine-thousand pounds a year) and altars, as well as devotions at the north door's Rood and the Great Rood at the entrance to the choir and veneration of numerous relics. These religious establishments were well maintained and endowed, many recently rebuilt and enlarged, especially to add chantries, usually with support from parish fraternities that were less political than craft guilds. Religious feasts and celebrations were an important part of London life, and Londoners delighted in sermons as well as processions and festivities. The large number of religious foundations meant many clerics, proportionately more than ten times as many as today. As Chaucer's portraits in the *General Prologue* indicate there was not always the dedication commonly associated with most clerics today. Indeed one of the complications of London life was clerical privilege, which meant milder punishment than laity received for the same crimes, as well as many seekers of personal advantage through benefices and other common abuses in the Church of the fourteenth century. Chaucer's idealized portrait of the Parson, sharply contrasted with the obvious failings of the Friar, Summoner, and Pardoner, shows how great was the discrepancy between expectation and behavior.

Also dominating the riverside was the Tower of London built in Norman times, a royal fortress whose defenses were updated in the fourteenth century. Here were not only armorers and a base for some ships; the Tower also provided storage of valuables for the exchequer and early in the century for the wardrobe, the king's household financial office. So extensive did royal operations become that the "Great Wardrobe" was moved in 1361 to a spacious townhouse near St. Paul's, and many smaller wardrobes for queen and prince were established in smaller houses. There was, then, much evidence of court business in Chaucer's London. Earlier division of the government, to York for example, had proved unsatisfactory, and in midcentury administration began to cluster at Westminster. The exchequer became permanently located there in 1339, and the court of common pleas accompanied it. Similarly, by 1345 the chancellor and the chancery sat normally in Westminster. By the time of Richard II, the court of the king's bench also heard cases in Westminster Hall. Similarly, during the fourteenth century Westminster was established as the meeting place for Parliament. Between 1327 and 1338 it met there thirteen times, while seventeen Parliaments were held elsewhere. But between 1339 and 1377 all thirty-one Parliaments were held at Westminster. Thus by the end of the reign of King Edward III this location was perceived as the normal place for meetings, the Painted Chamber of Westminster Palace for full parliaments, and the chapter house of Westminster Abbey for assemblies of the Commons. Chaucer was elected to Parliament in 1386 to represent Kent.

Associated with the royal court were, of course, nobility. The patronage of a chivalric court fostered the prosperity of London, not least through purchases of fine clothing, supplied by merchants. There were fine houses like the Savoy, a palace rebuilt by Blanche's father, Duke Henry of Lancaster, at a cost of more than thirty-four-thousand pounds. Located on the Strand, a road that was filled with bishops' inns built from Charing Cross to Temple Bar because of easy access to the river, the Savoy Palace was the great prize raided by the mob during the Peasants Revolt of 1381 as an act of vengeance against John of Gaunt, in memory of whose first wife, Blanche of Lancaster, Chaucer wrote *The Book of the Duchess*. At this time Chaucer was living at Aldgate, an entry through which thousands of rebels surged into the city. Many were killed in the Vintry area where Chaucer had lived as a boy. In a rare precise reference to contemporary events Chaucer recalls the occasion in the *Nun's Priest's Tale* (VII.3394–97), when he compares the noise made when the fox seized the cock to that made when Jack Straw and his men killed Flemings. A poll tax and ineptitude provoked the uprising, but one of the youthful King Richard II's finest moments was his show of personal bravery and levelheaded response, marked by a generosity in allowing no violence against the rebels after the immediate conflict ended. This popularity soon waned, however, when good governance was not subsequently combined with personal charisma.

The city was largely neither a place of nobles or peasants but of merchants and craftsmen who governed it and lived in town houses that were the urban equivalent of manor houses. To this merchant class Chaucer belonged, and its way of life was rich and varied. His family's house was on Thames Street along with other large houses and a mansion, La Réole, owned by Queen Philippa, where Joan of Kent and Richard II had both stayed. Merchants conducted much of their business in their houses and freely mingled with the nobility. Living in the same area were Italians, Europe's most advanced merchants; thus Chaucer very likely knew Italian before he made his journeys to Italy. There were also Flemings, who came for the cloth trade. A merchant's house was typically large and on the sides of its central hall usually contained windows, a sign of seeking more light than afforded by the barred windows on the street side. Ordinarily the house was shaped like a quadrangle; the sides were a hall, a two-story wing to face the street, with an entrance to the courtyard, a second two-story wing across the back, and warehouses and outhouses on the final side. Heating was a fire in the hall; coal already polluted the air, as satiric writings testify. Furnishings were rather simple: a few chairs, occasional chests, curtained beds, large spits in the kitchen, a trestle table, benches, stools. Those who were very wealthy and preferred could buy food prepared by pastry cooks, especially meat and bird pies, rather than in the house's kitchen. The floor was covered with rushes, often sweetened with herbs. Hospitality was generous, and typically there were servants.

Most strikingly houses blazed with color—an effect vividly preserved in manuscript illuminations and stained glass windows—in the hangings, cushions, tapestries for the walls, which were sometimes painted. Fourteenth-century delight in color and finery also is manifest in the expansion of the clothes industry; the Mercers, Drapers, and Skinners (respectively supplying silks, linens, ribbons; heavier cloths; and furs) were among the most powerful guilds, developed through the delight in display that led to a first law in 1363 to control excesses. Chaucer's many descriptive details of costume, for example in the portrait of the Wife of Bath, suggest direct observation as well as literary convention. Colorful clothing (especially scarlet) was favored as a symbol of status. Both the choice of crafts and the emphasis upon livery "Of a solempne and a greet lyveree" (I.364) for the Guildsmen presented in the *General Prologue* reflect a growing concern with luxury and display among Londoners. The building of halls by guilds, as social centers and administrative offices, begins in the fourteenth century; the only two known in the time of Richard II were those of the Taylors and Goldsmiths, crafts notable for wealthy interests. Such prosperity did not come without hard work, and the usual working day for most trades was from six a.m. to eight or nine in the evening. Since family businesses were normal, and apprentices lived within, living and working were all in the same place.

The fourteenth century was a gregarious time when there was

more emphasis upon community, before the stress on the individual that burgeons in the sixteenth century and today remains the norm in Western societies. Among an extraordinary number of entertainments perhaps the most notable were processions, which were part of any royal, civic, or guild occasion, but that were also for other celebrations. Victories and coronations were richly marked. The Goldsmiths, for example, produced an extraordinary pageant for Richard II's coronation in 1377. On the route from the Tower to Westminster, at Cheapside, was built a castle with four towers on each of which stood a maiden who threw artificial gold coins before Richard and his horses and blew down leaves of gold. A gold angel bowed to the king and offered a crown, and wine flowed from two sides of the castle. Such "devices" became increasingly more elaborate and numerous: for example, when the citizens of London sought reconciliation with Richard in 1392. Kings, particularly Edward III, and their courts delighted in tournaments held in the streets, the jousts usually opposite St. Mary le Bow in the middle of Cheapside. There was a royal box for spectators, but others flocked to the spectacle; Chaucer's London apprentice in the *Cook's Tale,* for example, "whan ther any ridyng was in Chepe" left the shop "Til that he hadde al the sighte yseyn" (I.4377, 4379). Quintain contests tested the skills of accurate blow and riding; participants rode at the shield and tried to avoid being struck by the sandbag hung at the opposite end of a freely turning bar. On days of patron saints some guilds had as many as three processions, one by torchlight, on the vigil or eve, and then another to high mass, and finally a third to a hall for a feast. In June, Marching Watches, a combination of procession and feasting with bonfires in the streets, provided a variety of activities, just as today Mardi Gras parades in New Orleans entertain and amuse a large audience. In the summer there were also plays performed in the open air, and Chaucer refers to this vital part of fourteenth-century life in the *Miller's Tale.* In the Christmas season there was not only feasting, but also mummings, for which masks were worn and charadelike plays enacted as well as dancing. The sounds of trumpets, sackbuts, shawms, cornets, tabors were no less lively and colorful than the liveries and other fine dress. Illuminations in the margins of Gothic manuscripts, especially MS Bodley 264, preserve images of such pastimes and entertainments. Londoners could also seek coarser entertainments across the river in Southwark, where not all taverns were as respectable as the Tabard, and the district was known for its brothels, as well as bear gardens, cockpits, bullrings, fighting booths that provided bloody spectacles, involving bears, dogs, cocks, bulls, and also men. Tavern scenes in the *Pardoner's Tale* and the *Cook's Tale,* with dicing, talking, and cheap ale show something of this seamy side of London life. All (except clerics) carried weapons, and violence was a part of life, as accounts of frequent street brawling record.

The poor lived much less grandly than the noble or merchant class. Their accommodation was cramped, often no more than single rooms in alley tenements. All levels of society met in the bustling activity of London's noisy and crowded streets. Chaucer would have met many whom he knew as he walked through the city. The scene was animated and energetic, albeit dirty and often disorderly. There was a sewage system, and several public latrines, but liquid refuse still coursed through open channels, and pigs rooted in garbage in the early part of the century. Even with the city's proximity to the countryside disease in such crowded conditions spread easily. Smells were strong, as the references to attempts of the wealthy to mask these with herbs indicate. A poet living in London saw many types of people to combine for purposes of a pilgrimage that would frame the many stories he wanted to tell.[7]

Religious Belief

Chaucer's framing of his last great work as a pilgrimage focuses attention on a salient feature of fourteenth-century life that is not omnipresent today—religious belief and the authority of the Church. In spite of difficulties and complexities, medieval life is permeated by Christian influences, as the buildings, manuscripts, and visual arts manifest. It is not possible to imagine the Middle Ages without religion, but it is crucial to recognize that the surviving monuments are only one sign, which emphasizes serenity and poise. The history of the Church in the fourteenth century was one of turmoil and confusion. The so-called Babylonian Captivity lasted from 1305 to 1378; the papacy was located not in Rome but in Avignon and was subservient to the French crown, though important Italians like Petrarch were part of the papal court. This avoided the danger, even to personal safety, of turbulent central Italy but complicated Anglo-papal relations after the outbreak of the Hundred Years' War, especially with Pope Clement VI, who was extremely sympathetic to the French, given to personal excesses and easy sale of benefices. Pressures of public opinion forced a promise of return to Rome, and Pope Gregory XI did this in 1377, the year that Richard II became king of England. There followed (until 1417) the Great Schism, when the Italians voted Urban VI as successor and the French chose Clement VII. Thus Christian Europe witnessed a worldly altercation, and each faction held to its pope and voted new successors as needed. Although John Wycliffe and his Lollard followers responded with increasingly radical arguments for reform, the Great Schism was a time of some reconciliation for England, since Urban VI was English, and the young king sought a concordat. England never questioned the rightness of its being in a universal church. Church conflicts should be seen as essentially legal and diplomatic and also a rivalry between two systems of patronage, regal and papal. The spiritual supremacy of a pope and legislative acts of a church were not the major question. Among Chaucer's friends were a number of important men, identified as "Lollard knights," who espoused a moral fervency that was less dependent upon a hierarchy, but not perceived as heretical.[8] Chaucer's severest comments come, predictably, against the unpopular bureaucracy that carried out the jurisdiction of the Church, like the Summoner and Pardoner, or the itinerant Friar and Monk.[9] Against this is set the Parson, the best to be found in the medieval church.

There were about ten-thousand parishes in the eighteen dioceses of England, and only about five-hundred were in the forty or fifty towns, with London having more than a hundred as noted above. In the villages and towns parishes served from fifty to two or three-hundred persons, and town churches served even more. Parishes were not primarily concerned with the great theological arguments of centuries of medieval thought, particularly the late work of thirteenth-century Scholasticism, which assimilated Aristotelian logic, recently recovered by the Arabs, with Christian belief, and the systematic ordering of knowledge and debate of intellectuals. Indeed by the fourteenth century the rational resolutions of Aquinas were already perceived as not answering personal religious yearning, particularly for a newly educated laity. A vast literature, much written in the vernacular, was produced to fill the need: manuals of instruction for parish priests, treatises about the commandments, accounts of the virtues and vices. A dominant theme in much of this religious literature is the use of the sacrament of penance, an inevitable response to the legislation of the Fourth Lateran Council (1215) that required annual confession and communion and stressed preaching. In fact, the most popular of all Middle English poems is *The Pricke of Conscience;* it survives in 114 manuscripts, more than Chaucer's *Canterbury Tales* or *Piers Plowman*. An extraordinary range of literature pertinent to moral improvement, a rich variety of practical treatises, were very popular, and Chaucer shares this concern of his age. Modern editions (unless complete works) of *The Canterbury Tales* do not contain the *Parson's Tale,* a treatise on sin, a manual to prepare all for confession. This exclusion shows a changed interest of modern readers; it is the only tale chosen, for example, for illustration in one of the best manuscripts (Cambridge University. gg. 4.27). Similarly, Chaucer's *Tale of Melibee,* which is a cautionary tale about prudence, good counsel, wisdom, and a religious romance like the *Man of Law's Tale,* or even the *Clerk's Tale,* are rarely included in selections. These stories and *exempla* were offered without apology—in contrast to the *fabliaux* (I.3170–86), so relished by modern critics—and they share an emphasis upon moral fervor.

Rather different from practical instructions, but yet an expression of personal seeking, is mystical and devotional writing, which flourished in fourteenth-century England as at no other time in the country's history. Richard Rolle, Dame Julian of Norwich, Walter Hilton, the author of *The Cloud of Unknowing,* and many others are yet one more indication of a climate in which piety was manifest. Manuals of confession and treatises on virtues and vices provided a rigorous grounding for contemplation, and direct union with God. Mystics were read by devout laity as well as religious. The anti-intellectualism and individualism of this writing are also a reaction against organizational limitations. Similarly, the growing popularity of the Carthusian order is significant. This religious group stressed a life of study and quiet, an emphasis upon personal spiritual life and mystical experience of God rather than communal life with its labor and liturgical prayer. Such an expression of piety appealed to laypersons who rejected other monastic orders and contemporary abuses in the Church, and it provides another way of seeing the search for personal religious expression in a time of public institutional disarray. Perhaps the simplest perception is a recognition that religious belief persisted in spite of abuses and individual inadequacies. No image more fully expresses the idea than that of pilgrimage, a seeking that is for Chaucer both personal and a communal activity.

2

"God's Plenty"—*The Canterbury Tales*

Geoffrey Chaucer is best known as the author of *The Canterbury Tales,* the work most widely read, and in recent years also available to a general audience as a musical and as a film. Literary critics and theorists focus attention on both the whole work and its many parts as well as many different contexts. The pilgrims are diverse, vividly described in the *General Prologue* and gradually developed as characters, with varying fullness, through the tales that they tell and the interaction among pilgrims provided by the connecting narrative links. Their "tales of Canterbury"—as Chaucer calls them in the Retraction—are a treasury of medieval story telling that engagingly evokes the Middle Ages but frequently delights with ideas and moments that seem quite contemporary. The range of subject matter, from bawdiness to high religious sentiment and affirmation, is extraordinary. *The Canterbury Tales,* more than any other work, is thought to provide a "picture of fourteenth-century life," its literature and learning as well as its people. Chaucer's wide reading of literary works, his delight in experimenting with genres, self-conscious use of the English language and rhetoric, and creation of authorial personae, were combined with current knowledge of science, philosophy, scripture, and theological questions, as well as court fashions. Thus any discussion is necessarily selective and limited, especially amid a plethora of modern interpretations.[1]

Distinguishing several characteristics is a helpful approach to this complex and various work. *The Canterbury Tales* is a collection of stories placed in a framework that is established in the *General Prologue* and sustained through prologues and links that record interaction between pilgrims before many of the tales. There is, then, a fiction that contains fictions. A group of pilgrims makes a journey from London to Canterbury, and they entertain themselves by telling stories as they travel. This procedure is, of course, not realistic; they number twenty-nine and proceed on horseback, "we ryden forth oure weye," (I.856), an unlikely situation for listening to long stories. Yet pilgrimages were frequent in the fourteenth century, and Chaucer creates an impression, through many authenticating descriptive details and with lively exchanges, that the pilgrims are very "real." Dramatic interplay is one of the poem's interests, particularly the quarrels between pilgrims, like the Miller and the Reeve or the Friar and the Summoner, or the self-revelation in the extended prologues of the Wife of Bath and the Pardoner. There are twenty-four tales, three of which are incomplete, and Chaucer sustains interest by constantly balancing genres, themes, and styles. The tales of the first fragment are explicitly conceived as a unit: *The Knight's Tale,* a chivalric romance, is contrasted with *The Miller's Tale,* a *fabliau,* to which *The Reeve's Tale,* another *fabliau* replies as the attempt of one rival pilgrim to "quite" (repay) another, and the fragment ends with the *Cook's Tale,* which is incomplete but also probably another *fabliau.* Several tales can be read as a sustained discussion of marriage, while a theme of greed unites others, and the idea of pilgrimage, the Christian's spiritual seeking, offers a way of interpreting the whole.

The portraits of the pilgrims and their responses to each other are vivid, but the stories told are at least as memorable. Some of the tales were written before Chaucer got the idea of *The Canterbury Tales,* whose unfinished state, incomplete and not revised, suggests that there might have been others. Chaucer's writing of many different narrative genres, often with several examples, shows his fascination with story telling. Exact definition of genres is difficult and constricting, particularly since Chaucer is often transforming conventions; however, I find this approach more illuminating than discussing the tales in the order in which they are usually printed because it gives emphasis to the stories told as well as to the drama of the pilgrims. Similarities suggest five combinations: Secular Romances, *Fabliaux,* Tales with Satiric Warnings, Religious Romances and Saints' Legends, and Sermons. Within these groups is variety but also commonality of interest. However, before looking at specific tales, it is useful to consider several general characteristics.

The Text and Order of the Tales

Those who study the Middle Ages constantly reiterate the limitations of knowledge about so distant a period; many tangible records have been lost, and the capacity to interpret what survives is further confined by the experience and authority of intervening centuries. This commonplace is especially applicable to *The Canterbury Tales,* a work both compelling and apparently accessible, particularly since it is not heavily didactic as is so much medieval literature. Nevertheless, there are numerous uncertainties, not least identifying a text for *The Canterbury Tales*. Although there are eighty-two manuscripts, the oldest is early fifteenth century, and many come late in the fifteenth century. Thus none was supervised by Chaucer, and there are many textual differences. The first printed text was that of William Caxton in 1478, based on a now-lost manuscript.[2] In practice the beautiful Ellesmere manuscript, Huntington Library El. 26. C 9, is the one most widely used.[3] Its equestrian portraits are the finest pictorial illustrations of the pilgrims and certainly the best known. Placed at the beginnings of individual tales, they show detailed knowledge of the descriptions in the *General Prologue.* The Ellesmere manuscript is one of the earliest copies, probably written by the same scribe responsible for the Hengwrt manuscript, National Library of Wales, Peniarth 392D; both are dated 1400–1410. A lively scholarly discussion centers about the Ellesmere "tales of Caunterbury compiled by Geffrey Chaucer." The precision of the manuscript and regularity of dialect suggest careful editing, so that Hengwrt is regarded by some as closer to Chaucer's original intention. Thus some editors urge Hengwrt's advantages. However, the completeness and careful arranging of Ellesmere make it *The Canterbury Tales* usually preferred.

Such considerations are crucial because the manuscripts are used to determine not only the exact text but also the arrangement of the poem, which survives in a number of fragments (I-X, indicating at least nine breaks) that typically contain internal linking. The poem appears to be an unfinished work; indeed there are early additions in the fifteenth century, *The Tale of Beryn* and Lydgate's prologue to *The Siege of Thebes,* which present the activities of the pilgrims in Canterbury and on the return journey. Different sequences in manuscripts provide several possible orders, and another arrangement has been suggested by references, in the prologues and links between tales, to places along the Pilgrims' Way from London to Canterbury.[4]

The pilgrims meet in Southwark, across the Thames River from London, at the Tabard Inn (I.20), where they spend the night. They get an early start—"whan that day bigan to sprynge" (I.822)—and about two miles along the way they stop at the "Wateryng of Seint

Thomas" (I.826), where the Host proposes they begin a telling of tales. Within the same fragment another reference is made to location, Deptford and Greenwich (I.3905–06), respectively about five and five and a half miles beyond London. This suggests an intention to provide an itinerary for the pilgrims' journey; it is paralleled by another clustering of geographical references at the end of the journey. Having seen the pilgrims depart from their hostelry in the morning (VIII.587), the Canon and his Yeoman overtake them at Boughton under the Blean Forest (VIII.556), which is about five miles from Canterbury. And *The Manciple's Prologue* notes that they have moved through Blean Forest to reach a little town "Bobbe-up-and-doun" (IX.1–3), Harbledown, which is but two miles from Canterbury. Today this is one of the better vantage points on "Canterbury Wey" for a view of the Cathedral. The end of the pilgrimage is signaled in *The Parson's Prologue,* which directly follows the *Manciple's Tale* and gives the time as "Foure of the clokke" and warns that "the sonne wole adoun." (X. 5, 70). In the intervening fragments there are two additional references: Rochester, a midway point, about thirty miles from London, is sighted in the *Monk's Prologue* (VII.1926), and Sittingbourne, which is about forty miles from London, midway between Rochester and Canterbury, is twice referred to by the Summoner. At the end of the *Wife's Prologue* the Summoner promises two tales of friars "er I come to Sidyngborne" (III.847), and he concludes "My tale is doon; we been almoost at towne" (III.2294).

References to places are sometimes combined with the time of day, but this detail is less exact. Traditionally the pilgrimage has been dated 1387, the time when Chaucer was writing the *General Prologue* and a year that would avoid a pilgrimage in Holy Week. Although initially only "Aprill" (I.1) is specified, a scheme has been worked out for a four-day journey of sixty miles, the normal time taken by horseback. The most precise reference is in the *Man of Law's Prologue:* ten o'clock on April 18 (II.5–6, 14). In this mimetic reading assembly occurs on the evening of April 16, early departure on the morning of April 17, a somewhat uncharted April 19 but for a reference to "prime"; finally a cluster of references for April 20—both to early morning, when the Canon and Yeoman catch the pilgrims who have gone only five miles (VIII.555, 584–592), and the Cook is not awake (IX. 4–19), and again to four o'clock as the last tale is begun (X.5). Alternatively, a symbolic single day may be the intention.

The reversal of the positions of Rochester and Sittingbourne is the basis of arguments for an order other than Ellesmere. By emphasizing the incompleteness of *The Canterbury Tales,* one can argue that there would have been revisions to make the central links as consistent as the opening and closing. The Wife of Bath, for example, begins her long *Prologue* without an invitation from the Host, and the *Physician's Tale* occurs without prologue or link. Alternately, one can give less weight to a "realistic" scheme of pilgrimage, so that one inconsistency does not warrant change from the order of the superior Ellesmere manuscript.

The two orders most favored can be shown in parallel columns:

Ellesmere			Chaucer Society, Skeat with "Bradshaw shift"
Fragment I	Group A	General Prologue, Knight, Miller, Reeve, Cook	I. A
II	B[1]	Man of Law	II. B[1]
III	D	Wife, Friar, Summoner	VII. B[2]
IV	E	Clerk, Merchant	VI. C
V	F	Squire, Franklin	III. D
VI	C	Physician, Pardoner	IV. E
VII	B[2]	Shipman, Prioress, Sir Thopas, Melibee, Monk, Nun's Priest	V. F
VIII	G	Second Nun, Canon's Yeoman	VIII. G
IX	H	Manciple	IX. H
X	I	Parson	X. I

Collections of Tales and Framing

Collections of stories were very popular in the Middle Ages. The earliest come from the East, an Egyptian fragment that is sixteen or eighteen centuries before Christ, and two very popular framed collections from India, *The Seven Sages* (fifth century) and the *Arabian Nights* (tenth century) that were widely known in medieval Europe. Many collections filled a didactic purpose: to provide inspiring lives of the saints as in the *Legenda Aurea* (c.1280) or *South English Legendary* (c.1300), or enriching examples for sermons, like the fourteenth-century *Gesta Romanorum,* which conclude with a moral but are also often quite worldly. Chaucer's friend and fellow poet John Gower in his *Confessio Amantis* (1390) uses stories to illustrate Genius's instruction to the author-lover. Italian literature, much admired and a strong influence on Chaucer, is distinguished for its *novelle*, short pieces of fiction. A large number were collected by Chaucer's contemporary Giovanni Sercambi (1347–1424), who was imitating Giovanni Boccaccio's *Decameron* (1348–53) but also introduces a pilgrimagelike frame and varied social classes. Sercambi probably wrote after Chaucer rather than before. Centuries earlier, Latin authors, notably Ovid in the *Metamorphoses,* which Chaucer knew well, had collected stories. There is, in short, no need to seek examples of collected stories as a precedent for *The Canterbury Tales,* since collections were widespread. Chaucer himself had earlier combined stories in *The Legend of Good Women* and in the *Monk's Tale,* written before the *General Prologue.*

Chaucer's admiration and use of Boccaccio's other works, the brilliance of the *Decameron* and similarities of frame, make it the most often cited analogue. There are, however, significant differences, and a brief comparison shows Chaucer's originality. Boccaccio's stories are all told by young aristocrats, initially seven young women and then three young men, who flee from plague in Florence, accompanied by four maidservants and three menservants. The stories are told at two palaces and a garden, not on the road, and other entertainment is singing and dancing. Not every day is devoted to story telling; the group is absent for two weeks, and there are ten days of stories, a total of one hundred, the perfect number used for the number of cantos in Dante's *Divine Comedy.* In the *Decameron* different persons preside over the story telling sessions, for each of which there is a set topic. There are some intervening links, including a quarrel between servants, who are not given an opportunity to tell stories.

Chaucer establishes his framework in the *General Prologue,* which is 858 lines in length; it has always been enthusiastically praised but variously interpreted. There are two essential parts: (1) an explanation of a pilgrimage to Canterbury and agreement to make story telling a part of the journey and (2) descriptions of the pilgrims. The opening 42 lines and the concluding 144 lines frame the central 672 lines, which—apart from 5 lines of narrative summary (I.163–64, 542–45)—describe the individual pilgrims, who are identified by the work that they do in society and only occasionally given personal names. This epitomizes the feature most commonly recognized in Chaucer's presentation, a combination of the typical and individual. Similarly, the spring invocation and statement about pilgrimage with which the poem begins are both conventional and made particular by Chaucer.

The time of year is April, identified as a period of change, specifically the occasion for rain after drought. This cyclic occurrence is reinterpreted by T. S. Eliot in *The Waste Land* (1922), probably the most famous modern poem, in the opening line "April is the cruellest month" because it is a time of awakening. For Chaucer the circumstances are transforming, a time of natural resurgence, marked by the greening of plants and singing of birds, signs of spirits energized. The human response is simply and emphatically stated: "Thanne longen folk to goon on pilgrimages" (I.12). The word *pilgrim* comes from French *pelegrin*, which derives from Latin *peregrinus*, meaning both stranger and traveler. There is, then, an interest in physical journey; a trip is made from London to Canterbury. More elemental is the idea of a pilgrimage of life, the basic metaphor of spiritual quest, a traveling in the self prompted by the sense of foreignness that comes for the believing person because of being in the world yet seeking the divine. This need is intensified by spiritual dryness, a metaphor favored by mystics, and evoked by the opening lines of *The Canterbury Tales*. Chaucer's indebtedness for the spring invocation has, of course, also been identified as the rhetorical tradition of the Mediterranean, basic to medieval literary expression. Close correspondences to specific works have been suggested, especially a passage in Book IV of Guido delle Colonne's *Historia Destructionis Troiae* (1287), the principal medieval source for the Troy legend, used by Chaucer in his *Troilus and Criseyde*. Similarly, records of climate indicate that March was a dry month in late-fourteenth-century England, a dramatic change from many extraordinarily wet years experienced early in the century. Thus the opening verse paragraph supports several alternative interpretations: poetic style, realistic observation, and spiritual metaphor.

Pilgrimage

Pilgrimages are familiar both as idea and as event in the Middle Ages. Pilgrimages, of course, antedate the Latin word and are not limited to Christendom. Benares has been a holy place for Hindus for more than three thousand years, and Mecca is Islam's holy place. Jerusalem is sought by Jews, Christians, and Moslems. Chaucer's Pardoner has come directly from Rome, and the Wife of Bath has visited not only Rome but also Jerusalem three times; in addition, she has journeyed to the other great pilgrim sites, Compostela in Spain, Cologne in Germany, as well as the less-important Boulogne in France. In the early Middle Ages physical journeys were recognized, particularly by Irish and English missionaries in the seventh and eighth centuries, as a way to spiritual improvement, typically a withdrawal or exile with a hope for redemption. By the twelfth century people increasingly thought of life as a pilgrimage, a seeking and journeying rather than merely enduring the hardness of life.[5] Pilgrimages also had significant economic impact, enriching the religious houses and towns adjacent to shrines. Offerings, payments for accommodations, and sales of mementos like pilgrim badges enriched local resources.[6] The fourteenth century is the great age of pilgrimage narratives, of which more than five hundred survive from the period 1100–1500. Chaucer, then, chose for his framework a rich metaphor and popular experience.

In England pilgrims went to Canterbury, where Thomas à Becket, the Archbishop, was murdered in the Cathedral on December 29, 1170, by four knights of King Henry II who thought they were carrying out the wishes of a ruler exasperated by the piety of Becket, Henry's former chancellor and appointee who unexpectedly championed the Church. Canterbury, already established from the late sixth century as the Church's see in Britain, thus acquired a special aura. In Christianity pilgrimages are connected with relics and bodies of saints. The cult of the saints developed after the fall of the Roman Empire as a means of joining temporal and eternal. Graves of saints became centers of piety in Late Antiquity, and the custom developed astonishingly, embraced by all levels of society and education.[7] This breadth of appeal was sustained on religious pilgrimages, an occasion when the usual distinctions of class and sex did not matter, as we see with Chaucer's pilgrims. At shrines miracles are associated with the saints, about whom collections of stories developed. A miracle was thought to be a part of the City of God on earth and was an integral part of life. A significant number of thirteenth-century stained glass windows in Canterbury Cathedral tell stories of miracles performed by St. Thomas, who also can be seen in windows at Coutances in Normandy.

"The Miracles of St. Thomas Becket" are the largest collection in the Middle Ages. Over seven hundred miracles are recorded in official accounts, kept by two monks, Benedict and William, during the first fifteen years after his death. Devotion and miracles were not confined locally; his shrine became dominant, indeed comparable with Rome and the Holy Sepulchre at Jerusalem in attracting pilgrims. The moment of Thomas's being struck down in his own cathedral, an act that scandalized Christendom, is preserved in manuscript illuminations and on many beautiful enameled reliquaries, the craft of Limoges. Such internationalism was unusual. The first to seek the tomb, after the monks opened it for devotion, were the poor. However, prosperous and prominent people soon came; indeed miracles are recorded more often for them, perhaps because the poor were less articulate or had not the means to memorialize. Almost immediately pilgrims came from all over Europe, already having experienced the power of St. Thomas. His popularity was increased by use of relics—especially "water" into which a little of his blood had been added and bits of his clothing—away from the shrine. Quickly throughout Europe festivals were introduced and churches dedicated to St. Thomas, who within a year was recognized as one of the three greatest saints in England (along with Cuthbert and Godric). Chaucer mentions only the most frequent miracle, the power of healing by the "hooly blisful martir," who helps when folk are "seeke" (sick, I.17). So great was his influence that the shrine even recorded an occasional failure, a cure not being achieved. Thomas à Becket began, then, as the most traditional center of a cult, a martyr venerated at the place of his death. In 1173 he was canonized, with extraordinary rapidity even by twelfth-century standards. In 1174 King Henry II was a public penitent at the tomb, and the invading king of Scotland was captured at the moment he completed the penance. Canterbury quickly became a place of pilgrimage to which thousands flocked, including Chaucer's "sondry folk." Pilgrims numbered two-hundred thousand annually in the fourteenth century, when the magnificent cathedral was enlarged by the addition of the finest Gothic nave in England to accommodate the crowds seeking cures, forgiveness, and salvation, but also the pleasures of the journey. One of the best descriptions of Becket's shrine at Canterbury was written by Erasmus, when he visited in 1510, a century after Chaucer's death. In 1520 King Henry VIII accompanied his nephew and guest Emperor Charles V to the shrine; this was the year before the pope named Henry "Defender of the Faith" because of his opposition to Luther. But in 1538 Henry VIII ordered the destruction of the shrine as part of the Reformation.[8] The gifts of pilgrims, jewels, and precious metals offered through four centuries, required twenty-six carts to be hauled away. These details suggest something of the strength of the idea of pilgrimage and its practical consequences in the Middle Ages and its subsequent relative demise. Nevertheless, the powerful appeal of the pilgrimage persists, albeit allegorized for an autobiographical and spiritual guide in which the journey is interiorized.

John Bunyan's *The Pilgrim's Progress* (1678) is a great Protestant work second only to the Bible in popularity, translated into more than a hundred languages.

The Pilgrims

In the *General Prologue* the first pilgrim mentioned is the narrator. Chaucer's personae are of great interest; pilgrim, poet, and man have been distinguished, and indeed the "I" of the poem is certainly the most elusive and intriguing figure. Several characteristics are noted in the opening: he is making the pilgrimage "with ful devout courage" (spirit, feelings, I.22), which does not mean ascetic withdrawal. By nightfall he has spoken to every one of the twenty-nine pilgrims assembled by chance at the Tabard and quickly become "of their fellowship." Further, he has spent this time in observation, for he is prepared to tell the circumstances, social class, and dress of each. Thus the initial framing concludes, and Chaucer proceeds with the large central section in which the other pilgrims are introduced. When all have been presented, the "I" of the poem resumes his self-portrait. He claims a systematic account truly rendered (I.715–16), promises to tell how they behaved, but then interrupts courteously with an *apologia* in which he explains his role in the poem: he will tell each tale as he heard it, not altering the language, however "rudelich" and "large" the account. This disclaimer has several characteristics: the pilgrim "I" assumes control but notes his limitations; he is reporter, not creator, of the stories; constrictions of language will not be allowed, and fastidiousness is eschewed. Christ and Plato, Christian and pagan, are cited as authorities to justify this attempt at accuracy. These are high claims for story telling; however, claims are immediately muted by an apology for already erring in not citing the proper "degree" (social rank, I.744) for each pilgrim; "My wit is short" (I.746). Nevertheless, pilgrim Chaucer does not lack discrimination and appreciation, since he notes that they ate the best food and were pleased to drink the best wine (I.748–750). The discretion of the pilgrim narrator is further developed by counterpointing his humility to the self-assertiveness of the Host.

With the Host, whose name "Herry Bailly" is given by the Cook in his *Prologue* (I.4358), Chaucer's emphasis becomes very much of this world. A "bailly" is a steward, manager of affairs. The Host is the first person to speak directly; he illustrates immediately the qualities of the narrator's observation, "Boold of his speche, and wys, and wel ytaught" (I.755). His manner is hearty, and he has devised a plan that assures his personal advantage. Identifying the assembled company as "myrie," he flatters them by first acknowledging their religious intent in making the pilgrimage, but then quickly makes the practical observation that a long journey to Canterbury would be tedious without some kind of amusement. His proposal, of course, is that they tell tales; this is immediately acceptable, not even requiring discussion before consent (I.784, 817). Harry Bailly next offers a specific plan: each pilgrim is to tell two tales on the outward journey and two on the return; a prize will be given—a supper at the Tabard, paid for by the other pilgrims, and a profitable business for the Host's Tabard Inn. The Host's contribution will be to accompany the group as a guide—at his own cost (I.804)—and to serve as judge. Another rule is that anyone who gainsays his judgment "Shal paye al that we spenden by the weye" (I.806). The limitations of such commercial interests are clear at the end; the pilgrims finish not in a tavern but at the cathedral with its shrine. Nevertheless, there is a strong case for authority and obedience, a medieval sense of order, since the narrator notes that the pilgrims' decision to comply is unanimous, and he restates the terms of the agreement to which all "swear oaths." Thus the enterprise begins harmoniously, and the evening at the Tabard concludes with a last drink and early rest. This tone carries over to the next day, albeit reinforced by the Host's reiteration of the obligation of vows and costs of rebellion (I.833–34). The drawing of lots is a practical device, but also a comment on established social hierarchy; the Knight is first, then the Prioress, followed by the Clerk. Ordinarily, in the Middle Ages, clerical figures would come first and women last, whatever their occupation. Chaucer's ordering suggests an alternative hierarchy: secular chivalry, with its concomitant respect for women, and a respect for learning, even if the person is materially impoverished. Some of these values are discernible in Chaucer's other works, but the choice was made by the Host. At least in the judging of stories, which are the present occasion, Harry Bailly identifies himself as an orthodox critic. The prize will go to the one that tells "Tales of best sentence and moost solaas" (I.798), that is, those that combine meaning with pleasure. The Host is, then, "prudent," for all his superficial worldliness. Nevertheless, he is overly ambitious; thirty pilgrims would tell 120 tales. Unlike the narrator, the Host fails to recognize human limitations. Alternatively, the large number of pilgrims is necessary to show a full range of society, and one of Chaucer's concerns is precisely that. His selection of characters, their exclusively English nationality, argues the poet's interest in analyzing that social world. Further, he presents an alternative to many values long held, just as he explores "gentilesse" (nobility of birth/rank and of character) in several tales and a lyric. The *General Prologue* concludes with a statement of order, the falling of the lots, so that the Knight is the first to tell a tale, just as he is the first to be reported in the portraits.

Chaucer presents the portraits in a lively manner. The verse form, imitated from French models, is five-stress lines in rhyming couplets that are arranged in verse paragraphs, varying in length from nine to sixty-two lines, but averaging thirty lines. The poetry has a fine flexibility because Middle English allows more light syllables, most notably the sounding of final -e and -ed endings. The use of verse paragraphs, rather than a stanza pattern, suggests conversation. This effect is supported by casual phrases like "I trowe," "I gesse," "I telle," "I woot," "I seyde," that allow, indeed encourage, the audience to respond thoughtfully. The narrator thus also contrasts himself with the authoritarian stance of the Host. This could reflect Chaucer's own social circumstances, a highly talented civil servant and gifted poet but not a noble at court. Although everything is being presented through his observation—and Chaucer the poet is writing *The Canterbury Tales* —there are disclaimers of control. There is a point of view, but there are also humble qualifications to avoid its imposition. Each pilgrim is presented in a single verse paragraph, which encourages a pause and response before moving to the next; the briefest account is of the Cook and the longest of the Friar. The effect of the form is to evoke the experience of meeting a large group of strangers: register a first impression and then perhaps speculate a bit about the person. But the details provided offer much more. Like the spring invocation, the portraits are deeply rooted in several literary traditions.

The most obvious point about the pilgrims is that they are identified by their work. Usual first questions upon meeting someone today are: What is your name? and What do you do? The implied distinction was not so obvious in the fourteenth century. Interestingly, some of the earliest and most common English surnames—Smith, Tyler, Mason, Thatcher—are simply statements of work done and reflect the growth of the building trades in late medieval England. Chaucer's own name, as noted, suggests an older family occupation of shoemaker, but there is no evidence for this. In short, a person's work is crucial in self-definition, both the development of personality and a perception of the world. A commonplace of medieval social structure is a tripartite division into clerics, nobles/warriors, and peasants. These categories are clear in England at least as early as King Alfred's translation of Boethius in the ninth century. However, this ordering of society was never adequate as a practical comment on social life; it was an ideal way of defining functions: prayer and ministry to spiritual needs; protection of the weak, upholding justice and the Church; and providing for physical needs through toiling on the land. Chaucer's pilgrims include a Parson, a Knight, and a Plowman—significantly, all among the idealized figures—but the greatest number do not fit easily into the threefold categories, any more than did Chaucer himself.[9] Nevertheless, thinking about the *General Prologue* as a comment on the conditions of society is crucial; Chaucer directs the reader when the narrator concludes his portraits by saying that he has given briefly the "estaat" (I.716) of the assembled company. An indebtedness of the *General Prologue* to "estates satire" has been cogently argued.[10]

The pilgrims can be arranged in several groupings; one combines estate, quality, and work: (1) nobility—Knight and Squire, with Yeoman; (2) religious—Prioress, Monk, Friar, Nun, Nun's Priest; (3) middle class, largest group—Clerk, Merchant, Sergeant of Law, Franklin, Guildsmen, Physician, Wife of Bath, Chaucer the pilgrim; (4) lower orders, but ideals—Parson and Plowman; (5) rogues—Reeve, Miller, Manciple, Summoner, Pardoner, Cook, and Shipman.

Chaucer's interest in the world is expressed through his showing what people do, but he omits a judgment of the effects of their work that is typical in estates satires. The response of many readers is an acute awareness of how the descriptions seem to express and certainly evoke continually shifting attitudes. This can be identified as tension between instinctive emotional reactions and rationalized moral judgments; there is no simply positive or negative way. Like Shakespeare in *Measure for Measure*, Chaucer follows the Gospel text: "Judge not that ye be not judged" (Matthew 7:1–5). Nevertheless, there is one repeated judgment. Just as the narrator qualifies and defers, shying away from assertiveness, when describing his own responses, so the individual portraits often express opposition to self-importance and pompousness. An obvious example is the Sergeant of the Law: "Nowher so bisy a man as he ther nas, / And yet he semed bisier than he was" (I.321–22). These lines illustrate

Chaucer's technique of introducing a sudden thrust, a startling shift, that alters the incipient judgment of the reader/hearer. The governing value is explicit in a line describing the Parson, identified as a good priest: "He *waited after no pompe and †reverence" (*expected, †ceremony, I.525).

Just as a pilgrim is identified by his work, so a focus on a single quality is one technique of Chaucer's portraiture. The Parson's priestliness, the Pardoner's hypocrisy, the Friar's wantonness are examples. Sometimes a picture is exaggerated, as in the repetition of "worthy" to describe the Knight, or the extraordinary "delight" that defines the Franklin. Or a portrait is built with conglomerate detail, as with the Monk where facts are piled up in disordered fashion. Chaucer adds interest to some pilgrims by identifying those traveling together: the five Guildsmen, who really stand as one, and their Cook; the Knight, Squire, and Yeoman entourage; another family group, the Parson and his brother the Plowman; the Prioress and her attendants, and the unsavory pairing of the Pardoner and Summoner. Others, like the Wife, Shipman, and Physician travel alone. For most of the pilgrims Chaucer blends physical description with details about character. Often physiognomy comes from the authority of medieval science, as with the Wife's gap-tooth, the Pardoner's waxlike yellow hair, or the Reeve's small legs—all signs with sexual meaning. The conjunction of planets is given to show influence upon behavior. In addition, Chaucer provides interaction of the pilgrims as they proceed on the pilgrimage.

Dramatic Interplay and Authorial Suggestions

The Prologues, Links, and Epilogues make a kind
has led many readers to focus attention on the
tale and an idea of dramatic pilgrimage in *Th*
Others have objected to this interpreta
ization is limited, flat rather than rou
social interaction and audience resp
portions, so that it is useful to ex
poem. As indicated in the pre
tales, not all of the fragments
related, there is a variet
formal courtesy towar
and prior acquainta
justification, mor

As exemplar of the noble estate of warriors the Knight both tells the first tale, appropriately about chivalry but also philosophical, and provokes the initial attempt to "quite" (pay back, revenge) through story telling. With the Miller's challenging response, Chaucer establishes a tension between ideal and mundane, exemplified through the contrasting genres of romance and *fabliau,* of "worthy" and "churlish" pilgrims, that recurs. The Knight does not participate in the lively and aggressive exchanges that follow his tale. Indeed his interventions are as a peacemaker. He forces the reconciliation of the Pardoner and the Host after a violent exchange of personal insult (VI.941–68), and he saves the company from the tedium of the Monk's long series of tragedies (VII.2767). The latter is a double example of concern with hierarchy, since the Monk belongs to a respected way of religious life in an older tradition and offers a tale of falls from high place. The usually aggressive Host is forced to "kiss" and make up; briefly lacking command, he is reduced to reiterating the need for an end of the Monk's tragedies, so that he can resume control of the story telling. The Knight's authority prevails.

A parallel to the Knight's intervention is that of the Parson, who

"Straw for your gentillesse!" (695), rejecting high sentiment and style, or at least the Franklin's attempts at a higher social level.

Further deference to social class comes with the Host's courteous request that the Prioress tell a tale (VII.446). The comment is brief and recognizes her womanliness as much as her work as the leader of a group of religious women. This suggestion neatly refers back to the duality of the Prioress's description in the *General Prologue.* In addition, the remark comes at the conclusion of the *Shipman's Tale,* an exposure of a monk's dishonest behavior that provokes the Host's warning against monks. Indeed one of the strongest themes in the linking material is the Host's lack of respect for the pilgrims who are members of religious communities, particularly his antagonism to clerical celibacy.

The Host's pressing remarks to the pilgrim Monk make clear his opposition. Although he asks the Monk to follow the Knight with a tale (I.3116–19), it is the Miller who "quites" the first tale. When the Monk is later recognized, there is no polite deference. Developing the *General Prologue*'s description of him as a man committed to hunting and wearing fine clothes, the Host heartily notes the Monk's fine physique and sexual potentiality (VII.1943–62), and his brief disclaimer of "pleye" and "game" does not offset the intensity of the remarks. One of Chaucer's neatest strokes of contrast is to follow the Host's long and aggressive harangue with a gentle response, "This worthy Monk took al in pacience" (1965). The tragedies that follow urge patient acceptance, but their number exceeds the patience of the pilgrims in listening and Chaucer thus both amuses and challenges an easy response.

The fullness of this dramatic interaction is contrasted with the Host's modest request that the Nun's Priest, for whom no description is given in the *General Prologue,* tell something to gladden the company. Chaucer, then, introduces one of his most brilliant tales with no fanfare and a modest comment identifying Sir John as "this sweete preest . . . this goodly man" (2820). Much of the tale's power comes from the contrast between its brilliance and the pedestrian recitation of tragedies that it follows and "quites." The tale can be read as a revelation of its teller's personality, but the prologue does not assist such interpretation. However, the Epilogue (preserved in only a few manuscripts but generally accepted) returns to the Host's explicit commentary on the sexuality of celibates.

The grossest example is the Host's insulting reply when the Pardoner, after an extraordinary self-exposure of duplicity and cupidity, attempts to sell him relics (VI.946–55). Harry Bailly's comments to the Monk and to the Nun's Priest may be seen as teasing, albeit with a hard edge, and perhaps even compliment; to the Pardoner he is vicious and threatening. Castration, not robust sexual experience, is what he wishes for the Pardoner, who is thus silenced. The Host's preoccupation with sexuality is not a subject of high sentiment, but typically an occasion of human failure.

Set against his statements about aggressive masculinity are remarks that show an uneasiness about women; more specifically his own situation as a husband whose wife is not as tractable as he would like. After the *Clerk's Tale* of patient Griselda, the Host exclaims that he wishes his wife had heard the "legend . . . a gentil tale" (IV.1212_a–1212_g). Similarly, he wishes that "Goodelief" had heard Chaucer's *Tale of Melibee,* in which the wife Prudence is a model of "pacience" (VII.1889–96). This is followed by a lively description of his own wife's behavior that ranges from energetic participation in the beating of his employees, to a resentment of her calling him coward, to a fear that she will murder him someday (1917). The Host here develops the earlier picture of his wife in the *Epilogue of the Merchant's Tale,* where after decrying women for their deceitfulness, he calls his wife "a labbyng shrew" (blabbing, IV.2428). This, of course, is not as extreme as the view of the Merchant, married only two months, that his shrewish wife could defeat the devil himself (1219–20). The Host just says his wife is guilty of a heap of other vices, so that he wishes he were not wed. From irritation he has progressed to paranoia, and the admissions provide a gloss on his own aggressive exercise of authority over the pilgrims. The man's tension is made explicit when he is moved by the *Physician's Tale* of Virginia, slain by her father to save her from ravishment, a deed of male authority as well as an example of pious martyrdom. The Host says that her youthful beauty, a gift of Fortune and nature, led to her death. (VI.294–97). At this point, his pity and stress are acknowledged by a need for drink before going on to another tale.

Thus the fullest dramatic articulation of a negative view of women, very much tied to their sexuality, comes through the Host. However, it is initiated by the Miller, who insists upon a reversal of the Knight's idealism. This is the way of the "cherl." Although the Miller in his *Prologue* admits there are good wives, his carpenter and wife are introduced as participants in a tale of cuckoldry (I.3141–43, 3151–66), and he begins a sequence of three tales with increasingly unpleasant sexuality. The Reeve's "quyting" includes remarks about male impotence and old age and lacks the robust energy of the *Miller's Tale.* Its very unpleasantness so excites the Cook that he "clawed him on the bak" (I.4326) and introduces a "tale of a hostileer" (4360) that begins with an unsavory environment and a prostitute as principal. This is an obvious jab at the Host, who gets his own revenge when he later warns the Manciple of the Cook's thievery and treachery (IX. 69–75). The *Cook's Tale* is broken off, and there are no links to explain. However, the rivalry between pilgrims is the strongest interest in these dramatic interludes, and Chaucer repeats such competitiveness and animosity in two other pairings.

Like the Miller and the Reeve, the Friar and Summoner are tied by profession, for they are rivals for souls and money. The competition between mendicants and secular clergy was long standing, from the mid-thirteenth century when new religious orders developed to serve in cities, and centers on who has the right to hear confessions. The confrontation of these two pilgrims is carefully prepared. It begins as an interruption of the Wife of Bath, when the Friar laughs at her long *Prologue;* the Summoner objects, the Friar promises to tell a tale against summoners, and the Summoner counters that he will tell tales against friars (III.829–49). The Host intervenes, so that the *Wife's Tale* can begin. Attempts to mitigate their animosity have limited success, for the Friar is still lowering when his *Prologue* begins (III.1266). He briefly deflects his attention to the Wife, referring her exploration of authority to a clerical, school debate, but quickly returning to his attack on summoners. The Host urges him to behave courteously, but the Summoner welcomes a provocation against which he can retaliate. Again the structure is to have one tale repay another. Nevertheless, the Summoner gets more than he expected so that he rises up in his stirrups, shaking like an aspen leaf "for ire" (III.1665–67). In this fury he attacks friars, placing them in hell with fiends, more specifically under Satan's tail. This is powerful dramatic interplay, but it is inconclusive, since there is no epilogue or link after the *Summoner's Tale.*

Other treatments of rivalry are not so thoroughly developed. There is no indication that the two men were personally acquainted, as were the Miller and Reeve, and their professional antipathy thus appears sufficient cause. Subtle arguments can be advanced about the Nun's Priest; he echoes a line ("Mordre wol out" VII.576 and 3052) from the *Prioress's Tale* and tells a tale of a cock and hens, but there is no overt confrontation. He also tells a mock heroic version of a tragic fall as a reply to the Monk. These connections, however, depend upon reading the tales, not the links.

Chaucer's most repeated device for initiating confrontation is to have the pilgrims drink beyond their capacity. This is signaled in the first fragment; the Miller "for dronken was al pale" (I.3120), so that he can scarcely remain in the saddle, and he speaks in Pilate's voice, with the loudness of a performer in a mystery play. The friction between the Cook and Manciple begins because the Cook is asleep in the saddle (IX.5–15). Although alternative explanations are possible, his falling from the horse and incapacity to rise without assistance (44–55), as well as his pale hue and stinking, enforce the Manciple's judgment. The Cook's drunkenness is proven by the eagerness and skill with which he downs the draft of wine offered by the Manciple. Indeed the Host, obviously a seller of drink, praises it as a way of achieving accord. There is, then, a little drama of drunkenness, shown both as loud aggressiveness and as stupor. A more complicated experience is that of the Pardoner, whose tale of the three rioters contains a tavern scene and drinking habits. The Pardoner is introduced in the *General Prologue* with his loud singing, a sign of drunkenness; when he interrupts the *Wife's Prologue*, she remarks upon his drinking (III.170–71). He seems to drink to embolden himself; his extraordinary self-exposure is preceded by an *Introduction* that has two statements that he must have his ale (VI.322, 3228), and the *Prologue* notes that he is ready because he has "dronke a draughte of corny ale" (VI.456–62).

Elaborate dramatic action involving the Pardoner and the Wife is appropriate because their prologues are unusually long and self-revealing, respectively 134 and 828 lines. Each candidly presents a biographical account by which Chaucer whets an appetite for even greater knowledge of the personalities of the speakers. Not surprisingly, these two pilgrims have elicited more speculation than any others. The Pardoner has been called "the most abandoned character among the Canterbury Pilgrims,"[14] a critical judgment that suggests divine knowledge. The Wife of Bath is often named, along with Shakespeare's Falstaff, the greatest comic character in English literature. Their tales are similarly esteemed: the Pardoner's as a first great short story in English and the Wife's as a fairy tale, the first piece of children's literature.

Both prologues can be described as examples of a medieval form of confession, for the speakers admit and describe their actions. However, neither is expressing penitence nor a resolve to amend a life misspent; the intent seems to be self-vindication. The Wife describes her five marriages, explaining how she manipulated the men but also revealing something of her own frustration and unhappiness, and she voices objections to the Church's view of marriage and chastity. The Pardoner explains his techniques as a preacher, which include exploiting both his considerable skills as speaker and storyteller and the credulity of an audience desperate for some reassurance of salvation. He also illustrates these skills through his denouncing of familiar tavern sins—gambling, gluttony, blasphemy. A simplification of their confessions is to use the medieval designations of the Seven Deadly Sins; the Wife declares her "luxurie" (lust, III.28, 45–46, etc.), and the Pardoner admits his avarice (VI.446–51). However, both Prologues go beyond any personal revelation. The Wife's opening lines pose a debate between authority and experience (1–2), an intellectual and theological subject as the Pardoner's calling her "a noble prechour" (165) explicitly recognizes. At the end of her tale, the Friar reiterates that "autoritees" belong to "prechyng and to scoles of clergye" (1276–77) and notes that she has presented matter appropriate for university debate (1271–72). The Wife's text is "wo that is in marriage" (3), and modern critics generally agree that there is a group of tales (the number included varies) that address the idea of marriage from various points of view.[15] Thus a university debate continues. The broad issue raised by the Pardoner is more exclusively theological and moral. While admitting his own duplicity, lack of belief in what he preaches and in the indulgences and fraudulent relics he sells, the Pardoner yet argues that he can do good, since a vicious man can tell a moral tale (VI.459–60). Guilty in his own sins, he can still lead others to repentance; confession is not invalid because the priest lacks grace. In other words, the sinful condition of someone who holds a religious office does not invalidate the good that he inspires and the forgiveness that comes through his office but from God. Since the occasion is story telling, the relation between the moral nature of the teller and the morality of the tale is also a crucial literary issue, as will be later noted.

Through the Wife of Bath and the Pardoner Chaucer poses some of the most difficult questions for formal religion. Particularly significant in the fourteenth-century context of abuses in the Church are issues of a necessary distinction between failures of the institutions of organized religion and the needs and desires of the person seeking union with God. It is necessary to remember this context while recognizing also the extraordinary complexity of Chaucer's creation of the self-revelation of the Wife and Pardoner. Examples of "literary confession," these texts anticipate stream of consciousness in the novel and provide a rich basis for modern psychological analysis. Always a critical challenge, the Wife has never been more thoroughly analyzed than in the last twenty years with the advent of formal feminist criticism, and the Pardoner's sexual nature has also become increasingly a subject of discussion as definitions are sought.

The fascination evoked through self-revelation is clear by a brief noting of the relative lack of interest in the other long distinctive dramatic link, the *Canon's Yeoman's Prologue.* A hurried arrival of two additional pilgrims enlivens the dramatic framing of *The Canterbury Tales.* In this late development—the pilgrims are only about five miles from their objective (VIII.556)—Chaucer repeats some of the techniques of earlier links, notably a confrontation between two who are professionally tied. The innovation is the exposure of the Canon's craft by his Yeoman, who not only describes something of his master's alchemy, but quickly establishes its quality by reference to the disreputable suburbs in which they dwell and through the hellfire imagery (666, 705). The Yeoman's telling of trade secrets provokes the Canon's attempt to stop the slander (695), and when he realizes that the Yeoman will make a long confession, he "fledde awey for verray sorwe and shame" (701). The *Canon's Yeoman's Tale,* then, becomes an analogue of the *Pardoner's Prologue* and *Tale,* for it is a revelation of professional craft and secrets. A difference is the subordinate role of the person confessing, one who has served a worldly master rather than himself initiating the procedures and practice of deception. Because it explores ideas about knowledge and its uses, the *Canon's Yeoman's Tale* is related to the Wife's questioning of authority, one of Chaucer's main interests.

A number of references have been made to learning and moral purpose as well as to merriment; these can now be brought together by looking at ways in which Chaucer the pilgrim addresses such ideas, especially in relation to literature. Having established in the portraits of the *General Prologue* how complicated and diverse are the details of appearance that can be perceived about persons, Chaucer goes on to consider what is told. The critical issue is introduced in the *Miller's Prologue* , when the drunken Miller insists he will "quite" the *Knight's Tale* and the narrator anticipates that his will be a "cherles tale" (I.3169). In the *General Prologue* (I.725–46) Chaucer offered an *apologia,* casting himself as a recorder and reporter of exactly what is said. His texts were justified, however disconcerting, as an attempt to avoid being "untrewe" (735), and his authorities were Plato and Christ, classical and scriptural models. Here he extends definition of his role with an explanation and defense of variety in *The Canterbury Tales* (I.3167). First, there is an acceptance of the circumstance of not being able to stop a drunken aggressor. Then a case is made for accurate recording, a rendering of what was said in the words of each speaker. This is, on the one hand, part of the dramatic verisimilitude of the link; it is also a plea that all voices be heard, a broadening of the scope of literature to include more than the obviously acceptable. The breadth includes both social class and moral import. The rationale for tolerance is threefold: there is variety—"storial thyng that touchest gentilesse, / And eek moralitee and hoolynesse" (3179–80) as well as "harlotrie"; any tale can be ignored—"Turne over the leef and chese another tale" (3177); and a plea is made to understand authorial intention by specifically recognizing a principle of play—"Men shal nat maken ernest of game" (3186). The last point is resumed in the *Reeve's Prologue* when the audience's response is specified; people laugh, then they show their differences by their various comments, but mostly they laugh. The exception is the Reeve, who introduces a serious note through comments about old age and failing potency. This is labeled "sermonyng" by the narrator (3989), and the Host argues against a tendency to "speke alday of hooly writ" (3902). Nevertheless, the Reeve's final words refer to scripture, with the figure of "stalke" (piece of straw) and "Balke" (beam). Echoing Matthew 7:1–5, this passage counsels against judging others, since all are sinners. The Reeve, of course, does not forbear; he not only exercises the judging that he argues against, but also he rates his own fault as the lesser and the Miller's the greater. Although the emphasis shifts, an idea of critical debate is reiterated in the *Cook's Prologue,* in the midst of Roger/Hogge of Ware's excited delight in the bawdy tale. This comes from two phrases, "a sharp conclusion / Upon his argument," which means a proposition derived from disputation, and a reference to "Salomon in his langage" that connotes wisdom and the importance of language (4328–30).

Chaucer's place in a debate about tales is reviewed in the *Introduction to the Man of Law's Tale* (II.46–89) in a substantial comment on his "rymes." They are so numerous, albeit limited in poetic skills, that the Man of Law is hard pressed to think of a suitable tale not told by Chaucer. The twofold interest is in style and matter.

Chaucer is identified as one who knows little about meters and rhyming but who has done the best he can in the English of long ago—a suggestion of the poet's choice away from French that was favored at the court after the Norman Conquest (47–50). Then follows a reiteration that Chaucer has written a great deal about lovers, more than to be found in Ovid. The Man of Law names worthy women included in Chaucer's *Legend of Good Women* and in the *Monk's Tale,* as well as *The Book of the Duchess*. In contrast, Chaucer has avoided tales of Canace and Apollonius of Tyre, which both include incest. Here is greater emphasis on subject matter than style. Chaucer's substantial productivity is recognized, and this provokes a question of originality for the Man of Law. Since all of the characters named are familiar ones, a use of traditional material is assumed. This suggests that the way of story telling is a basis for judgment, even if elements of rhyme and meter are not emphasized. Finally, the Man of Law says that he got his tale from a merchant. This choice, rather than a courtly or clerical source, evokes the strength of lay literacy, an educated middle and professional class to which Chaucer belonged.

Another specific naming of Chaucer comes after the *Clerk's Tale;* the meaning of *Lenvoy de Chaucer* (IV.1177–1212) is much debated, but traditionally read as ironic. This song follows upon the Clerk's urging "lat us stynte of ernestful matere" (1175); comment upon Griselda's patience and the unlikelihood of its occurring in the present combine with a noting that women's speech can pierce male armor to sustain the disputation. Its being assigned to Chaucer develops his role as a poet very interested in women. Chaucer's affinity to books is also shown in his association with a tale told by a Clerk, who provides more bibliographical information than other pilgrims. The Clerk identifies his source: "Fraunceys Petrak, the lauriat poete," (31) whom he met at Padua and who is now dead (26–29). Petrarch is praised as "a worthy clerk, / As preved by his wordes and his werk" (27–28). That last phrase, of course, applies to Chaucer himself, a man recognized both for poetry and public service. This dual role lies behind the most extensive dramatic interplay with Chaucer the pilgrim.

The Host addresses him in merry words, beginning to "japen" (joke, VII.693), looking at Chaucer, and asking "What man artow?" (695). Every other pilgrim is clearly identified by the work that he performs, so that Chaucer hints at an ambiguity in his situation and challenges the reader to think about his place in the social order. As one who looks at the ground, he is deferential in manner, but the Host also describes his countenance as "elvyssh" (703). Further, the Host says Chaucer the pilgrim is not sociable; this directly contradicts an earlier account in the *General Prologue* of his talking to each of the other pilgrims on the first night and becoming one of their company (I.31–32). Again the audience is acutely aware of diverse tellings of story and a need for interpretation. Similarly, the Man of Law's observation of Chaucer's prolific authorship is here changed to a statement that he has only one tale, "a rym I lerned longe agoon" (709). Then after *Sir Thopas* is stopped as "drasty speech" (worthless, 923), "rym dogerel" (925), Chaucer protests against not having his turn as well as any other man (926–28). Nevertheless, he remains affable, offering "a litel thyng in prose" (937), since one rhymed tale did not please. With *Melibee*, "a moral vertuous tale" (940), Chaucer supplants the Host's constant demand for a merry tale. His authority is the Evangelists—Mark, Matthew, Luke, and John—and his argument is about "sentence" (substance, essential meaning, 947, 952, 961, 963). Each version of the Gospels differs in particulars but not in essence; "hir sentence is al oon" (952). The Passion of Jesus Christ is what matters, not the details of the tellings. By analogue, pilgrim/poet Chaucer's version of a "litel tretys" should not be blamed, even if it differs from previous hearings of it, for as a reteller he keeps the right "sentence" (961–63). This argument contrasts sharply with the *apologia* in the *General Prologue*—"Whoso shal telle a tale after a man, / He moot reherce as ny as evere he kan / Everich a word" (732–33) and in the *Miller's Prologue*. There are, then, diverse kinds of tales told on this pilgrimage. Chaucer's final description of his contribution as a pilgrim is of "this murye tale I write . . . herkneth what that I shal seye, / And lat me tellen al my tale, I preye" (964–66). This acknowledges fourteenth-century practice of both listening to and reading a text. Further, the designation "murye tale" recapitulates the ideas of merriment and moral purpose that have interlaced throughout the dramatic interplay in *The Canterbury Tales*. Pilgrim Chaucer uses the Host's favorite description, but for a serious tale of "sentence" rather than frivolity. He thus reiterates the earlier argument for a level of meaning that transcends worldly interests and judgments.

Chaucer has already tied himself to the *Clerk's Tale* of Griselda and to the *Man of Law's Tale* of Constance by specific naming. His *Tale of Melibee* is thematically linked because Prudence is the third virtuous wife, or allegorical figure to present "pacience" and forbearance. The final placing of Chaucer the pilgrim storyteller is with the Parson, who comes last to tell a "myrie tale in prose, / To knytte up al this feeste and make an ende" (X.46–47). The *Parson's Prologue* has many echoes of Chaucer's comments to introduce Melibeus. The Host's request is for a "fable" (29), but the Parson refuses, citing the New Testament, specifically St. Paul's First Letter to Timothy (4:7), which says that foolish fables should be avoided. The Parson seeks to sow wheat rather than chaff (35–36). Niceties of style and dialect are not his concern, nor is textual sophistication that he leaves to clerkes (56–57). Taking "but the sentence" he will stand to correction on the other matters in his "meditacioun" (55, 69). The audience response is unanimously positive; all agree and formally have the Host communicate their belief that it is right for the pilgrimage "To enden in som vertuous sentence" (63). This is a positive fulfillment of the Knight's observation—"Whereas a man may have noon audience, / Noght helpeth it to tellen his sentence" (VII.2801–2).

Geoffrey Chaucer the poet has an audience far more extensive than the twenty-nine pilgrims who went together to Canterbury. The dramatic interplay has an urgent vitality, serves as a useful guide to some ways of approaching the tales, and provides an anticipation of Chaucer's Retraction. Nevertheless, the "tales of Canterbury" would make compelling reading even if there were no frame story. They must be read on their own to experience the richness of the fourteenth-century poet's story telling.

Connections through Subject and Tone

Any single tale, or indeed any work of literature, has a unique quality that makes generic classification only partially appropriate. Chaucer refers most often to "tales" and "stories" (histories), or to "rhyme" or "prose," so that modern designations are needed to create categories. Chaucer, for example, does not use the word *fabliau,* though he identifies "cherles tales" (low-born fellows', I.3169). He uses "lyf" (VIII.120) for stories of saints, which would be designated "legends" by many (outside the Catholic Church) as a modern distinction between history and legend that was not made in the Middle Ages. His naming of "tragedies" marks a story of a fall in a time when there was no secular drama. Nevertheless, designating a genre, a distinctive category where one tale can be read in comparison with similar tales, satisfies a need for ordering and provides a way of reading the tales to show the variety of Chaucer's narrative interests and styles of writing. It also allows a way of showing relationships among tales that are similar, both likenesses and ways in which Chaucer expands beyond the usual generic qualities. Finally, the numbers and effectiveness of tales in each grouping suggest something of the poet's concentration of attention. The five groups and the selection of tales for each provide, of course, only one of many ways of exploring the extraordinary variety of *The Canterbury Tales*.

Secular Romances, the *Tales of the Knight, Wife, Squire, Franklin,* and pilgrim Chaucer's own *Sir Thopas,* are the simplest grouping. Each tale is quite distinctive, and there are many different ways of defining romance. But Chaucer provides a start by referring to "romances of prys" (excellence, VII.897) and naming several popular examples, of which the most famous share common characteristics of chivalric interest and adventure. However, they differ in their interest in piety, literary excellence, and comprehensiveness, and the lengths and range of narrative interest are as divergent as those of short story and novel. The romance is commonly accepted as showing an aristocratic society, concerned with chivalry in some way, and often with the supernatural. These basic characteristics form a point of classification.

The "muryie tale" is often called for and commented upon in the connecting links, and many could be called simply "Comic Tales" because they make an audience laugh. Five whose comic episodes emphasize sexuality are readily identified as *fabliaux: Tales of the Miller, Reeve, Cook, Merchant,* and *Shipman*. Two others, the *Friar's* and the *Summoner's Tales* are considered in a third grouping because they add a sharper "Satiric Warning" to the comic exuberance. This is partially tied to an emphasis on the role of characters as members of religious communities, also strongly evident in the *Canon's Yeoman's Tale*. The *Manciple's Tale* is hard to place, but it treats a theme of sexual betrayal and offers a strong warning about speaking out, so that it forms a tidy summary of this group.

Another group is tales overtly religious in impulse, although they are somewhat dissimilar as examples of story telling. Two, the *Prioress's* and *Second Nun's* tales, are readily identifiable as saints' lives, while a third, the *Physician's Tale,* treats virginity, a popular topic in such narratives. Two others are similar; the *Man of Law's Tale* and the *Clerk's Tale* have a worthy woman as principal character, who in spite of extraordinary trials has a happy ending in this world, not a martyrdom. These stories have something of the adventurous qualities and multiple testings of romance. Looking at these five together as "Religious Romances and Saints' Lives" allows, then, some helpful comparisons.

The last group is "Sermons." Again two can obviously be placed in this category, the *Parson's Tale* and the *Pardoner's Tale.* To these are added the *Monk's Tale,* a kind of learned preaching, and the *Nun's Priest's Tale,* comic but also a virtuoso homily, rich in authorities and examples. Finally there is *Melibeus,* Chaucer's own prose moral treatise that is a rich basis for a sermon about patience and forgiveness.

Although Chaucer certainly did not patttern *The Canterbury Tales* with an attention to numbers as in *The Divine Comedy* or *The Decameron,* the division into five categories, each with five examples (short of one since there are but twenty-four tales), is perhaps not without significance. Five is an important number, obviously connected to the five senses. Five is also one way of naming the ages of man, based on the Parable of the Vineyard (Matthew 20:1–8).[16] This interpretation has a strong history in Christianity from Origen (185?–254?), through Gregory the Great (c. 540–604), and then to subsequent homilists, including several in Chaucer's time. This scriptural story records five specific times of day that represent the times that God calls individuals to his kingdom: early childhood, youth, maturity, age, extreme old age. The Parable of the Vineyard, included in *The Pearl,* a poem contemporary with Chaucer, provides a crucial statement about Grace, which is a gift of God not something that is earned by human effort. Each of the workers in the vineyard, however long or briefly he labored, is rewarded with a penny. Similarly, the many tales represent different human efforts, none of which can expect a reward for its own worth. Playing with fives, then, may be Chaucer's earnest way of looking to the Retraction. At any rate, to examine the tales in five groups makes them more accessible.

3

Secular Romances

The *romance*, called the most elusive of genres, has been variously defined, with many different kinds of narrative proposed as examples. Consistently included are stories of chivalry that recount adventures and trials, include rich descriptive details of aristocratic life and manners, introduce the marvelous and bizarre (giants, dragons, magic), often are quite suspenseful, seem primarily intended for entertainment, but also include serious moral concerns, typically an exposition of a system of value, usually an ideal that is beyond human attainment but intended as inspiration.[1] These qualities, at any rate, are found in the five tales that are here considered as secular romances: *Knight's Tale, Wife of Bath's Tale, Franklin's Tale, Squire's Tale,* and *Sir Thopas*. Each, of course, has been given alternate, or modified, generic description. For example, the *Knight's Tale* is usually termed a *philosophical romance;* the *Wife's Tale* has been called a *fairy tale,* the *Franklin's Tale* is termed a *lay*, a distinctive short form of romance; the *Squire's Tale* has been called a *composite romance* or *miscellany of motifs;* and *Sir Thopas* is usually read as a *burlesque of tail-rhyme popular romances*. The five tales vary in length from 2249 lines of the *Knight's Tale* to 206 lines of Chaucer the pilgrim's *Tale of Sir Thopas,* which is dramatically interrupted. The *Squire's Tale* is also unfinished; the other three are complete.

From these five tales emerge some interesting points about Chaucer's interest in romances, the genre created for a courtly audience but through the centuries gradually filtered down the social scale. The form was established by Chrétien de Troyes (flourished 1160) in France, and by the fourteenth century was flourishing in distinctively Middle English romances, many of which were translations, that appealed to a wider audience than the narrowly aristocratic that still favored French. *Troilus and Criseyde,* Chaucer's great completed poem, is another rich and highly imaginative example. A strong case has been made for the poet's direct knowledge of the Auchinleck Manuscript, which was produced 1330–40, in a scriptorium or bookshop in London and thus provides strong evidence of lay interests and taste.[2] The volume is a collection of romances and religious pieces, as well as a chronicle and topical poems; it was probably designed for a member of the aspirant middle class, perhaps a merchant, an increasingly significant and literate social group in Chaucer's day. The romances found here provide a diverse view of the genre, and Chaucer demonstrates his indebtedness to them for both subject and style. He also knew the Italian works of Boccaccio's highly individualized adaptations of romance materials, and these were the sources of his two romances of pagan antiquity.

The Knight's Tale

The opening line of the *Knight's Tale,* "*Whilom, as olde †stories tellen us" (*once, †histories, I.859), introduces a world of romance, where, under a patina of distant time, legend and history are not sharply distinguished. Chaucer and his contemporaries were fascinated by and attracted to pagan antiquity, and classical stories provide one of the Matters of Romance.[3] The *Knight's Tale* begins with Theseus, Duke of Athens, who is perhaps the most perfect of Chaucer's pagans, one who shows a wisdom of age and experience that go beyond the chaos of the world to a perception of order. His presence gives meaning to the story of youthful protagonists, Palamon and Arcite, cousins who are also sworn brothers, and their love for the maiden Emily, Theseus's young sister. In the *Knight's Tale* Theseus is a constant figure, providing a counterpoint to the youthful excesses and disturbance occasioned by the volatile young men. The import of Theseus is indicated by Shakespeare's re-creation of his role as wise ruler who establishes order, not only in *Two Noble Kinsmen,* his version of the *Knight's Tale*, but also in *A Midsummer Night's Dream,* another story of unwise young men competing in love. For Theseus's understanding Chaucer draws on Boethius. *Troilus and Criseyde,* which was written a few years later, shows the same influence. Although both of Chaucer's romances retell stories of Boccaccio, Boethian philosophy is crucial because it transforms the narrative. Characteristically, romances are not sustained by statements about order and stability, though as a genre associated with the aristocracy they foster a conservative and traditional view of life.

The *Knight's Tale* is only about one-fifth as long as Boccaccio's *Teseide,* its primary source. Not only does Chaucer eliminate the epic design and mythological machinery of Boccaccio, but he also lessens the intense personal feeling of the Italian love story. The poem is written mostly in a high style, but there are numerous authorial comments that are direct and colloquial. Several passages describe the enormity of the task of telling this tale. An early comment to the audience notes: "I have, God *woot, a large feeld to †ere, / And ‡wayke been the oxen in my plough. / The remenant of the tale is long ynough" (* knows, †plow, ‡weak, 886–88). Another admits inadequacy: "Who koude ryme in Englyssh proprely / His martirdom?" (1459–60). Such rhetorical questions are conventional, but the detail about writing in English is particularized, and the cumulative effect affords a glimpse of concerns about writing that tempts readers to regard the *Knight's Tale* more as Chaucer's than the Knight's. Certainly the tale was written long before the pilgrim character of the *General Prologue.* The style of the *Knight's Tale* is enlivened by a number of proverbs; for example, "That 'feeld hath eyen and the wode hath eres.' " (1522), Emily understands no more than a cuckoo knows of a hare (1810), "We faren as he that dronke is as a mous" (1261). In such lines Chaucer shows the influence of English romance, which is more straightforward, direct and homely, than its continental counterparts. Often the effect is a quick contrast, as when the description of Arcite's suffering of mortal injuries concludes briskly: "Fare wel physic! Go ber the man to chirche!" (2760).

The tale is divided into four parts, which mark the narrative development. Since the poem is written in five-stress couplets and larger units of verse paragraphs, rather than short stanzas, this is helpful. In Part 1 a conquering Theseus returns to Athens with his Amazon wife Hippolyta and sister Emily. He is met by grieving widows who ask mercy and help against the tyrant Creon. As a worthy knight he agrees; in the ensuing battle Theseus is again victorious and captures Palamon and Arcite, two young Theban knights, whom he imprisons. From their tower they look down upon a garden, where on a fine day in May they first see Emily. Both fall in love, Palamon worshipfully claiming her first and then Arcite because he recognizes her as a woman, not a goddess. Thus they quarrel. A friend secures a release for the more aggressive Arcite, and there is much dispute about the advantages of being in prison but seeing one's love, or being free but apart from the lady. In Part 2 Arcite returns to Athens, disguised as Philostrate. Meanwhile Palamon has escaped, so that the two cousins meet in a grove and arrange to fight the next day. While hunting, Theseus comes upon them and stops the fight. Again the Duke is moved by the plea of women; Hippolyta and Emily and all the ladies ask for mercy. Thus he spares the lives of those who have broken his law and decrees that the quarrel will be settled in chivalric manner, with no bloodshed (2537–60).

Part 3 is devoted to the building of the lists and other preparations. The splendid descriptions, reflecting both Chaucer's literary knowledge and practical experience as clerk of the king's works (when he supervised the building for two tournaments at Smithfield) are a glowing presentation of knightly circumstances. However, they include details of pain and sorrow, a somber tone that is always the counterpart of chivalric grandeur. There are three temples, and each of the principals prays: Arcite to Mars, for victory; Palamon, to Venus, for Emily's love; Emily, to Diana, for virginity, or at least that the man who loves her most be victorious. Lycurgus accompanies Palamon, and Emetreus is with Arcite; each company has one hundred knights, and respectively they are allied to Mars and Saturn, father of Venus. The pagan gods are, then, involved with strife on earth, vying for the success of the humans who pray to them. Conflicts are resolved in Part 4 because the prayers of both young men are answered. Arcite wins the victory; however, as he rides in triumph, his horse is startled by a wind sent by Saturn. Arcite is thus cast down and dies of fatal injuries, but not before reconciling and urging that Emily marry Palamon (2783–97).

A great ceremonial, Arcite's pagan funeral, and "matrimoigne or mariage" complete the story. Theseus's most eloquent speech urges reconciliation, a way of continuing in this wretched world, making virtue of necessity, creating one perfect joy of two sorrows (2987–3089). Arcite's death is accepted, and Emily is asked to agree on the same plea of "womanly pitee" that Theseus has earlier responded to when women urged him. Emily's own prayer to Diana acknowledges her acceptance of life in the world, specifically that marriage was obligatory for a woman of her station. This human resolution is strengthened because Theseus speaks not only as an individual but for a "parlement." Marriage is society's sign of unity, a conjunction of opposites both personal and public; it provides an assurance of the continuity of the human race, a way of passing on the thoroughfare of woe that is the world. Theseus's marriage to his captive Hippolyta begins the poem; here another union of former enemies offers hope in an instable world, albeit a place of certain passing from joy to woe.

Any summary of the plot of the *Knight's Tale* falls far short of indicating the extraordinary accomplishment of this romance. Its episodes are limited—in contrast with novelistic romances like *Guy of Warwick,* which influenced Chaucer in many ways—but many traditional themes of fighting (single and group combat), sworn brotherhood, love, gardens, wise kingship, and ceremony are included. Few poems evoke more powerfully the beauty of medieval pageantry, the magnanimity of a great ruler (Theseus is perhaps an evocation of King Edward III at his best), the highest chivalric virtues of fidelity, honor, knighthood, wisdom, humility, quality of social rank, high kinship, nobility of character (2789–91). Yet the poem is also a gloss on pagan antiquity that goes beyond the choice of subject matter and the introduction of deities, who are also planets. In prison Arcite declares that "Fortune hath yeven us this adversitee." (1086), and he blames the planet Saturn, traditionally in enmity with Thebans. Later Palamon blames the "crueel goddes that governe / This world" (1304–05) arbitrarily and wantonly, treating man as another beast. Yet he affirms the moral quality of man, his feeling of grief, that increases his "penaunce." Thus although the two young men appear to be equal, mere agents of providence, there is a correlation between their behavior and their fate that illustrates Theseus's belief in free will shown by his constant responsiveness to appeals for mercy.

Arcite, who is allied with Mars, a god associated with worldly princes and tyranny, dies. His prayer is not for love, but for victory, which indicates a primary commitment to the bellicose. Indeed his passion first introduces enmity, disordering the harmonious kinship and warrior brotherhood with his companion. Palamon's prayer puts love before victory, and he lives to marry Emily, to carry on the harmony espoused by the wise and mature Theseus. In a very simple way is shown the felicity of the modern slogan "Make love, not war," if one defines love in relation to community. A tension between the roles of warrior and lover characterizes many medieval romances, and the *Knight's Tale* can be read as a treatment of this theme. By marrying Hippolyta Theseus loves his enemy, but the opening scene shows the complexity of ongoing choices. The widows appeal for his help, and he responds properly as a knight. Nevertheless, his championing of them leads to another war with Thebes. From the carnage of that conflict come two young prisoners, who are spared but severely treated; they are to dwell perpetually in prison with no opportunity for ransom (1023–24). They remain "in angwissh and in wo . . . yeer by yeer and day by day" until their situation is transformed by seeing and loving Emily. Theseus is generous when he releases Arcite to his friend Perothesus, "withouten any ransoun" (1205); humans thus can make choices about how to treat others. Theseus's generosity and favoring of life is further shown at the grove, when he again agrees to preserve life. The tournament is a community action that moderates impulses to fight; not only the two protagonists, but also other warriors, are thus safely employed, a characteristic achievement of chivalry.

Chaucer goes far beyond ordinary practices, for the tale offers explanations and counsels order. Arcite dies, but his last words are a remarkable confession (2765–96). Lamenting his own end, he admits his ire and jealousy in struggling against Palamon, to whom he attributes all the knightly virtues. Formerly devoted to Mars, he now commends himself to Jupiter (2786), associated with peace, the god thanked by Theseus (3069). Such penitence comes as an answer to Arcite's question,"What is this world? What asketh men to have?" (2777). Arcite learns only as he is dying, but others attain wisdom sooner. Often challenged, Theseus grows increasingly able to detach himself, putting aside personal impulse for the good of others. If Theseus is seen gradually manifesting this maturity, his old father Egeus is identified as one

> That knew this worldes transmutacioun,
> As he hadde seyn it chaunge bothe up and doun
> Joye after wo, and wo after gladnesse,
> And shewed hem ensamples and liknesse. (2839–42)

Egeus provides the most pertinent image; granted the world is a path of woe, "We been pilgrymes, passynge to and fro" (2848). This is a consolation for death; however, the need for those in the world, especially those who have chosen chivalry, is to continue. Thus the elaborate description of the preparation for the funeral becomes a litany of the things of creation, beautiful goods made by man but also the fruits of the earth, as in the catalogue of trees and naming of creatures of the forest. This anticipates Theseus's paean to the First Mover, stable and eternal, and his argument for acceptance through necessity. (The oak [2921, 3017] ties the two passages together.) Arcite dies with fame; he is "of chivalrie flour" (3059), and this is comforting and an argument for calm resignation in a pagan ethos. The marriage will sustain such achievement, and the *Knight's Tale* celebrates this wisdom of classical antiquity, but Chaucer also notes what is missing. Arcite's last words are "Mercy, Emelye!" (2808), a poignant cry for the beauty and love of the world. Then follows an authorial observation that makes explicit the limits of this inspiring story:

> His spirit chaunged hous and wente ther,
> As I cam nevere, kan nat tellen wher.
> Therfore I stynte: I nam no divinistre;
> Of soules fynde I nat in this registre, (2809–12)

Theology is not to be expected in a secular romance, but the freedom of the genre allows Boethian philosophy and a thorough analysis of pagan excellence, as well as engrossing details of medieval life and a good story. Chaucer included several other versions of romance in *The Canterbury Tales,* but none is so richly textured and deeply thoughtful.

The Squire's Tale

The seriousness found in the *Knight's Tale* is rather limited in the *Squire's Tale,* for this romance is incomplete in several ways. Not only does it break off in the middle of a section, but also it lacks a clear story and philosophical argument. Neither element is a requirement for romance; indeed the *Squire's Tale* is interesting because it is such a different kind of romance, one that is arresting and very charming but obviously inconclusive. Much of its attraction lies in its ease, an apparent lack of argument but many memorable details and scenes. The tale was sufficiently intriguing and affecting to inspire admiration of Chaucer's successors, Edmund Spenser in his chivalric epic *The Faerie Queene* (1589) and John Milton in "Il Penseroso" (1631?), a lyric written by a youthful poet to celebrate learning and voice a wish for the symbolic powers of Canacee's ring. Although some modern readers are delighted to think about possible ways that the tale could have continued, most are less keen about the *Squire's Tale,* or view it as a satiric treatment of romance. Again this illustrates how crucial is audience response, especially in reading romances; a popular genre in the Middle Ages is now highly regarded only for a few gems. In the development of types of romance the *Squire's Tale* seems a bit before its time, since it is closest in form to *composite romances,* like *Valentine and Orson,* which became increasingly popular in the late Middle Ages, and which favored blending disparate elements, especially the exotic. At this the Squire excels, even if no subtle interlacing occurs, as in the best completed composite romances.

The tale is set in the East, in Tartarye or the Mongol Empire. European exploration of the Far East was significant in the thirteenth century; Marco Polo is only the best known of numerous merchants and adventurers. By the fourteenth century a writer like John Mandeville wrote *Travels* that were imaginary, and a manuscript like Bodley 264 contains rich illustrations of the "marvels" that Polo saw, as imagined by English illuminators. Prester John's descriptions were also famous. The Squire appeals to such interests, placing his tale at the court of King Cambyuskan or Genghis Khan. In fact, apart from names the scene seems familiar. The court with its bustling, noisy conversations, music, rich food and wine, too much imbibed, appears distinctly Western. Like King Arthur, Cambyuskan holds a feast in hall, into which a knight rides in a manner similar to that of the challenger in *Sir Gawain and the Green Knight*. The knight's courtesy is compared to that of Gawain (V.95), and the narrator wishes for Lancelot's expertise to explain dances and courtly dissimulation. But the story is really very simple: the knight's purpose is to bring gifts. These are quite remarkable: a metal horse that provides aerial transportation and is operated by turning pins in its ear and speaking commands, a magic mirror that allows a glimpse into the future, a magic ring that permits the wearer to understand the language of birds and to converse with them, and a magic sword that can pierce any armor and with a stroke heal wounds. With these special effects come many possibilities for narrative action, but only the ring is used.

After the feast, brilliantly described in Part 1, all retire to sleep. The king's daughter Canacee wakes after a first sleep, happy with thoughts of the ring and mirror, the gifts just bestowed on her. She rises refreshed and walks out, coming upon a falcon in a tree. This wretched creature cries out piteously and has so beaten herself that she is bleeding. Through the magic of her ring, Canacee asks the cause of the bird's grief, a pain like that of the Furies in hell. The remainder of Part 2 contains a moving story of the female bird's gradually evolved trusting love and abrupt betrayal by a tercel, the male bird who wants "newfanglenesse" (V.610), so that he leaves her for a kite, a scavenger bird. A sorrowing and compassionate Canacee prepares medicinal remedies for the desolate creature. The Squire interrupts this story, providing only a brief promise that the formal's love will return repentant through the intercession of Canacee's brother. Then he says, it is time "To speken of aventures and of batailles" (V.659), and Cambyuskan's victories provide great marvels. These, however, are never recounted, for Part 3 breaks off after two lines.

The *Squire's Tale,* then, has several lively and skillful passages: the feast that is a nice bit of social realism (the menu includes swans and herons; minstrel entertainment follows the third course), fascinating magic items, and a poignant episode that sharply analyzes male lack of trustworthiness in love. Such literary finesse contrasts with the tale's structure, a loose stringing together of pieces. No specific source has been identified, and this suggests Chaucer is experimenting. A lack of causality is not unusual in romance narrative, where events just occur: a knight is riding through a forest and meets a giant, or comes upon a dragon and lion fighting, or finds a lost lady, or baby, meets a hermit, and so on. It is largely because of the Squire's frequently interrupting his tale to apologize for his limitations that he is regarded as inexperienced or lacking in skill. Yet the topos of cutting short a description ("What nedeth yow rehercen hire array?" V.298) is commonplace. However, a specific disclaimer of poetic skill, a modesty topos as in the failure to tell of Canacee's beauty (V.34–41), does not usually identify missing poetic skills. As in the *Knight's Tale,* a point is made about the vernacular: "Myn Englissh eek is insufficient." Further, a "rhetor" (master of eloquence) is needed, one who knows the colors or devices of rhetoric. These two points are fundamental in translation from French to English, for example, of Anglo-Norman romances like *Bevis of Hamtoun* and *Guy of Warwick*. There is also a consideration of oral delivery. The knight who brings the gifts delivers his message in "a manly voys" (V.99), uses his language correctly, and reinforces this with an appropriate facial expression, "As techeth art of speche" (V.103). The style is a higher one than the Squire can manage. Indeed the tale comments on levels of sophistication. Many theories about the magic items are aired, the less educated doubt things that are subtler than they can comprehend, a dull man cannot set forth something unless he has directly experienced it (V. 220–24). Thus Chaucer is exploring the nature of romance—its subject matter and story telling and stylistic devices.

The Franklin's courteous interruption of the Squire and praise of his rhetorical eloquence can be interpreted as gestures of goodwill to protect youthfulness and inexperience. But the same circumstances of too many elements that are not connected and an interruption of the tale recur in Chaucer's own *Tale of Sir Thopas*. Close ties between the tales of the Squire and Franklin encourage a dramatic reading. However, to see the tale as an engaging exploration of composite romance is to recognize how challenging was the romance form. Chaucer was more at ease in very sharply focused stories.

The Wife of Bath's Tale

Just as the *Squire's Tale* relies upon magical elements, so the *Wife of Bath's Tale* opens with an evocation of fairyland. The story begins "In th'olde dayes of the Kyng Arthour" (III. 857), "many hundred yeres ago" (863). After a brief digression by the Wife against the abuses of friars that have made fairies flee the land, the tale resumes "And so bifel that this kyng Arthour" (882) . . . "That on a day cam ridynge . . . And happed that. . . ." (884–885). Thus there is a feeling of the remote past and of events occurring without identified reasons. Later, the effect is reiterated, "And in his wey it happed hym to ryde," (989), when the knight comes upon twenty-four ladies (fairies) who are dancing in the forest and then vanish as he approaches, so that only an "olde wyf," a foul or Loathly Lady remains. The tale is a popular and traditional one, Celtic in origin. There are many versions from the eleventh century on, some associated with the Arthurian cycle, notably *The Weddynge of Sir Gawen and Dame Ragnell* and a related ballad *The Marriage of Sir Gawain*. Chaucer's friend John Gower retold it in the *Confessio Amantis*. The basic theme of transforming an ugly hag into a beautiful maiden is appealing, not least as a gloss on much that the Wife of Bath argues in her extraordinary *Prologue*, especially since it is generally agreed that the assigning of this tale to the Wife was a late decision in the making of *The Canterbury Tales*. Thus it is important to recognize but also to separate the initial attack on friars and the concluding half-dozen lines in which the Wife prays for "Housbondes meeke, yonge, and fressh abedde" that will be governed by their wives, who will also outlive them (1259–64). Although useful in an argument for a group of tales that form a Marriage Debate, these remarks shift the tone of the *Wife's Tale*, which is one of idealism, and foster a reading of the tale as an argument for female sovereignty over men. The story itself is much more complex and of broader import. It is another of Chaucer's explorations of the romance as an argument for a virtuous life, especially difficult in a world of chivalry, and its seriousness comes close to that in the *Knight's Tale*. However, the meaning is enriched by Christian belief, since among the Nine Worthies Arthur is one of the three Christians.[4]

Perhaps the boldest indication of Chaucer's intent is his changing the occasion for the knight's quest to find the answer to the question "What thyng is it that wommen moost desiren" (905). The *Wife of Bath's Tale* is the only one in which the knight's fault is rape; since his victim is a peasant maiden, the crime is both sexual and sociopolitical, and the argument is intensified. The law requires that a man lose his head for this offense, but as in the *Knight's Tale* women plead for mercy, not the justice of law, and the king grants the queen's request that the knight be spared. The question, which must be answered after twelve months and a day, is an attempt to rescue the knight, to provide a way in which he will not only survive but also live a nobler life. The story, then, combines the popular tale of the Converted Knight with the Loathly Lady. The sinner can be saved, to use the terms of a sermon. The urging of mercy to a rapist by a woman is unusually compelling because the crime is the most personal against women. Indeed in this tale the male is saved only through the generosity of women, for what the queen initiates the old wife, whom the knight is forced to marry against his will, completes. So proud and self-centered is the young man that he tries to renege on his plighted vow to the old wife that her reward for the answer to the question will be the first thing she asks. His grieving cry "Taak al my good and lat my body go" (1061) is an outrageous one for a convicted rapist. Compelled to wed, he yet persists in supercilious abuse, often protesting against the hardship of a young knight marrying an old widow. There is no evidence that he recognizes that without her help he would be dead. Further demonstration of mercy and generosity come in her forbearing, and in the process he receives a remarkable education, which is the real point of the story.

The central passage is a speech made on the wedding night, when the smiling old wife explains the meaning of "gentillesse" (nobility, 1109–1212). This comes after she mildly and wittily chides her husband for his lack of interest on such a night, followed by a further quiet tolerating of his abusive remarks about her appearance which, he argues, justifies his "walwe and wynde" (writhing and tossing about). Like Theseus's great oration about the chain of order in the universe, the old wife's explanation of gentillesse provides a way of responding to disharmony that is the nature of the human condition. But instead of a fine pagan resignation, admirable in its realism and power, here is articulated a belief in the strength of the human person through Christ's giving. The old wife begins by observing the falsity of an attitude that gentillesse comes from birth or riches, for "Crist wole we clayme of hym our gentillesse" (1117); nevertheless, human action is significant, for the noblest is he that does "the gentil dedes that he kan," a trust in faith and good works, basic to Catholic belief. Human character, not worldly inheritance is important in Christianity, a system that is essentially democratic as many other religions are not because it embraces all. The Christian context is signaled by citing Dante as the first authority: God wills we claim nobility from Him, for from our elders we can claim only temporal things (1132). Then follow pagan authors—Seneca, Valerius, Juvenal and of, course, Boethius—who argue that one can be called "gentil" when one lives virtuously and abandons sin. A large section of the lecture deals with poverty, which taken "in pacience" can be a source of strength and thus is not cause for reproof. About one-fourth of the tale is given to this explanation of "gentilesse," and its powerful argument is clear from the major alteration in the Knight's behavior. Previously insisting upon his own impulses and needs, particularly in relation to women of whom he is brutally contemptuous, he now recognizes and admits his limitations. The end of the old wife's speech poses a question to the reluctant husband, a nice repetition of his initial seeking of an answer. She explains that he has a choice: he can have a wife foul, old, true, and humble, or young, fair, and chancy in her response to others. And he does at last know the answer; he leaves the choice to her. This is not a simple matter of male submission; in fact, the wife does nothing to dominate but rather asks a kiss and declares that she will be both fair and good. Then there is a moment of magic transformation, for when he lifts the curtain he sees that what she has promised is true. His release of control, an insistence that he determine everything, admits limitations, as does Arcite's penitence. The result is "parfit joye" for the rest of their lives, or as a fairy tale would say, "They lived happily ever after." This, then, is the most romantic of romances, including a conventional ending with a marriage that promises continuity, again as in the *Knight's Tale,* but here achieved in an intensely personal growth of knowing, not a resignation to fated circumstances.

Noting the serious moral argument of the *Wife of Bath's Tale* should not inhibit delight in its entertaining qualities. The narrative is tightly focused, and the story develops rapidly with a concentration upon the knight's quest for an answer in the first part and the more serious test posed by the old wife in the second part. Since she is seeking both love and wifehood, there is a dilemma. Chaucer includes a tidy bit of suspense, for the knight knows the answer before the audience does. They learn only when he gives his reply to the queen at court. This is a fine illustration of how oral presentation can build excitement and empathy. Much is told through dialogue, and the tale is less given to elaborate rhetorical expression. There are fewer cries of "Alas!" and questions are addressed to persons rather than being exclamatory. Authorities and examples are moderate in number. The style is closer to that of simpler Middle English romances, and simplicity is appropriate to the story's fairy-tale quality. It is significant that the authorial comment about detail neatly illustrates rhetorical convention. The formula for not including elaborate description of the wedding—"To tellen yow the joye and al th'array / That at the feeste was that ilke day" (1075–76) is not rhetorical modesty, but precise statement, followed by "I seye that ther nas no ioye ne feeste at al" (1078). A private wedding was followed by the reluctant husband's hiding himself as an owl, a bird that flies by night out of sight of other birds.

The happy ending of the *Wife's Tale* somewhat obscures the hard questions posed by the tale. The queen's setting of the conditions is a challenge, and when the reply is given the court situation is formally set. Many women are present, noble wives, maids, and widows, and "The queene hirself sittynge as a justise" (1028). The scene evokes the Courts of Love supposedly held during the Middle Ages, for example by Marie de Champagne, patron of Chrétien de Troyes, by her mother Eleanor of Aquitaine, wife of King Henry II of England, and at Paris in 1400. Another romance, the *Franklin's Tale* ends with a question to the audience, again about generosity of human behavior.

The Franklin's Tale

The *Prologue of the Franklin's Tale* announces it as a "lay," a form of brief romance that most often tells of love but also of wondrous things and adventures of long ago. If Chaucer saw the Auchinleck manuscript, he found there some of the most famous Middle English lays, *Sir Orfeo, Lay le Freine,* and *Sir Degare.* All have happy endings; even the classical story of Orpheus finishes with husband and wife reunited and a good steward. This is an important characteristic because it forestalls anxiety in the *Franklin's Tale,* as does

Arveragus's reassurance at the worst moment in the story, when he sends his wife to Aurelius to keep her "trouthe" (pledge): "It may be wel, paraventure, yet to day" (V.1473). An attitude of confidence comes quickly, for the story begins with a happy love that leads to marriage. The *Franklin's Tale* has often been read as the culmination of the Marriage Group or Debate, a resolution of conflict between men and women for sovereignty. Nevertheless, the marital relationship remains at risk; there is always a garden of temptation, and moral choices are constantly called for. The *Franklin's Tale* continues the discussion of "gentilesse" that the *Wife of Bath's Tale* finally realized. Its purpose is to argue for virtuous living, teachings that are expansive but familiar in Chaucer. Not only nobility, but also loyalty, fidelity to one's word, patience, avoidance of excess, and generosity are advocated and illustrated. The happy ending is cumulative, a kind of great chain of behaving well, one person's generosity inspiring another's. Again there is confidence in an essential goodness that prevails, in spite of serious and widespread lapses that can be offset by mercy and kindness.

The plot is fairly simple, but the treatment and questions posed are not. A handsome young couple, Dorigen and Arveragus, equals in age, class, beauty, and love, wed happily. One of the most idealistic passages in *The Canterbury Tales* defines love as "free" (generous and unconstrained), sustained by "pacience," recognizing that forbearance is necessary, not least because all are guilty of faults of some kind (764–90). However, even in so "perfect" a marriage there are difficulties. Marriage is both a private relationship and a public part of society. As a knight Arveragus must seek his arms, and thus he leaves for England after a year or so. Dorigen is left alone, a grieving wife who often thinks anxiously of the rocks below the castle. A Chaucerian addition, these rocks become a symbol of her fears about her husband's return, and she prays to "Eterne God" for their removal. Gradually, with the urging of friends, Dorigen modestly resumes some social activities. On May 6 she is in her garden, "the verray paradys," when a young squire Aurelius, who has secretly loved her for years, declares his feelings and asks her pity. Dorigen firmly asserts her fidelity as a wife, but as a gracious gesture makes a Rash Vow: she will love Aurelius when he removes the rocks. Clearly this is not a realistic promise, although it is interesting as a sign of her anxiety. Aurelius, however, takes the rash vow seriously; he proceeds to pray to the pagan god Apollo and, following his brother's advice, hires a clerk of Orleans for a fee of a thousand pounds. There are fine accounts of magical appearances and illusions, for the clerk's skill is redoubtable. In short, through his magical illusion the rocks seem to have vanished, and Aurelius claims Dorigen. In the years that Aurelius has worked to secure this magic, Arveragus has returned. Dorigen, then, first laments her fate at great length and with much emotion. Next she explains her plight, and Arveragus declares, "Trouthe is the hyeste thyng that man may kepe" (1479). He weeps but sends her to keep the vow, thus recognizing that his wife is more than a body; but he asks for discretion to avoid public scandal, an acknowledgment of the claims of community. When Dorigen meets Aurelius and explains these circumstances, he is inspired to "gentilesse" and releases her from his churlish bargain, even though he will now have neither the lady nor his money. The Clerk of Orleans, learning what has happened, also proves that he can behave "gentilly" by releasing Aurelius from his thousand-pounds fee. The tale concludes with a question, an invitation to discuss which character was "mooste fre."

In folklore a basic motif known as the Rash Vow appears in many Eastern as well as European tales, but there is no single source for Chaucer's tale. Rather he seems to have been experimenting, creating an example of a form popular in the fourteenth century. The center of the *Franklin's Tale* is a wife's rash vow, but the circumstances are not rash, nor are the consequences. As in other romances Chaucer favors a simpler plot to allow more provocative posing of moral questions. Deliberation is explicitly the tale's intention, for it concludes with a question "Which was the mooste *fre, as thynketh yow?" (*generous of spirit, 1622) that echoes the opening definition "Love is a thyng as any spirit free" (767). Many different interpretations of this tale, typically judgments of the characters, indicate that the *demande* is being fulfilled. Cynical readers think Dorigen a foolish woman given to emotional excess and not competent to look after herself, since she has to turn to her husband. Another way to view Dorigen is as the true wife, but living in a society that does not countenance her reclusiveness and where there are aggressive males seeking sexual favors from women who have no interest in them but must survive in the society. In short, life in this world is not simple or easy, even if one is happily married. Similarly, readers perceive Arveragus's action as ridiculous, sending his wife to commit adultery by honoring a rash vow. Or he is praised for thinking of his wife as one with "trouthe" that must be kept and that is not simply physical chastity, a frequent male view of women. Aurelius often receives less notice. A would-be courtly lover, of the adulterous variety, he begins with little except self-interest, and pride in his own attractiveness, even though he is polite. His insistence upon the rash vow is a legalistic approach, a view of the bond that shows no comprehension of the New Testament's advocacy of mercy. He has only blind devotion, and that is both false and impermanent.

Seeing, perception, is a crucial theme in the *Franklin's Tale,* which begins with a clear affirmation of love, gentilesse, truth, and so on. The values are easy to define, but seeing how to embody them is another matter, for there are many appearances that prove false. Dorigen sees the rocks as a threat, an occasion for shipwreck, and as part of the natural world rocks can injure. However, her anxiety makes them a real threat, first because she is presumptuous in praying for a world that is without danger—a distortion of what "eternal God" has created as well as a proud belief that she knows what will happen—and second because she names the rocks as the only obstacle to Aurelius's passion, when in reality there are quite different oppositions. A garden in Maytime seems pleasant, a beautiful enclosed area that suggests safety. Actually it is a place of temptation and potentially of sin, the biblical archetype. The magic of the Clerk of Orleans, highly praised and sought after, is another example of mistaking appearances for essences; his capacity is to create illusions, ways of distracting and helping people to secure their self-interest. The eager students at Orleans who seek, in every nook and cranny, to master the arts of magic are far from truth. They are specifically identified as pagan, foolish, and no longer viable: "For hooly chirches feith in oure bileve / Ne suffreth noon illusions us to greve" (1133–1134). In the midst of the Clerk's astrological calculations comes a reminder: "For swiche illusiouns and swiche *meschances / As hethen folk useden in †thilke dayes" (*evil practices, †those, 1292–94). Arveragus may seem proud and/ or a fool, but his decision solves the dilemma; "trouthe" is preserved, and all emerge a bit wiser and more likely to behave with "pacience" and compassion.

Although the Franklin protests that he "lerned nevere rhetorik" (718), the tale is replete with elaborate and formal utterances that reveal a penchant for set pieces to convey the extreme emotional states that occupy many of its 916 lines, again ten-syllable couplets that are more elevated than the octosyllabic lines favored in many lays. Dorigen's complaint to Fortune (1355–1456) is very long, with examples of women who have been raped or committed suicide, or preserved their chastity. Summarized from Jerome's *Adversus Jovinianum,* previously cited by the Wife of Bath in her

Prologue, it is part of Chaucer's exploration of rhetoric. Aurelius's addresses to Dorigen (and her reply) and his prayer to Apollo and through this god of the sun to his sister, Lucina, goddess of the moon, are similarly extravagant, in high style. And the reader is told that the clerks speak Latin (1174), another example of inflation beyond the ordinary. In contrast, the exchanges between the Clerk and Aurelius are in a low style, closer to ordinary speech, and are about supper and money (1210–18; 1227–34). And Arveragus's words to his wife are simple and straightforward (1469–86), a restrained style that she learns (1512–13). The poem's language serves, at least partially, to reenforce its warning against appearances, the simple being surer than the grand apostrophes. Chaucer in his pilgrim's attempt at romance explored this further.

The Tale of Sir Thopas

Chaucer's interest in romance is supported not only by the number and variety of examples that he wrote, but also because the first tale presented by Chaucer the pilgrim is a romance. The difficulty is discovering what kind of romance *Sir Thopas* is. The Host's interruption predisposes a negative response to the "rym I lerned longe agoon" that was supposed to be "A tale of myrthe" (VII.710, 706). For sophisticated readers it has been a source of merriment, an exquisite comic turn, described as burlesque or parody, in which Chaucer the poet reveals the absurdities of romance by writing an example that is a horror. But any edition of the tale is replete with references that show Chaucer's indebtedness to some of the most popular Middle English romances, particularly *Guy of Warwick* and *Bevis of Hampton,* which lost a sophisticated audience only in the Renaissance. Other more recent critics have found in *Sir Thopas* an argument for Chaucer's advocacy of antiwar, which is one theme of the *Tale of Melibee* told by Chaucer the pilgrim after the Host calls *Sir Thopas* "rym dogerel" (VII. 925) and "*drasty rymyng" (*worthless,VII. 930), and cuts it short. As noted in the discussion about the *Knight's Tale,* antiwar is an unlikely sentiment for the fourteenth century, when chivalry and war are major occupations of the ruling classes. The Host's critical acumen has also been seen as questionable.

An immediate response to *Sir Thopas* comes from its different verse form. Chaucer uses a tail-rhyme stanza, here six octosyllabic lines rhyming *a a b a a b* or *a a b c c b,* including some looser rhymes and occasionally a "bob" (one-stress line) that leads to an additional three lines. Most metrical romances have a twelve-line stanza, but the effect of the short line is a trotting movement and the simplicity associated with a short and popular form. Contrast with the elegance of Chaucer's favored iambic pentameter couplet is startling, one way of showing his extraordinary poetic skill in comparison with much of what was being written in English. Chaucer, who at least began his career writing for a courtly audience, here allies himself with the minstrels that performed for bourgeoisie and tavern. The hero's birth in Flanders suggests trade and industry associations. *Sir Thopas* begins with the oral formula: "Listeth, lordes, in good entent / And I wol telle" (VII.712–13) and repeats at the start of the Second Fit: "Yet listeth, lordes, to my tale / Murier than the nightyngale" (VII. 833–34).[5] This suggests a little joke by a court performer lowering his style for an audience of pilgrims, a bit of self-mockery since Chaucer wrote all of the tales, many in elevated style and all higher than this. The opening of the Third Fit confirms: "Now holde youre mouth, *par charitee,* / Both knyght and lady free, / And herkneth to my spelle" (VII. 891–93). Here is evidence of a restive audience, and the performer's soliciting both female sympathy and religious mercy.

Not only is the style familiar, but also the contents of *Sir Thopas*. Indeed the tale seems largely a compendium of romance motifs: a description of the hero, including a scene of his arming, riding forth for adventures ("And so bifel upon a day . . . He priketh thurgh a fair forest" VII.748, 754), lovelonging, seeking a fairy mistress, feasting, encountering a giant and promising to fight on the morrow. In addition, Chaucer twice places himself in the minstrel tradition. First, Sir Thopas asks that his "mynstrales and geestours" (musical entertainers and tellers of gestes or stirring adventures) come to tell tales during his arming; these are to be royal romances and of love, but also of popes and cardinals (VII.845–50). The latter is not clear, but perhaps refers to pious stories. Then in the last section, as a desperate or conventional (?) appeal to authority, comes a list of six "romances of prys" (excellence, VII. 897), a not untypical motif, usually with some of the same heroes. Horn Child and Ypotys are both presented as excellent children: one reclaims his inheritance, and the other piously instructs the emperor Hadrian. Sir Thopas in the encounter with the giant is called "child," and his feast features sweet wine, ginger and licorice, and cumin with sugar. Then there are Guy of Warwick and Bevis of Hampton, the two great English heroes. Both romances have Anglo-Norman originals and are very long—even called "novels" by modern critics—presenting a remarkable series of adventures both in love and war. No Pleyndamour romance has survived, but the name suggests a lover. Lybeaus Desconus (the Fair Unknown) is a youthful kind of folk hero with a career rather like that of Perceval, again a youth trying to discover himself and demonstrating both knightly and amatory skill with a magic (serpent) lady. Finally, the last comparison is to Percyvell (VII. 916), an Arthurian type of the awkward young and unknown knight—but also one who seeks the Holy Grail.

Much attention has been paid to Chaucer's playful tampering with traditional romance motifs, and some describe the tale as built upon a series of motifs suitable for satire. These include the name "Topas"—a bright gem connoting superlative excellence, both in men and women, and a power against lust, appropriate for the chaste hero—his pink and white complexion, his not noticing or at least not at first mentioning that the giant has three heads (not a conventional characteristic!), loving an elf or fairy queen when he has never seen her except in a dream, and so on. An underlying seriousness has been less discerned. For example, Percival provides a model for change from childish bumbling to religious quest; Chaucer begins with *Sir Thopas* and foregoes it to tell the *Tale of Melibee,* a prose work of serious moral argument, Prudence's counseling of mercy and forbearance. Because so much of Chaucer's tale shows the influence of *Guy of Warwick* in style and details, and in length that is oppressive to many modern readers, the poet is perceived as opposing this romance and others like it. It is worth noting that the action of *Guy of Warwick* is in two parts: in the first an ambitious hero, inspired by love, fights to become the best in the world and to win his lady, while in the second he fights as an unknown champion for the glory of God. There is a parallel with Chaucer's *Sir Thopas*, his own writing of frivolous romance, with no known source, and then finishing with *Melibee,* a pious argument, with a bit of story, that is a close translation. I freely admit my advocacy of Guy of Warwick that inclines to a particular reading.[6] But there is a very broad context for my argument.

An early advocate of chivalry and romance in the eighteenth century, when the Middle Ages were being recovered by antiquarians who approached romances without the prejudices of earlier humanist opposition, was Bishop Richard Hurd. He said, "Sir Topaz is all Don Quixote in little." This is a very helpful insight. Cervantes's great work, the first part published in 1604, came as the end of the tradition of medieval chivalric romance; and while it is a burlesque, it is also a lament for lost idealism so eloquently espoused for centuries through romances. *Sir Thopas* is written in the style of popular metrical romance, already a sign of movement down the social scale. The treatment of hero and episodes shows great enthusiasm for a chivalric way of life, knowledge of details about how a knight should behave, albeit not always precisely deployed, and the narrative is broken off, so that like the *Squire's Tale* it is inconclusive. Comparison with that attempt at romance suggests a similar enthusiasm for romance, but an incapacity to create a story in the old way, not because of lack of technical information but because of a lack of controlling vision. Both the Squire and Chaucer the pilgrim have a great desire to sustain romance, but they do not succeed. This may be seen as an affirmation of the values of chivalric romance but an admission of the unlikelihood of their achievement; high sentiment, idealism, remains compelling, even when not attained. A need persists: the old romances survive with a popular audience in the next centuries, and chivalry is reestablished in later ages, particularly with the Victorian formulation of the idea of a gentleman that persisted long into the twentieth century. Chaucer's *Sir Thopas* creates laughter about romance, but also great poignancy and nostalgia for a form early chosen for his great ambitious poem *Troilus and Criseyde*. There, as we shall see, he had already combined comic with serious. In *The Canterbury Tales,* then, examples of comic tales were inevitable, but the quality of their achievement would probably not have been predicted.

4

Fabliaux

While secular romances present an idealistic view of life, *fabliaux* show a coarse side with little that is noble. This French form of short versified narrative, designed to provoke laughter, flourished in the thirteenth century, but received its richest articulation from Geoffrey Chaucer, who revived and indeed transformed it. It is notable that a significant effort was devoted by the mature poet to writing these tales, which usually have indecent subject matter, presenting sexual or excretory functions that typically develop from some kind of practical joke or seeking of revenge. Although the first study of *fabliaux* was made by Joseph Bédier in 1893, early twentieth-century critics shied away from these tales. However, since the midcentury they have been read enthusiastically and become a focus for critical attention. Some see the *fabliau* as the center of Chaucer's artistic creation, finding in them a source for his artistic objectivity that others see rooted in his Christianity and study of Boethius. Similarly, most definitions describe *fabliaux* as "realistic" to contrast with an "idealistic" quality of romance; this implies a judgment that true and faithful representation of humans shows them as coarse and ignoble, self-seeking, and lacking consideration of others. Because Chaucer wrote so many romances, both secular and religious, it seems more appropriate to regard the *fabliaux* simply as a different part of his artistic achievement. A way of thinking about this is to equate the *fabliau* with marginalia in Gothic manuscripts, which not infrequently provide images of action from *fabliaux* as well as grotesques combining animal and human features. These figures not only accompany romances but also religious texts in manuscripts of great beauty. All indicate a medieval awareness that humans have both body and soul, as a popular poetic form poses in debate, that they live in a temporal world but this is only a shadow of the eternity that is to come. Great energy and vitality are present in what has been called the Gothic tension, the balance of these disparate "realities."

Chaucer explicitly recognizes that *fabliaux* can occasion a negative response. To the basic *apologia* of the *General Prologue* that argues the pilgrim Chaucer must report whatever he hears, is added a more precise statement to introduce his first *fabliau,* the *Miller's Tale*. Pilgrim Chaucer identifies the Miller as a churl, issues a warning that tales come in many varieties—a kind of fourteenth-century ratings of suitability—and frees himself of blame by indicating that the reader has a choice, "Turne over the leef and chese another tale" (I.3177). The tale is to be one of "harlotrie" (about rascals, ribaldry, or a dirty story), quite different from those that feature gentillesse, morality, holiness. By late twentieth-century standards much of the indecency in *fabliaux* seems mild; it may momentarily shock, but there is no lingering over detail, and most readers do not find anything pornographic or perverse. The comic brilliance, much dependent upon swiftness of action and verbal surprise, means that a first reading is often very startling but rarely less than hilarious. Intrigue and trickery, rejection of pretentiousness, cleverness that allows rascals to evade punishment—these are the appeals of *fabliaux*. So deftly do the stories unfold, that there is no (or very little) occasion for sympathy and involvement, except to laugh at the joke. As with the romance, Chaucer provided many examples, and the most brilliant comes first in *The Canterbury Tales*.

The Miller's Tale

Placement of the *Miller's Tale* directly after the *Knight's Tale* has long been recognized as Chaucer's deliberate contrast between romance and *fabliau*. The dramatic introduction contains the drunken Miller's statement that he will "quite" (pay back, revenge, I.3127) the tale that the Knight has just completed, the romance of Palamon, Arcite, Emily, and Duke Theseus. The *Miller's Tale* is about two young male lovers and one woman, and an older male figure, here the cuckolded husband. Thus it offers a view of sexual interest and behavior that is a far cry from the lovelonging, chivalric competition, and solemn acceptance of marriage as a way of binding both persons and community to assure order and continuity in the world of romance. Instead of years of seeking love, the characters in the *Miller's Tale* achieve their satisfaction and triumphs in a few days.

The motifs of the *Miller's Tale,* if no specific source, are to be found in folk tales. Three jests are fused: the man fearful of the flood, the misdirected kiss, and the revenge taken with a hot iron. Chaucer sets the tale in Oxford, and much of its richness comes from details of student life, or more specifically the conflict between town and gown. Nicholas, a clerk, is described (eleven times) as "hende," a word that has many connotations (courteous, gracious, pleasant; expert, skillful, clever; ready, skilled with his hands). He has rooms out of college, living with an old carpenter John and his sexy young wife Alison. Bred in the country, she is memorably described through animal imagery that conveys voluptuousness even in a black-and-white study. The charmer Nicholas overtly expresses his desire, and she does not repulse his personal advances. All that is needed is an occasion, and Nicholas devises an elaborate scheme. Feigning a trance and illness, he claims knowledge that the world will experience a second flood, so that the credulous carpenter becomes a kind of Noah. Specifically, he builds three large tubs, one for each of them. These are suspended from an attic ceiling, and there John and Alison and Nicholas await their fate. Exhausted by his labors, the old carpenter soon falls asleep and snores loudly. Alison and Nicholas get down from their tubs and go to bed, where they lie "In bisynesse of murthe and of solas" (I.3654). Their pleasure is interrupted by Absolon, a parish clerk who also wants Alison, whom he has admired at church. Thinking that the old husband is out of town—because the carpenter has been absent building the tubs—Absolon appears at a window and declares his love. Alison tries to send him away, but when he persists and demands a kiss, she decides upon an insult. She offers through the window "hir naked ers," and thus in the dark there is a Misdirected Kiss. A furious Absolon seeks revenge; he secures from the blacksmith Gerveys a hot "kultor" (plowshare, 3776) and returns to ask for another kiss. Nicholas decides that he will share the practical joke, taking it a stage further by a thunderclap release of wind, and is rewarded by a blow from the hot iron. In pain, he cries out for "Water! Water!" The old carpenter wakes, thinks the flood has come, cuts his tub from the roof, and falls to the cellar. The lovers rush into the street, declaring to the neighbors that John is mad, "And every wight gan laughen at this stryf" (3849).

The folly is so outrageous and such care has been taken to avoid any involvement with characters that the pilgrims also laugh (3855–59). The uniting of the plots with the cry of "Water! Water!" is an unsurpassed piece of plotting, so clever that the wildly comic scene leaves one breathless. Chaucer, of course, does not write tales that are no more than plot. The *Miller's Tale* is wonderfully textured, an occasion for precise local color, a town situation quite removed from court scenes. There is an evocation of Oxford, already renowned for its university, especially the sounds of bells that mark the hours and provide a counterpoint of church practice to the worldly activities of clerks and townspeople. Memorable is the description of Absolon, "jolif and gay," glowing with colors, a golden account that notes his biblical name, and hair that represents gentility, as well as the elegant clothes, which typify his fastidiousness and make his punishment the more telling, and his delight in dancing and musical skill. His little scene with the blacksmith is an easy exchange, a hearty joking about sexuality that shows tolerance between town and gown.

The plan of the carpenter's house reveals much about medieval city dwellings, down to the hole low on a board through which the cat creeps (3440–41). Nicholas's presence there shows relation between student and townsperson. One of the more diverting points is the antipathy between intellectual and working man. The carpenter resents his tenant's learning, voicing a familiar objection to study that seeks to know more than God intends (3449–64), and directly contrasting their two ways of life. There is a pervasive sense of John's working, making trips to nearby Oseney for business and skilled craftsmanship. When Nicholas comes from his trance, John is assertive: "What seystow? / What! Thynk on God, as we doon, men that *swynke" (*work, 3490–91). These vain details forestall emotional sympathy that might come for the loving doting husband, though in a January–May relationship the old man is already stereotypically foolish. As the work of Goliard poets[1] show, medieval clerks, nominally celibate and certainly poor, delight in endless stories of their success in pleasing women encumbered with such husbands. Chaucer himself pursued these themes in the second *fabliau* of *The Canterbury Tales.*

The Reeve's Tale

The *Reeve's Tale* contributes much to Chaucer's picture of noncourtly life, but lacks the vigorous zest and enjoyment found in the *Miller's Tale*. Again there are two clerks, both students at Soler (King's) Hall in Cambridge, but the action occurs in the country at a village mill in nearby Trumpington. Symkyn, the miller—obviously made unpleasant and foolish as the Reeve's revenge against the teller of the previous tale—is first described as "proud" (I.3926). He is also a bully and sly cheat, an old man who takes pride in besting others and in his family's pretensions. His wife is a parson's daughter, raised in a nunnery; there are two children, a twenty-year-old daughter Malyne, heavy and not obviously attractive but with a "fair heart," and a six-month-old baby, whose cradle is crucial to the plot. Aleyn and John are introduced as headstrong, seeking mirth and revelry, and thus trying to get out of college. They are also distinguished by their Northern accents, which show Chaucer's linguistic astuteness, and are an early use of regionalism to indicate provincialism and boorishness.

An occasion for adventure presents itself in the illness of the manciple, a kind of business agent who purchased college supplies; the college warden thus sends the two young men to the mill to have the grain ground. Determined that the miller will not cheat them, they carefully monitor the grinding. However, "This millere smyled of hir nycetee" (foolishness, 4046), for he knows that he can outwit them. He simply sneaks out and unties their horse, which rushes out into the fens, excited by the mares. A lively scene follows as John and Aleyn scurry to capture the horse. Before they succeed, night has fallen, and the miller has taken part of their flour for his gain. The two young men are angry to have been thus bested, and because it is dark they have to remain—and pay for their keep. Complacent Symkyn provides a meal (a goose) and becomes drunk on ale. All retire in the same big room, where there are three beds—a large one for Symkyn and his wife with baby's cradle at its foot, one for Malyne, and a third that John and Aleyn share. Already indignant, the two clerks are angered by the loud snoring, "As an hors he snorteth in his sleep" (4163), and seek revenge. Aleyn goes to the daughter's bed "And shortly for to seyn, they were aton" (together, 4197). Resenting his own lack of advantage, John gets up and moves the cradle to the foot of his bed, anticipating that Symkyn's wife will get up to relieve herself. She thus returns to John's bed, and he vigorously imitates his fellow. Before dawn, when it is still dark, Aleyn returns to what he thinks is the bed with John and gleefully describes his night's activity. This awakens the miller, and bedlam ensues. The scene is as outlandish as the central one of the *Miller's Tale;* there are shouts, rushing about, and a misdirected blow when the wife hits her husband with a staff. The clerks give the miller a thorough thrashing before riding away, taking the cake made from a half bushel of flour that he had stolen and which kindhearted Malyne had told Aleyn about as a parting gift with the words, "And, goode lemman, God thee save and kepe!" (4247).

The moment of Malyne's farewell is one gentle touch in a tale so frequently disagreeable that the fun is mitigated. Sexuality is exploitative and calculated for revenge rather than pleasure; indeed the tale notes more struggling effort than satisfaction for John and Aleyn. The natural impulses of the horse and wild mares are more appealing than their vicious and brutal sexual exploitation of women for whom they feel only contempt. The contest for the half bushel of grain has more to do with vanity than need. There are no simple impulses; pride and vengefulness are constantly in evidence, and the Reeve concludes his tale reiterating that "the proud millere [is] wel ybete" and thus has he repaid the pilgrim Miller (4312, 4324). This conclusion is very different from the Miller's "This tale is doon, and God save al the rowte!" (3854). It has a didactic ring, but there is nothing inspiring, only a grim picture of avarice and bitterness that prevent admiration for cleverness.

Like other *fabliaux* the *Reeve's Tale* provides vivid pictures of nonaristocratic life. The circumstances of living in a single large room in the mill, the significance of a mill in medieval economy, securing provisions from a town, the struggle to secure a horse that has bolted, enveloping darkness and how this determined behavior—these are very different from paved gardens and great halls and a private curtained bed. They are also different from the setting of the third *fabliau* in the opening fragment of *The Canterbury Tales*.

The Cook's Tale

The connections among the tales in Fragment I are the most completely realized among the various links. The Cook is hysterically enthusiastic about the Reeve's "jape of malice in the derk," a nice piece of audience response that shows Chaucer giving loud approval for a bitter *fabliau* to a churlish pilgrim that is himself given to excess. Inspired by what he has heard, the Cook begins what seems to be a third *fabliau*. Roger of Ware introduces Perkyn the Revelour, an apprentice whose name and youth suggest affinities with university clerks. However, his trade is victualing, the selling of food, and the scene is London, where there is just a glimpse of taverns, processions at Cheapside, and of Newgate Prison before the tale breaks off. There is no interruption, as with the incomplete *Squire's*

Tale and *Sir Thopas*. There are hints of what the tale might have contained: Perkyn's master decides that it is a good idea to get rid of a rotten apple before it spoils the rest. Perkyn's next companion loves dicing, reveling, and pleasure, and is married to a prostitute.

Responses to the *Cook's Tale* emphasize regret at the incompleteness of the picture of London life, and there is speculation about why Chaucer stopped. A third story of this "realistic" type of comedy is perhaps more than anyone could approach with eagerness. Contrast with one romance has been well made by two complete *fabliaux*, and an incomplete example forms a strong conclusion to Fragment I. Chaucer's fascination with such comic and bawdy stories reappears later in *The Canterbury Tales*.

The Shipman's Tale

The *Shipman's Tale* more obviously shows indebtedness to its French origins than do Chaucer's other *fabliaux*. The tale is of a merchant who lives at Saint Denis, which is just north of Paris, and there is even one French bit of dialogue, when he asks, "Quy la?" (Who's there? VII. 214). There is also a significant difference in tone, a cool detachment rather than broad, farcical humor or bitterness. The sexuality is discreet; by comparison with the other *fabliaux* it is refined. This seems closer to the pure *fabliau*, but perhaps stems from the point of view taken in the tale. Many details indicate a woman teller, and it is generally agreed that Chaucer's original intent was to give this tale to the Wife of Bath. Indeed the *Shipman's Tale* can be read as an account of "woe that is in marriage," the theme of the *Wife's Prologue*, and there are many statements about what women want from their husbands. The wife in the *Shipman's Tale* takes a view of sex and money that is very like that of the Wife of Bath's attitude toward her first three husbands. Her uninhibited sexuality resembles that of Alison in the *Miller's Tale*, though she is not a country girl. In addition, the woman in this tale is shown to be much more in control, not only not a victim but a manipulator who knows what she wants, strikes a bargain and keeps it, recovers quickly and smoothly extricates herself when threatened with exposure.

The plot is a simple one. The wife of a wealthy husband finds him niggardly, and she turns to his friend and cousin, a monk called Daun John, for a loan of one hundred francs to pay her debts. The monk agrees and borrows the sum from her merchant husband, who is setting out on a business trip. The monk gives the one hundred francs to the wife, who rewards him with a night of pleasure, a simple equation of sex and money. When the merchant returns he stops to see his friend the monk, who tells him that he repaid the loan to his wife. At home, the merchant, who has been successful in his business enterprises, enthusiastically makes love to his wife, another equation of sex and money, and chides her about not telling him that Daun John returned his money. She quickly replies that she thought the money a gift and has spent it; however, she offers to repay the debt to her merchant husband through sexual favors, again an equation of sex and money. The hapless husband, who does not know that he has been both cuckolded and financially defrauded, sees no remedy but to forgive the loss, yet he urges his wife "But, by thy lyf, ne be namoore so large. / Keep bet thy good, this yeve I thee in charge" (430–31).

The plot conveys little of the sophistication of the tale. The scenes are vividly presented, the dialogue subtle and witty. When Daun John first speaks to the wife in the garden, his tone is light and playful, but his testing is deliberate. He notes that she is pale and attributes this to lack of rest because of enthusiastic marital sex, and then comes the narrative detail that he blushes at his own thoughts (106–11). The technique is successful, for she answers with a hint that her life as a wife has left something to be desired. This prompts his declaration of love, and she responds with disclosures of her personal life, however disloyal this is to her spouse, whose principal fault is lack of generosity. Her ideal husband sounds very like one sought by the Wife of Bath; he should be vigorous, wise, rich, generous, obedient to his wife, and fresh in bed (175–77). These qualities are what women desire, as the knight in the *Wife's Tale* discovers from many replies to his question. There is, then, a closer correspondence between this *fabliau* and romance; "gentilesse" is, of course, not the subject, but there is no rudeness or coarseness, and there is no rape.

This tale, along with the *Merchant's Tale*, completes Chaucer's study of the noncourtly in *fabliaux*. It is notable that two are centered on merchants, a class with whom Chaucer most came in contact. Indeed one of the great attractions of the *Shipman's Tale* is its picture of medieval commerce, particularly the household, which provided both office and dwelling. The garden suggests prosperous circumstances. There is a vivid scene of the merchant retiring to his countinghouse, where he is not to be disturbed while he creates an annual financial report, whether he gained or lost. The intensity of his efforts is indicated when his wife knocks at the locked door and chides him: "How longe tyme wol ye rekene and caste / Youre sommes, and youre bookes, and youre thynges?" (216–17). The merchant's reply is an *apologia;* beginning with a sexist remark that women cannot understand male preoccupation with business, he proceeds to describe the anxieties and uncertainties of being a merchant, a constant fear "Of hap and fortune in oure chapman hede" (238). Merchants traveled extensively, and this one, accompanied by his apprentice, goes to Bruges, a major commercial center. His business is buying and obtaining credit, and he is not deflected from his work by entertainments. The venture is successful, for he returns to Paris and buys back his bond from Lombard bankers. The vignette vividly evokes a sense of merchant activity. Following an emphasis upon the indefinite nature of merchant enterprises, Chaucer concludes with a nice detail about the merchant's return. Confident because of his success—he is now rich and out of debt—he becomes a passionate lover (375–81). The picture of business argues its importance, but there is a serious defect in husbandly behavior. Not only does the merchant assume his wife's ignorance of his work, but also he is very firm about expenses, demanding "a thrifty household" (246) in his absence and reiterating that she must manage better and be less free-spending in the future. Indeed this forbearance comes only because she has silenced him with her long justification and promises that she will repay the lost money as his wife: "score it upon my taille" (mark it on my tally, charge to my account, 416). The choice of language is significant, for there is a pun that reaffirms the association of sex and money. This meanness and calculation contrast sharply with the merchant's oft repeated generosity toward Daun John, to whom he freely lends the one hundred francs, does not ask for a return, and is anxious that he not be thought to press for a return of the loan. In short, with a male cousin he behaves with largesse worthy of a knight. In fact, merchants were often wealthier than knights and imitated their behavior. The *Merchant's Tale* is of a knight; this most complex and difficult of Chaucer's *fabliaux* shows another view of connections between knight and merchant.

The Merchant's Tale

Consideration of the *Merchant's Tale* as a *fabliau* should begin with a recognition that this designation is only partially adequate to identify a remarkably complex work, which provokes many contradictory responses and is not easy to describe. The narrative is about twice as long as the other tales considered in this section, and only the final Pear Tree episode (about a hundred lines, a twelfth of the total) uses a traditional *fabliau* plot, the deception of an old husband by a young wife in somewhat grotesque circumstances. The opening section contains arguments about marriage; the middle portion is an account of the wedding of old January and young May and the beginning of May's responsiveness to a young squire Damian. The three parts are neatly related. January, an old knight, decides at the age of sixty that he will wed. Advantages, especially legitimate sex and an heir, are reviewed, but much is said against marriage, particularly the demands of wives. At January's request two friends, Placebo (I shall please) and Justinus (the just one) articulate cases for and against marriage. As in a scholastic debate, authorities are cited: Theophrastus, who attacked marriage, the moralist Seneca, examples from the Old Testament, Cato. There is no reconciliation between the points of view presented by January's two male companions. In practice, January is really only trying to justify his decision, especially his choice of a young bride, a creature who will fulfill all his fantasies (IV.1610). Thus even Justinus accepts his "folye" (1655). The extent of the old knight's illusion is shown in his anxiety about his salvation, since with the young wife he expects to have perfect bliss and he worries that man cannot have such felicity on earth and in heaven. Wryly, Justinus suggests that May will perhaps be January's "purgatorie" (1670). The second portion of the *Merchant's Tale* begins (1689) with the marriage, a sacrament in which "wysdom and trouthe" are the ideal. Wedding feasts are not usually described in detail; here attention goes to January's eagerness and anxieties about the wedding night and to Damian's lovesickness. The teller is explicitly noncommittal about May's reactions. In the third part of the tale all strands come together. January has built a garden, where he enjoys May and also tries to confine her. He is now blind, a physical sign of his folly in thinking that he can control his wife. She and Damian communicate by letters—read and disposed of in a privy—and a meeting is arranged. May takes an impression of January's key, which Damian copies and uses to get into the garden. At a sign from her he climbs a pear tree. May expresses a desire for fruit, which may be a sign of pregnancy; her blind husband helps her into the pear tree, where she meets Damian, who immediately takes her. All has been observed by the king and queen of the underworld, who take sides according to gender. January's sight is restored through Pluto's power; however, through Proserpine's intervention May talks her way out of being caught flagrantly in adultery. The influence of these rulers of fairy is crucial; their conflicting advocacy of male and female points of view that can only be reconciled through mutual tolerance parallels the disputation between Placebo and Justinus that was not resolved. The attitudes of Pluto and Proserpine foreshadow the conclusion, and the dispute also is a device for building suspense, since it delays May's joining Damian in the pear tree, even leaving their encounter in doubt. In the end January does not insist upon what he has seen, the only occasion when he defers from having absolutely his own way; he helps May from the tree and embraces her; no more is said of Damian.

The *Merchant's Tale* is generally recognized as part of the so-called Marriage Group, providing a kind of interlude between opposing attitudes in tales of the Wife and Clerk and the resolution of the *Franklin's Tale,* and continuing the discussion of "woe that is in marriage" in a cruder fashion. The discourse of the Wife of Bath is specifically noted (1685), and January is reminiscent of her first three husbands—old, lusty, rich, and doting. This reading relies heavily upon the role of the teller, the Merchant who in his *Prologue* describes himself as an old man unhappily wed to a wife that could defeat the devil. The teller and his hero January are then both aged lovers, *senex amans,* and interpretation is conditioned by the teller's personal bitterness. The tale is then read as a bitter account of the foolishness and ugliness of male sexuality, desire lingering after potency and repulsive physicality, in which an old lecher is punished by his shameless young wife. January, for example, takes an aphrodisiac on his wedding night (1807–12). His gleeful dance of anticipation and his sitting up in bed and singing after the consummation of the marriage linger in one's mind, as does the description of his old, freshly shaved bristly face against May's tender face.

An old husband is a familiar figure in *fabliaux;* he appears in each of the previously completed tales. What is different are attempts to explain male sexuality, why an old husband behaves as he does and what his life was like before he became a sixty-year old cuckold. Damian, a squire, suggests a youthful January, the kind of promiscuous man who plays the courtly lover—he is so ill that he will die but recovers quickly when the woman responds—takes other men's (friend's) wives, yet has but fleeting pleasure, to judge by the minimal encounter in the pear tree. Old January shows greater awareness and concern for women. He worries obsessively about his sexuality, but he also has qualms about how his bride will react to it, and his wish not to hurry the wedding night is at least partially a concern for May (1828–41). January is desperately possessive, but he perceives that such jealousy is a fault, and his settlement of property on his young wife is generous. Here, then, is some feeling beyond simple desire and self-interest. Whether May has feelings is not clear. On the wedding night, "The bryde was broght abedde as stille as stoon" (1818), and her later experience of sex is also indeterminate, "wheither hire thoughte it paradys or helle" (1964). Apart from her Proserpine-inspired defense, May's longest speech is a reply to January's anxiety that she will be false. May notes the double moral standard that men are "evere untrewe" but constantly accuse women of being so (2188–2206). Young Damian makes an impression on May, so that she has "pity" and encourages him; there is nothing explicit about pleasure. Her return to January can thus be seen as genuine, an enactment of the Woman Taken in Adultery (John 8:3–11) when men, themselves not without sin, are taught not to cast stones. The complexity and mixed tones of the *Merchant's Tale* encourage interpretation more than hearty laughter.

Each of the other *fabliaux*, as noted, contains descriptions of noncourtly life. Here the principal character is an old knight, who lives in Lombardy, a center of finance and international banking, so that there is an interest in money as in the *Shipman's Tale*. Old January lives in a palace, his wealth brings him the young bride that he wants, and he spends lavishly for feast, garden, and May's inheritance. A description of the marriage ceremony and opulent wedding feast are the fullest pictures of these events in Chaucer's works. However, such straightforward realism is balanced by the appearance of Pluto and Proserpine, rulers of fairyland, who intervene on behalf of January and May in the garden, a highly symbolic setting. January's calling forth his wife in a reworking of the celebratory Song of Songs is only one of many uses of convention. Chaucer's interest in genre is perhaps most fully expressed in the *Merchant's Tale* because he forces analysis by setting a *fabliau* episode in the midst of a fuller narrative and by creating a tone that involves the audience but never allows a simple response. There is so much emotional bitterness that the usual detachment and emphasis upon clever action do not occur. Yet there are some humane moments, so that a purely harsh reaction, a negative view of behavior, is not allowed. The tale, then, poses many questions about the *fabliaux* and a major theme in *The Canterbury Tales*—marriage. There are, however, no answers. From the beginning January's decision to wed is questioned: "Were it for hoolynesse or dotage / I kan nat seye" (1253–54). January's seeking a wife combines "Heigh fantasye and curious bisynesse" (1577), "But natheless, bitwixe ernest and game, / He atte laste appoynted hym on oon" (1593–94). The audience has the same dilemma. The inspiration for the narrative is sexual desire, a worldly interest and pleasure, but January becomes affectionate and caring. He is blind for a time, but so are any who judge only by appearances, and appearances are often all that is available. *Fabliaux* seem to be outrageous and comic stories, but they can become very serious and thought provoking.

5

Religious Romances and Saints' Legends

Middle English romances usually are preserved in manuscripts that also contain religious pieces, and this suggests a common didactic interest. Similarly, legend and history are not sharply distinguished. Several of the *Canterbury Tales* show characteristics of melding that set them apart from "purer" examples of romance; they are also related by an explicit emphasis upon Christianity. In this section five tales are included. Two are clearly Christian saints legends: the *Prioress's Tale* of a little boy murdered by the Jews in an Asian city, which is tied to the martyrdom of young Hugh of Lincoln, and the *Second Nun's Tale* of St. Cecilia, a Roman Christian martyr who converted her husband Valerian to Christianity and chastity. A third, the *Physician's Tale,* is an episode from the Roman historian Livy, recast in medieval terms, that tells of the death of Virginia, a pagan martyr to virginity. Two others, the *Man of Law's Tale* and the *Clerk's Tale,* contain elements of romance, notably hagiographical or exemplary. However, the heroes are not knights but married women, Constance and Griselda, who embody allegorical Christian virtues of constancy and patience. Chaucer's naming of himself in both the *Prologue of the Man of Law's Tale* and "Lenvoy to the Clerk's Tale" may indicate a special interest in virtuous women. The *Prioress's Tale* is about a young boy, but it is a Miracle of the Virgin. Thus a common characteristic of these five tales is the nobility and strength of women, sometimes sealed in martyrdom and other times tested and proven to inspire others in the world. Also of interest is the early Christian context of the tales; all but one (*Clerk's*) are explorations of the time at which Christianity was being established in a pagan world.

The Man of Law's Tale

The story of Constance was a popular one in Chaucer's time. Its principal source is "historical," the Anglo-Norman chronicle of Nicholas Trivet, a Dominican friar, written c.1334. However, this accounts for only about one third, and there are significant changes as well as additions, notably from Innocent III's *De miseria condicionis humane.* Two themes from folk tale, a princess exiled for refusing to marry her father and a queen exiled for giving birth to a monstrous child, are combined. Constance is only one of many accused queens; her story occurs in a number of Middle English versions, including Gower's *Confessio Amantis* (Bk.II. 587–1598).[1] There are also pictorial representations, of which the bosses at Norwich Cathedral most obviously indicate a hagiographical value. Chaucer deletes any idea of incest and adds much description and dialogue. Most memorable is the pathos in Constance's characterization—when she is plotted against, accused and attacked, shown as especially vulnerable in a rudderless ship with her baby son—and powerfully evocative rhetoric. The tale is unified by her journeying in the rudderless boat, an image of the Ship of the Church to show the spread of Christianity in the early Middle Ages.[2]

Constance, daughter of the emperor of Rome, is a Christian. However, her father accepts the marriage proposal of a pagan Sultan of Syria, who has learned from traveling merchants of Constance's beauty and virtues—humility, courtesy, generosity, holiness. With prayer Constance accepts her fate. As was often the case in the early centuries, a ruler converted because of his wife's faith, and the people followed. However, the Sultan's mother objects to a change of religion. Feigning conversion, she plots and accomplishes a slaughter of all at the wedding feast, except Constance, who is put into a rudderless boat that sails through the eastern Mediterranean, the Straits of Gibraltar, and finally reaches the Northumberland coast. There Constance is befriended by the constable of the castle and his wife Hermengyld, who so loves the virtuous castaway that she converts to Christianity and accomplishes a miracle. Soon Satan makes a young knight lust for Constance. After he is repulsed, he slips into the chamber where the two women are asleep, cuts the throat of Hermengyld, and puts the bloody knives by Constance. Thus once again her life is threatened; she is brought to trial before Alla, the local king. Such pity does Constance evoke that Alla tests the false knight by having him swear on the Gospels.

Again Constance's prayers are answered and another miracle occurs; before everyone the false knight falls down and his eyes burst out, as a voice proclaims his guilt. The knight is executed; Alla converts and weds Constance. The narrative pattern is repeated: Donegild, a pagan mother-in-law, is furious but bides her time. When a son is born, she intercepts the messenger and substitutes letters telling of a monstrous birth. Alla is grieved but as a Christian accepting, so that he hurries home to be with his wife. However, before he arrives, Constance has been set adrift in the same rudderless boat, this time with her infant son. Appropriately, she prays to the Virgin Mary, and they sail for five years. Once a would-be rapist from a heathen shore enters the boat, but Mary protects Constance. Finally the boat is discovered by a senator who brings Constance and her son to Rome without knowing that she is the emperor's daughter. Meanwhile Alla has angrily slain his evil mother, but soon repented and gone as a pilgrim to Rome, where all are reunited. Alla and Constance return to Northumberland, and the emperor names his grandson Maurice as successor. After Alla's untimely death Constance goes to live with her father in Rome.

Several episodes in the tale are specifically identified as "miracles": Constance's escaping the slaughter arranged by the Sultan's mother, the blind man's recovering his sight through Christ with Hermengyld as agent, Constance's demonstrated innocence at the trial before Alla when a voice is heard, the falling overboard of the would-be rapist. In contrast, there is a realistic detail; provisions for five years are put into the boat for the second voyage. Further, miracles occur in realistically sketched scenes with rich dialogue. The name "Constance" is allegorical and a fit description of her unshaken acceptance of whatever happens and reliance upon prayer. Constance's life is her witness to living as a Christian, persecuted but resilient and always hopeful. The tale is one of abiding faith, which is reiterated in Alla's Christian devotion. Though his killing of his mother is a significant sin, he is immediately penitent. Few passages in *The Canterbury Tales* are more memorable than those describing Constance's pale face as she quietly expects death at her trial (II.645–51), and when she weeps before being put out to sea with her baby son and gently quiets his crying (822–40).

The *Man of Law's Tale* provides a moving account of a woman falsely accused, which is always a powerful narrative theme. Her vulnerability is emphasized because as a woman she is helpless against the will of men—her father, who arranges the first marriage, and two lustful male attackers. But the constable is moved with pity at her plight, as is Alla. Further, two women, the evil mothers-in-law, are responsible for Constance's severest trials; they oppose her Christianity and resent loss of their pagan heritage more than their sons' marrying. Constance's tale is then not primarily about an oppressed woman who triumphs but a showing of the constant difficulty of living in the world as a Christian; it is distinguished by the care with which context is established. Her two voyages represent missionary ventures of the early church, more successful in the West than in the Middle East. The establishment of Christianity in Britain, reintroduced by Pope Gregory the Great in the sixth century, provides the central episode. Communication in "corrupt Latin" (519–20) is a reminder of an early hold of Christianity before the Romans left, and the detail of a British Gospels book recalls the splendid manuscripts of the Northumbrian flowering.

Although the *Man of Law's Tale* uses many rhetorical strategies common to a saint's legend, an essential difference is an absence of the heroine's martyrdom. Constance lives in the world rather than dying for the faith. She resembles virgin saints—marital sex is tolerated, not sought—and like the Virgin Mary she has a son. However, Constance's motherhood, a manifestation of femininity, is central, and this ties her to earthly experience. Alla is a loyal convert, but he is also a devoted lover/husband of romance. As in a saint's legend, the structure is episodic, for conflicts are repeated. High sentiments abound, and these are eloquently reinforced by the rhetoric of the tale's laments, exclamations, devout prayers. Question and answer suggest the style of a lawyer, but also a response to religious belief. Faith must constantly be reaffirmed; even the nobles are frequently tested by circumstances that pose doubts about God's goodness. Constance is an extreme characterization, an ideal, and in the *Clerk's Tale* this virtue is further explored with an emphasis upon patience.

The Clerk's Tale

As part of the Marriage Group the *Clerk's Tale* is usually seen as an argument for male dominance, an answer to the Wife of Bath's insistence upon female sovereignty. The long tradition of Griselda's story as an example of wifely subjection—in a sixteenth-century play, eighteenth-century chapbooks, as a type for twentieth-century feminists—encourages this reading. An alternative is to emphasize

Walter's transformation, a freeing of himself from male selfishness, first by agreeing to marry and thus provide an heir for his kingdom, and then to recognize that testing his wife is not necessary, that he can accept her goodness, best identified as "pacience in adversitee."[3] Seen in relation to the *Man of Law's Tale*, the *Clerk's Tale* is another story of constancy. Chaucer often exemplifies this virtue in women and also sympathetically records its loss in Criseyde. The concluding moral supports this interpretation, for it notes that wives are not capable of Griselda's humility, but that everyone "Sholde be constant in adversitee" (IV.1146). A Latin gloss for this passage, one of several that accompany the tale in important manuscripts, expands the idea that all should imitate Griselda's "constancy" by transforming it into what "they might dare to do for God."[4] Some kind of allegorical and exemplary meaning is necessary for acceptance of Walter's behavior, which is monstrous. The type for child sacrifice is Abraham and Isaac, frequently represented in visual arts, where obedience is being tested and God preserves life.

The origins of the *Clerk's Tale,* as with the *Man of Law's,* are in folklore; actions in tales of "Monster Bridegroom" and "The Patience of a Princess" are similar. Chaucer's immediate source, explicitly given in the *Clerk's Prologue,* is Petrarch "the lauriat poet." Indeed the passage (26–56) is his richest comment about an experience of Italy, combining both topographical references and praise of the author. In fact, Petrarch's Latin prose *De obedientia ac fide uxoria mythologia* (A fable of wifely obedience and faithfulness) is translated from Boccaccio's *Decameron* (X.10).

Unlike Constance, Griselda is very poor indeed, living in a village with her old father Janicula, not as daughter of the emperor of Rome, but as one who is never idle. One theme of the tale is "gentilesse," that goodness comes from God and is not dependent upon wealth or birth. This argument is advanced by Walter, a marquis in Lombardy, who has resisted marriage until his people forcefully urge it upon him. He exercises residual power by insisting upon his own choice of bride and revealing only on the wedding day that she is Griselda; the marriage agreement included her promise of absolute obedience. This tale, then, illustrates "gentilesse" in the two main characters: nobly born Walter lacks the quality, while poor Griselda is truly noble. Putting off her poor clothing, she behaves with the elegance of an emperor's daughter that increases her virtue and the people's love. A daughter is born, and Walter's first testing soon follows: arguing that his people resent Griselda's humble origins, Walter orders her to surrender their daughter. Griselda meekly gives the child to a sergeant, but shows sadness. Walter is moved to pity and secretly sends the child to his sister at Bologna. Four years later, Griselda bears a son, and when he is two years old Walter repeats the testing. Again Griselda is obedient to her lord, and Walter is struck by her constancy and patience (667–72). The boy joins his sister, and Griselda says nothing in recrimination, though she believes that her children have been slain. Walter's final testing comes when the daughter is twelve years old. With a false papal bull the marquis declares he will put aside Griselda as his wife to marry a young noblewoman. Ever obedient and humble, Griselda makes all the necessary preparations for the wedding, patiently accepting this latest change in Fortune. She asks only that she be given a smock to cover her nakedness when she leaves to rejoin her father; this will be payment for her lost maidenhood. On the day of the supposed nuptial sister and brother return from Bologna, and all are happily reunited. Only with this "pitous joye" does Griselda swoon and then embrace her children (1079–87). The dominant response of bystanders to these events is pity. Griselda resumes her finery and life with Walter, who has finally learned to behave gently. And they all live happily ever after. . . . Again Chaucer includes a tale, from one of his more ideal pilgrims, that argues for Christian virtues through a woman who is utterly self-effacing and dedicated to something beyond herself, in short saintly. Her unwavering faith contrasts sharply with the vagaries of popular attitude.

The conclusion of the *Clerk's Tale* is one of Chaucer's most elusive and ambiguous in *The Canterbury Tales*. The moral, as noted, asks an allegorical interpretation in which wifely obedience represents subservience to God, a model of humility that should be cited more than Job (932). Clerks are remiss in their praise of women, who are twice as humble and true as men. This is probably ironic, since the final stanzas ruefully note the absence of women like Griselda and specifically ask God's blessing on the Wife of Bath and all like her. Then "Lenvoy de Chaucer" adds a final comment that shifts the argument: a warning to husbands not to test their wives, not least because women's angry eloquence can pierce man's armor. Such songs often serve to connect story and life. Thus Chaucer's "Lenvoy" can be read as further irony, or as a counterargument to the Clerk.

The Physician's Tale

The story of Virginia, a martyr for purity, was also very popular in the Middle Ages and is often viewed as a secular saint's legend. Although Chaucer's most immediate source for the episode is the *Roman de la Rose,* the opening of the *Physician's Tale* cites Titus Livius, and later the episode is identified as "no fable, / But knownen for historical thyng notable" (VI.155–56). Thus it can be interestingly compared with the historical context for the *Man of Law's Tale* as a story of Roman times that explores the relation between justice and mercy. Although frequently used in other medieval versions as an example of evil government, Virginia's story in Chaucer's handling does not emphasize a political dimension. There is popular response to the plight of Virginius: "a thousand peple in *thraste, / To save the knight" (*thrust, pushed in, 260–61). However, they act "for routhe and for pitee," not as social protest. Similarly, Virginius intervenes "of his pitee" (272) to save Apius's servant Claudius, who is thus exiled rather than hanged. A hint about audience response to the *Physician's Tale* comes in the *Prologue to the Pardoner's Tale* that follows. Here the Host describes Virginia as "pitously" slain and his own heart as lost "for pitee of this mayde" (317). A compelling interest, as with Constance and Griselda, seems to be woman's story.

Here she is young, just fourteen. The name Virginia is not just a patronymic from Virginius, but also an epitome of her character. A knight's daughter, she is introduced by Nature's description of her as a creature who could not be counterfeited by the greatest artists. Virginia's physical beauty is surpassed by her "gentilesse" and virtues, notably virginity, humility, temperance, patience. Modestly she avoids social gatherings that are occasions of dalliance. Nevertheless, she attracts the attention of Apius, a justice who lusts for her. He engages the service of a churl Claudius to bring false charges that Virginius has taken his slave girl and passes her as his daughter. The case is heard before Apius, who awards Virginia to Claudius as his servant. The distraught Virginius believes that only death can save his daughter from shame. Moved by "fadres pitee," he urges Virginia to accept her death "in pacience" (223). After a brief complaint, formal lamentation, she concludes, "Yif me my deth, er that I have shame" (249). Virginius cuts off her head and sends it to Apius. He is, however, not hanged since the people protest and cast the wicked judge into prison, where he hangs himself. Virginius intervenes to reduce Claudius's sentence to exile, and all the other guilty are punished.

The tale poses many difficult questions. Such an absolute defense of virginity seems distorted by modern standards; indeed Chaucer's handling, as of a wife's chastity in the *Franklin's Tale* and *Merchant's Tale,* makes the reader examine values. The tale, then, has much to say about justice, or rather its lack in a corrupt official like Apius. Yet young Virginia's first words are: "O mercy, deere fader!" (231). The authority cited in her complaint is Jephthah, an Old Testament figure who pays for his victory by sacrificing his daughter, then asks for two months to lament her virginity before she is killed (Judges 11:30–40). Jewish and Roman fathers are analogous. Virginius does not show mercy to his daughter; however, after her death he intercedes for Claudius and shows "pitee" at the end of the tale, manifesting Christian forgiveness. The young woman could only be responsive to male attitudes, which are specifically identified as sinful. Apius's lust is inspired by the "feend" (devil, 130), and the moral of the tale is "Forsaketh synne, er synne yow forsake" (286). A larger theological explanation is provided: Envy, as defined by "The Doctour," provokes sin, destruction of beauty and goodness (112–17). A Latin gloss identifies St. Augustine as the authority for "Envy is the hatred of another's good fortune." Innocence, then, suffers in the world, but evil is punished: "Heere may men seen how synne hath his merite" (276).

The magnitude of the problem is further complicated. Virginia is not just a victim. Like Isabella in Shakespeare's *Measure for Measure* she practices a conspicuous virtue, noted in her withdrawal from human pleasures (61ff) that precipitates disasters in a sinful world. Women like Constance and Griselda are not so assertive, and they survive, albeit after great trials. Virginia's mother, it is worth noting, appears in a meager but significant way; mother and daughter go together to temple, a sign of acknowledging a divinity to which they are subject. In contrast, Virginius insists upon his own knowledge and power; by killing his daughter he assumes a godlike function. Yet as in other tales with saintly women, the man is forgiven, allowed to live a penitent life chastened by his mistake.

Indeed this theme explains two long digressions in the *Physician's Tale* that have provoked critical speculation, the exhortations to governesses (72–92) and to mothers and fathers (93–103). The first has been variously interpreted as a comment tied to John of Gaunt, either because Katherine Swynford, his third wife and Chaucer's sister-in-law, was governess to Gaunt's children and his mistress, or because of the elopement of Gaunt's second daughter. These suggestions provide a topicality for commonplace sentiments. In the first is a recognition of Christian repentance; governesses may be chaste, or if fallen, they have given up their earlier misconduct. Thus the female mentor's chastity is distinguished from the virginity that is the subject of the tale. The second address urges the responsibility of parents, which is to be exercised in two ways: providing a good example by how they live and chastising firmly when the child errs by analogue with a shepherd who can only protect his lambs from the wolf by not being negligent. Christ, of course, is the Good Shepherd. Taken together these two warnings provide a context for Virginius, a too-severe father with an absolutist view of the virtue of virginity, a Roman patriarch who ignores the human. An alternative understanding of virginity, explicitly Christian and expanded, is explored in another tale.

The Second Nun's Tale

Saint Cecilia is a virgin, but her "life" is very different from Virginia's. The *Second Nun's Tale* is a saint's legend, best known in a collection *Legenda aurea* (Golden Legend) of Jacobus de Voragine. Such stories easily blend historical and miraculous, and the *Second Nun's Tale* shows characteristics of the genre: religious dedication, conversion, an angel, miracles, persecution, martyrdom. The tale is inspiring, permeated by Christian belief, part of the account of the early centuries of opposition in pagan Rome. The historical St. Cecilia is recorded sometime between the second and fourth centuries. Her virginity is less a denial of sexuality than a commitment to loving many in the Christian community, the kind of loves espoused by members of religious orders. She is both free and deeply committed to work. Cecilia combines characteristics of the women in the three tales just discussed. She is married but remains a virgin, yet loving others and converting them.

There is no surrounding dramatic interplay for the *Second Nun's Tale,* but its *Prologue* establishes ways to read the tale. First is an urging against Idleness, to which the devil always draws human beings. This prepares for an emphasis upon good works, necessary to support even the greatest faith. Then comes an invocation to the Virgin Mary, "Mayde and Mooder," that reiterates the necessity of both, while stressing the distinction between body and soul. The significance of Marianism in the history of Catholicism is manifold. Acknowledgment of Bernard of Clairvaux (VIII.30) marks the fervent veneration also shown in numerous cathedrals that bear Mary's name, endless representations in religious art, liturgical celebrations, and many tales of Miracles of the Virgin that share with romances excitement and unusual situations as well as idealism. In addition to answering prayers for help, Mary out of "pitee" aids even before she is asked. A third section of the *Prologue* provides several etymologies for Cecilia's name, derived from the *Golden Legend* (85–119). Although not linguistically accurate, these provide a moral explanation. Cecilia signifies virginity, but also a teacher; combining holiness with busyness, she follows the active life.

Like Constance, Cecilia is a nobly born Roman, "And from hir cradel up fostred in the feith / Of Crist, and bar his gospel in hir mynde" (122–23). Her closeness to God and confidence of how she is to serve never falter. At the appropriate age she is married to Valerian, while wearing a hair shirt next to her skin and with a prayer that she will not be defiled. Such asceticism is, however, not entirely negative. Unlike the male St. Alexius, who conforms to family expectations of marriage but leaves to become a severe ascetic, Cecilia remains accepting of life in the world as do Constance and Griselda. On the wedding night Cecilia explains to Valerian that she is guarded by an angel that will slay him if he consummates the marriage, but guard him if he lives purely. The young husband asks to see the angel, and Cecilia takes him along the Appian Way to meet Pope Urban, who lives in the catacombs to escape Roman persecution. Urban oversees Valerian's conversion, but an "oold man" that holds the Gospels (probably St. Paul) indicates further divine intervention and emphasizes that grace comes from God and humans need only to accept. Shortly after this, Valerian converts his brother Tiburce. Arguments are precisely put, with an emphasis upon the life to come. Cecilia explains the Trinity by analogue to man's three mental facilities—memory, imagination, judgment. She is an effective preacher and converts many to become "Christ's knights" (353, 383). Thus, like Constance, Cecilia spreads the Gospel. Roman authority is, of course, threatened. Even Maximus, officer of the prefect, is converted and subsequently executed. Finally Almachius summons Cecilia and offers a choice: sacrifice to the pagan god Jupiter or be executed. In rigorous cross-examination Cecilia is a strong apologist: Roman power and authority are only of the world, and pagan gods are but images, mere stones, while Christian faith knows that "God is high in his heavens." Almachius orders Cecilia burned. Placed in a caldron over flames, she remains cool, without even a drop of sweat, for a day and night. Next she receives three strokes against her neck, but she does not die for three days, the time she asked of God. Thus Cecilia has time to preach again, to leave her property to Urban, who buries her with other saints and makes her house a church. Cecilia is finally described as one whose "good werkynge . . . perseverynge" (constancy) burn ever "in charite ful brighte"—the essential Christian virtue, as St. Paul explains (1 Corinthians 13).

St. Cecilia's life is, then, one lived entirely in service to Christ. Faith is not a private virtue (though often lived in solitary circumstances as during Constance's sailings in the *Man of Law's Tale*) but given witness in the harshness of the pagan world. Christianity requires strength, here expressed in the language of chivalry, for those converted are knights, armed in brightness, that do battle against darkness. Pitted against the worldly power of Rome, they accept martyrdom and triumph in it. Contrasting values are indicated, for example in Valerian's statement that before conversion he and his brother lived previously in dreams but now in truth, as the angel's presence makes explicit. There is also the "miracle" of the two crowns, snow white and rose red betokening virginity and good works; sweet-smelling garlands replace the traditional marriage crowns for Cecilia and Valerian and, as St. Ambrose explained, foreshadow the palm of martyrdom. Belief in the Trinity is affirmed in Cecilia's explanation, and the three days before Christ's Resurrection are recalled by the three blows against her neck and her prayer for three last days of life to reaffirm and provide for future conversion. A salient characteristic of St. Cecilia's life is its continuous expansion of Christianity. The climax of the *Second Nun's Tale* is certainly her martyrdom, but this fills only the last six stanzas, and ongoing good works are the main interest, not physical torment. Just as Cecilia's asceticism is a minor theme to the major idea of professing and living faith in the world, so her "life" stands as a model, virtue shown in deeds that inspire and do not require a final exhortation.

The Prioress's Tale

Although its principal character is a "litel clergeon," a schoolboy aged seven, the *Prioress's Tale,* like Chaucer's religious romances and saints' legends, also emphasizes the importance of women in Christianity. Like the *Second Nun's Tale* it begins with an invocation to Mary, and many details come from the Little Office of the Virgin. Again Chaucer uses the *Prologue* not for dramatic interplay of pilgrims but for devotion. One stanza (VII. 467–73) gives Mary's relation to the Trinity (Father/ Power, Son /Wisdom, Holy Spirit/Love): through the Holy Spirit she conceived Jesus, God the Father's Wisdom. Mary is praised as a magnificent and bounteous helper of man, coming to aid before asked; her purpose is to lead humans to her Son. Finally the prayer declares an inadequacy to praise, like a child of one year who can scarcely express itself. This image returns to the opening stanza that declares children give homage to Mary. The *Prioress's Tale* is of one small boy, utterly devoted to the Virgin and martyred for this love, who provides a saintly model and evokes responses of pity; it also explores maternal love.

The story takes place in a great city of Asia, a Chaucerian specificity that ties the *Prioress's Tale* to the *Second Nun's Tale* and the *Man of Law's Tale* through presenting the opposition between Christianity and other religions, here Judaism. While the *Man of Law's Tale* and the *Second Nun's Tale* show hardships and dangers during the early centuries of Christianity, the *Prioress's Tale* suggests religious conflict in the later Middle Ages. Inside the city is a Jewish ghetto, allowed by a lord of the country for worldly gain, since the Jews practice usury, "Hateful to Crist and to his compaigne" (492). Through the streets of the ghetto the little boy walks to school, singing the *Alma redemptoris* (Gracious [mother] of the Redeemer) on his way. Taught by his mother to love Mary, he has independently learned this hymn to honor Our Lady. Like Virginia he is innocent, but such conspicuous virtue provokes evil. Satan inspires Jewish hatred, and the Jews conspire to murder the schoolboy. His throat, like St. Cecilia's, is cut, and the body cast into the pit of a privy. The boy's mother becomes anxious, prays to Mary, and searches for her son in the ghetto, a new Rachel bewailing the Slaughter of the Innocents. The Jews deny any knowledge, but "Mordre wol out" (575). The boy begins to sing *Alma redemptoris* loudly, and his body is found. After the Jews are executed, from his bier the schoolboy continues to sing, explaining the miracle to an abbot in attendance: Mary intervened to keep him from dying so that he could sing, and only with the removal of a "grain" from his tongue can he stop. This the abbot does, and the schoolboy dies, a "martir" (680). A final stanza offers a context; the analogous slaying of young Hugh of Lincoln in 1255, recorded by Matthew Paris, is a recent work of "cursed Jewes."

Many readers and critics fault this tale as anti-Semitic, often seeing this as crucial to a satiric portrayal of the Prioress. Others recognize the attitude as commonplace in the Middle Ages, especially notable in cycle plays that emphasize Christ's Passion and in Miracles of the Virgin that tell how Mary rescues many from sin. There are numerous extant versions of tales about a child murdered for his faith, often in a Jewish ritual reenactment of the Crucifixion. Much of the interest of the *Prioress's Tale* is the compelling account of the seven-year-old. Chaucer provides a vivid picture of the early schooling that complements scenes of university life in the *Miller's* and *Reeve's Tales*. The child studies his primer, an elementary text that usually contained alphabet, basic prayers, and elements of faith (Lord's Prayer, Apostles' Creed, Graces, Psalm, Ten Commandments, Seven Deadly Sins, Devotions to Mary, Works of Mercy). The smallness of the school, where different ages are together—as in some rural schools today—makes it possible for the seven-year-old to hear the lessons of his older fellow students. Thus although he does not know Latin, he learns the *Alma redemptoris* by rote, after one of the older boys explains that it is a devotion to Mary. His singing while he walks alone through the ghetto is, then, an extension of the school day. More crucially, it illustrates the simplicity of faith, Christ's statement that believers that are as little children will enter the kingdom of heaven (Matthew 18:1–4).

A combination of piety and young innocence gives poignancy to the *Prioress's Tale*. This is heightened because the schoolboy is a widow's son; mother's "pitee" seems stronger when the woman is alone. The scene of her "with face pale of drede and bisy thoght" (589), searching first at the school and then learning that her son was last seen at the ghetto, builds dramatically. There she stops every Jew to ask about her child; the reply is always "nay." The loss of this widowed mother echoes Mary's loss of her Son and reiterates the point of the *Prologue*. Although the tale is Marian, Christ is very evident; through His grace the mother is led and hears the schoolboy sing "with pitous lamentacioun" (611). Not Mary but God's might glorifies martyrs; the provost praises Christ and then His mother; the abbot questions in the name of the Trinity, and the boy recognizes the will of Jesus Christ. The role of Christ's mother is to be a "welle (source) of mercy," an intermediary to

God, from Whom mercy—thrice noted (687–88)—comes "For reverence of his mooder Marie."

In all of the tales considered as religious romances and saints' legends, Chaucer shows women's strength in expressions of constancy, patience, humility, innocence, obedience, and piety that relies upon God and not human resources. The exceptions are the evil stepmothers in the *Man of Law's Tale* who plot and initiate evil actions to secure power—traditional male behavior—and their sins seem greater because so divergent from the ideal. The virtuous women—virgin, wife, mother, widow—because of their experience and greater sense of human limitations rely upon and receive God's mercy in large measure, triumphing as did Christ through suffering. The message of the Gospels is reiterated in several other tales that provide satiric warnings and in a final group that are best called sermons.

6

Tales with Satiric Warnings

Because each tale strains the bounds of a conventional genre, whether romance, *fabliau*, or sermon, the designation of this section simply indicates tales that are overtly satiric and provide explicit warnings. The *Friar's Tale* and the *Summoner's Tale* are often deemed *fabliaux,* and usually considered primarily as two sides of a quarrel, a seeking of revenge by members of rival professions with religious duties, which parallels the opening quarrel of the Miller and Reeve. Much can also be made of a link with the Wife of Bath, whose tale delights the Friar and thus triggers the Summoner's enmity. Nevertheless, the *Friar's Tale,* notable for its liveliness and folk origin, is mostly satiric in effect. Similarly, the *Summoner's Tale* contains scatological elements that resemble those in *fabliaux,* but reiterates a warning against avarice. Both are anger-filled and vituperative. Direct professional attacks, against friars and summoners, as well as revelations of their working techniques, tie these two tales to the *Canon's Yeoman's Tale,* which is an exposé of alchemy, but also a comment about damnation with references to hell that tie it to the *Friar's* and *Summoner's Tales.* The *Manciple's Tale* is most difficult to place. Both another representation of anger and a fable about a bird, its most distinctive passage is a long moral observation about using restraint in speech. This can be read as a warning and an anticipation of the concluding homily of the *Parson's Tale* and the Retraction.

The Friar's Tale

The opening of the *Friar's Tale* suggests generic mixture. It begins "Whilom ther was dwellynge in my contree" (III.1301), but the person named is an archdeacon, not a knight or a fairy. His activity is to carry out the law, to punish those guilty of a variety of sins, beginning with fornication but also including usury, refusal of the sacraments, and so on. In the process, of course, money is gained. Carrying out the archdeacon's work is a summoner who is the main subject of the tale. The pilgrim Summoner objects to the Friar's obvious plan to defame his activities, but the Host restores silence, a captive audience for the Friar. Initially his satire seems directed against sexual failings as the tale's summoner collects information, especially from a "retinue of wenches" who expose their clients. Intimidation and bribery are a summoner's trade. With this establishment of context, there is a return to story telling, "And so bifel that ones on a day" (1375), and the tale evolves through vivid scenes and lively dialogue with only occasional reiterations of the evil of the profession of summoner (1392–94), 1639–44, 1663–64).

The folk elements of the story, for which there is no exact source, are the heartfelt curse, forest green, and the devil. A summoner who is setting out to secure payment from an old widow meets a yeoman dressed in green. The two quickly agree to ride together, becoming "sworn brothers" (1405). Gradually the yeoman identifies himself; he comes from the North, where he hopes some time to see his new companion. The aptness of this wish is clear after the summoner explains that he is an extortioner and asks the yeoman's name. A direct answer is given, "Brother . . . / I am a feend; my dwellyng is in helle" (1447–48). Rather than fleeing the devil, the summoner, like Faustus, is fascinated to discover more of his nature. Like Mephistopheles, this devil is a shape changer, taking different bodies through feigning and even inhabiting dead bodies. More pointedly, the yeoman-devil explains that he is sometimes an instrument of God, when evil is converted to good. Utterly candid, the devil acknowledges that he is only an agent; man's free will allows resistance to temptation. Here, then, is a vigorous affirmation of Christian belief in the power of God, but also a true understanding coming from the devil, a satiric warning. Authorities are cited, first the scriptural example of Job, then Virgil and Dante, the classical and Christian poets who most memorably recounted experiences of the underworld and hell. This long description of the way of the devil concludes with his offering a choice to the summoner who is free to decide whether to continue to ride together "Til it be so that thou forsake me" (1522).

This rich exposition establishes the free choice of the summoner in allying himself with the devil. In practice, lacking discrimination, he is more wicked than the devil, albeit less clever. The remainder of the tale describes two episodes of curses, a demonstration of the all-too-frequent and human exclamation, "Go to hell/the devil." They first meet a carter who curses his horse and cart that are caught in the mud. The avaricious summoner exults in a gain for the devil, but the devil denies it on theological grounds. At issue is a question of "intente," what is really desired in the heart (a consideration of conscience). Or, as the devil observes, "The *carl spak oo thing, but he thoughte another" (*fellow, 1568). Such subtlety is far beyond the summoner, who persists in his attempts to secure money. He orders an old woman to appear before the archdeacon, not relenting when she explains that she has been ill and asks a representative. The only alternative is to pay twelve pence, a sum far beyond her means. The summoner's angry persistence, "the foule feend me fecche" (1610) prefigures the old woman's curse, "Unto the devel blak and rough of hewe / Yeve I thy body" (1622). Unlike the carter's momentary impatience, this heartfelt curse, as the devil verifies, is made "in ernest." Yet there remains a chance for salvation; the old woman will remove her curse if the summoner repents. Again his self-righteousness and avarice make him persist. Thus the fiend/devil seizes his sworn brother and takes him off to hell.

Concluding with a statement that additional authority could be cited from scripture, the *Friar's Tale* becomes very like a homily preached to those with simple understanding. Both carter and widow are ordinary people in everyday situations; their examples and the notion of converse with the devil, as well as the urgency about salvation, are commonplace. The irony of the tale indicates a subtlety of mind. The summoner is trapped by his vanity, a proud confidence that his own salvation is secure. The tale argues, then, for a need for humility and alertness, as well as against the evils of some ecclesiastical authorities who seek money. Although salvation comes through the grace of God, free will is crucial; temptation is not avoidable, but sin is, "For Christ wol be youre champion and knyght" (1662). By showing a clever and proud summoner pitted against the devil, but giving to the devil a strong assertion of this Christian theology, the *Friar's Tale* is indeed a satiric warning to all.

The Summoner's Tale

The *Summoner's Tale* is tied to the *Friar's Tale* by an ongoing quarrel, a response of unmitigated anger expressed through scatology that is introduced in the *Prologue* through an anecdote about hell. At first there are no friars, but then they are discovered in great numbers—twenty-thousand—nested beneath the tail of Satan. So intense is this crude attack that none replies. However, dramatic interplay occurs in the tale itself when the pilgrim Friar objects to the Summoner's account of a begging friar in Yorkshire (north country) who takes money but, when he leaves, erases the names of those who have given. The Host intervenes, and the *Summoner's Tale* continues. Thematically similar, it is very different from the *Friar's Tale* in tone and effect. Deft cleverness and sound theology yield to a coarse, nasty joke of humiliation that is unrelieved by the energy of a *fabliau* like the *Miller's Tale*. Relentlessly, friars are presented as guilty of seriously evil behavior. Like the summoner of the previous tale, the friar is money-seeking, playing upon anxieties about salvation. However, here ruthless intimidation is reinforced by a combination of intellectual judgment with contemptuous physicality.

The object of the friar's begging assault is Thomas, who has on earlier occasions been generous. Thomas is ill; he is in no mood for "false dissymulacioun" (III.2123), especially since he perceives no benefits from previous charity and the avowed efforts (prayers) of this friar and his chapter to regain his health. At the outset of their meeting, Friar John identifies his professional skill: "Glosyne* is a glorious thyng, certeyn" (*interpretation, 1793). As a university graduate, a Master of Arts, Friar John knows theology and is skilled in methods of argument. These, and his hypocrisy, he proceeds to demonstrate. At the same time that he is flirting with Thomas's wife and eating delicacies, he claims that friars are noted for purity and fasting. Repeatedly he cites Christ as his authority, as when he quotes the Sermon on the Mount as a gloss to exalt his claim of poverty, or claims greater knowledge of Christ and more answers to prayer than laypersons experience. The manner recalls that of the pharisees that Jesus attacked. Confronted with Thomas's anger, the friar adds Seneca and Fortune to his argument with an exemplum of knights and the example of Cambises' drunkenness. Moreover, his begging is repeatedly blasphemous; Thomas is asked to help "for hym that harwed helle!" (2107).[1]

The friar claims spiritual superiority, an understanding and influence with God lacked by laypersons. There is, then, vengeful savagery in Thomas's punishment of Friar John's pride. Exhilarated by his rhetorical and theological skill in glossing, Friar John does not suspect that Thomas will tolerate no more. Without suspicion, greedily eager, he follows the directions of the bedridden man, gropes beneath his buttock, and finds a "gift," which has sound and smell but no substance. An angry friar is chased away from Thomas's bedside; he who has preached against ire is very angry indeed. The tale, however, is not at an end, for the quick shock and joke of the *fabliau* are supplemented by academic explanation. Friar John was to divide Thomas's gift among members of his order. Furious, he goes to the lord of the village and explains how he has been insulted. The lord and his lady are not able to solve the problem of division, but a squire, Jankin, suggests a cartwheel with a friar's nose at each of twelve spokes and Friar John at the hub so that each can receive a fair share of "sound and stink." Such belaboring makes the tale satirical rather than humorous, and the issues are deeply serious. Thomas is on his deathbed, and he has no spiritual comfort; Friar John, highly educated and facile, is shown a likely candidate for hell, as is an ecclesiastic in another tale.

The Canon's Yeoman's Tale

A seeking of material advantages thematically relates the *Canon's Yeoman's Tale* to the retaliatory tales of the Friar and Summoner. Again the main characters are in religious orders, so that there is a strong cumulative effect of satiric warning against the seeking of wealth by those who have professed poverty and the credulity produced by greed. Further, there is a continued exploration of the misuse of intelligence and knowledge, and this is tied to hell and damnation. The Canon's Yeoman explains his master's pursuit of alchemy and the ways in which a desire for goods ensnares others, notably himself and a London priest.

Because there is again no specific source for the tale, it is tempting to argue Chaucer's use of personal experience. The poet could have known William Shuchirch, an alchemist and canon of the King's Chapel at Windsor, where Chaucer, as clerk of the king's works, worked in 1390 to repair St. George's Chapel. A man called Brumley, arrested for counterfeiting, said he learned from Shuchirch. It has even been argued that Chaucer had dealings with Shuchirch in which he lost money. If true, this would add force to the tale's moral: "A man may lightly lerne, if he have aught, / To multiplie, and brynge his good to naught!" (VIII.1400–1401). Several distinctive characteristics of the *Canon's Yeoman's Tale* encourage speculation. The tale is a late composition, perhaps originally written for a different purpose, like an audience of canons at Windsor. It includes an apology to religious canons that disavows an attempt to slander by urging that one evil canon does not make all guilty, as Judas's presence among the Apostles shows (902–1011). This seems necessary since the Canon's Yeoman so frightens his master with promised revelation of their work, that the Canon flees the company. There are other unusual interests, beginning with a dramatic introduction of the teller who rides up with his canon to overtake the pilgrims very near the end of their journey. And, of course, extraordinary self-revelation invites comparison with the Pardoner and Wife of Bath. Whatever theory offered, there are in the tale itself many important ideas that tie it to others of warning.

Chaucer's interest in science is evident throughout his poetry. In the *General Prologue* are frequent uses of physiology and psychological corollaries. Dreams are crucial in many poems, and references to astrological signs abound. *A Treatise on the Astrolabe* shows precise knowledge of the instrument used for calculations and explains how to use it. Some attribute to Chaucer another treatise, *The Equatorie of the Planetis.* In the *Canon's Yeoman's Tale* the science is alchemy, precursor of modern chemistry. There is a disturbing quality: not just observation and understanding but also attempts to change substances, to alter God's creation, are activities of alchemy. Early in the fourteenth century because of disreputable practices alchemy was condemned by Pope John XXII. Stories about Roger Bacon, a Franciscan friar who worked experimentally at Oxford, indicate deep anxieties. Knowledge of alchemy spread to Europe in the twelfth century through Latin translations of Arabic treatises that came from Greek Hellenistic writings. One crucial idea was "the philosophres stoon, / Elixer" (862–63), the changing of base metals into gold. This is the subject of the Canon's Yeoman, who first presents methods and materials and then a specific application—by a trickster, one example of a false canon and a greedy London priest. Grave misgivings and anxiety about such pursuits are early stated, and a final condemnation comes when the tale finishes with the Canon's Yeoman urging that since God does not want man to have the philosopher's stone, there should not be a working against His will (1472–81). Thus the Canon's Yeoman's account of his master repeatedly indicates failure, the futility of such alchemical activities and the credulity of those who attempt them.

Like the two previously considered tales of satiric warnings, the *Canon's Yeoman's Tale* shows not only that those who seek a quick way to riches finish poorer but also that such behavior is hellish. Where the Friar and Summoner specifically tell of persons taken off to or resting in hell, the Canon's Yeoman equates alchemy with hellfire and his canon with Satan. However, its practice did not cease. In his *Prologue* the Canon's Yeoman says that unfortunately he is so accustomed to blowing the fire that his color has changed (665–66); at the start of his tale he elaborates, stating that his once fresh and rosy complexion is now "wan and leaden hewe" (727–28), and admitting also that the vigor of blowing the fire makes his heart grow faint (753). Nevertheless, he provides information adequate "To reyse a feend" (861) and describes the Canon's efforts, albeit marred by errors, at bringing the devil—though not visible—to their midst, where more woe and rancor exist than in hell (915–21). Part 2 of the tale describes the canon as himself a "feend" (979–84), one who is false, beguiling many. Later references reiterate that the canon is a devil (1071, 1158, 1304) and wishes that the devil will take him (1159, 1270). While the Yeoman admits that he is himself a victim (1172–75), he constantly explains the tricks and failures of the practice. Vividly convincing is the account of sleight of hand and placing of coals filled with the higher metal and plugged with wax that melts in the fire to release it. The ingenuity of deception, accompanied by facile explanation and calculated timing of illustration, seduce the London priest into parting with forty pounds to learn secrets known only to the canon—and a friar (1355–56). The canon, of course, escapes—perhaps by riding as violently as shown in the *Canon's Yeoman's Prologue*. Making the gulled victim a London priest, someone both more educated and with urban sophistication, reinforces what seems the basic theme, the misuse of knowledge or excessive learning. This, at least, is what the Canon's Yeoman announces when he explains his canon's shabby plight: "For whan a man hath over-greet a wit, / Ful oft hym happeth to mysusen it" (648–49). Placing limits upon the development of human knowledge is an idea that lost favor with Renaissance humanism; however, the myth of Doctor Faustus, which was widely disseminated as popular literature from the sixteenth century, shows a residual medieval belief that such ambition was consorting with the devil and ultimately led to damnation. The warning is very powerful, and another tale can also be seen as an exploration of the dangers of information.

The Manciple's Tale

Beast fables are a familiar way of commenting upon human actions, traditionally for purposes of satire. Chaucer's best-known example is the *Nun's Priest's Tale,* linked to the popular Reynard the Fox stories. In the *Manciple's Tale* he turns to his favorite poet Ovid, whose *Metamorphoses* chronicle changes. The account of how a sweet-singing white bird became a harsh-croaking black crow was adapted in the medieval *Ovide moralisé,* retold by Gower and Machaut, and included in the popular collection *The Seven Sages of Rome.* In addition to the main episode, there are other examples of beast lore—birds, cat, and she-wolf—derived from the *Roman de la Rose.* The basic story is quite straightforward. Phoebus Apollo lives on earth; he is renowned for slaying the serpent Python, the best example of his facility with a bow. More pointedly, he has musical skills, playing an instrument and singing as can no other. He also has a snow white bird that can "counterfete the speche of every man . . . whan he sholde telle a tale" (IX.134–35), a skill to which Chaucer aspires in *The Canterbury Tales.* The virtuous Phoebus has only one vice; he is jealous. This trait leads to an analysis of the futility of trying to constrain another. A wife, like a bird caged, or a pampered cat, or evil she-wolf, seeks alternatives. Thus Phoebus's wife is not satisfied with her husband and takes a lover of low reputation. The crow observes the adulterous union, and when Phoebus comes home, it sings, "Cokkow! Cokkow! Cokkow!" (243). The cuckoo is traditionally a bird associated with cuckoldry. Enraged, Phoebus slays his wife, but he immediately laments her death and his ireful action. Then he berates and punishes the crow: he turns its feathers black, takes away its sweet song and speech, leaving only a capacity to cry against rain and tempest, and commits it to the devil. Beast fables conventionally conclude with a short moral; here there are fifty-four lines, and the point argued is restraint in speech, a difficult idea for a poet. Scripture and Seneca are the authorities cited.

The *Manciple's Tale* is built upon satiric warnings. Idealistic expectations of sexual fidelity, as in many tales, especially those of the Marriage Group, are again explored. Phoebus's jealous response is vengeful, not the forgiveness and tolerance seen in the *Wife's Tale* or the *Merchant's Tale,* where the parable of the Woman Taken in Adultery is a crucial reference. A reiteration of the concept of "gentilesse" comes with a denial of class; lady or wench does not matter when adultery is committed. The Manciple's description of man's appetite—"Flessh is so *newfangel" (*fond of novelty, 193)—is a harsh contrast to Phoebus's nobility. A betrayed husband's ire leads to murder, and no amount of grief and penitence can restore the wife that is killed. Here is another warning against anger, a common theme among these satiric tales. All of these readings enrich and reiterate points made in the other tales.

The distinctive emphasis of the *Manciple's Tale* is its extended moral, a warning against speaking out. This concept is hardly credible to modern democratic societies, where "to tell it like it is" is deemed high virtue. Yet the tale is one that modern readers who stress language as the key to interpretation find a significant comment on Chaucer's role as a writer. The Manciple's statement "I am a man noght textueel" (235, repeated 316) asserts that the tale (story) is his concern, but the line has served to focus attention upon reiteration of ideas in the earlier literary explanations of *The Canterbury Tales.* The Host comments in the *Prologue* about the Cook's drunkenness by declaring that Bacchus, god of wine, "kanst turnen ernest into game!" (100). An *apologia* before the scene of adultery again cites Plato's argument that words and deeds must be akin. The crow—though not the Manciple—provides proofs and "wordes Bolde," and these provoke Phoebus's rage. Not only does he kill his wife, but he also breaks his minstrelsy—harp, lute, psaltery, cithern—and his bow. Harsh "truth," then, leads to destruction and silence.

Nevertheless, there is a long *moralitas,* an extended statement that makes a didactic point, to offer a warning derived from the tale of the telltale crow. Restraint in speech is urged; more specifically "A wikked tonge is worse than a feend" (320). Here as in the previous satiric details human behavior is seen as diabolic. A crucial distinction is made; "wicked tongue" indicates speech that is intended to injure. Further, God did not intend utter candor when humans speak to and of others; such openness is reserved to His praise. The moral is couched in simple terms; its wisdom is that given to children, as the reiterated "My sone" (318, 320, 321, 325, 329, 335, 346, 351, 359) constantly affirms. Proverbial mother's advice "If you can't say something nice, don't say anything at all" is here evident. Given the proclivities of the pilgrims to quarrel and be personally and professionally abusive, this is indeed a pointed satiric warning. Explicitly, God finds "janglers" (chatterers) abominable. As in the *Canon's Yeoman's Tale,* excess in proclaiming knowledge is eschewed. Since what is said, stays, even if repented, the advice for those who would please God is to follow Christ's injunction: become as little children, here to be quiet. The moral seems hard, particularly from a poet who is "textuel" as well as a tale-teller, but it prepares for more elaborate sermons and the Retraction.

7

Sermons

In the fourteenth century *sermon* was still used with the meaning of its Latin root *sermonem* (talk, discourse, speech) as well as with the more particularized meaning of a talk given for religious purposes, usually based on Scripture and delivered from a pulpit. Although they are all very different, five of *The Canterbury Tales* can be helpfully considered as sermons because they share common characteristics of preaching. The tales of the Friar and Summoner contain some qualities found in sermons, as previously indicated, but are more easily read as satiric warnings. Four that I am identifying as sermons are by the professed religious—the tales of the Pardoner, Monk, Nun's Priest, and Parson—and one is Chaucer's own *Tale of Melibee*. Each cites authorities more fully than do other tales, each has a clearly stated didactic theme, and the responses of the pilgrims in prologues and links suggest reactions to preaching. Further, in the order of the tales is a suggestion of Chaucer's interest. The *Pardoner's Tale* comes in Fragment VI, and the *Parson's Tale* in Fragment X; the others are all in Fragment VII and are closely connected. In addition, Chaucer places himself as pilgrim teller, a lay preacher in the center of this group. A preacher is supposed to be a teacher, one who inspires his audience to live a good Christian life by explaining and by showing how this may be achieved.[1] Together these tales can be read as a consideration of the art of the sermon.

The Pardoner's Tale

Of the five tales being considered as sermons one is explicitly presented as an example of preaching, and it most fully explores the techniques of this popular art. The Pardoner begins, "Lordynges, . . . in chirches whan I preche" (VI.329). Reminding his audience many times that this is his work (329, 401, 414, 424, 426,

433, 439, 443), he devotes his *Prologue* to describing techniques of preaching. These include using a loud voice that rings out like a bell, knowing the speech by rote, presenting his credentials, including a sprinkling of Latin to add flavor and impress his audience, then showing his rich store of relics with claims for their effectiveness in setting right the maladies of farm animals and increasing the crops. These details indicate a rural audience, no doubt a credulous one. The Pardoner gains rapport with the pilgrim audience by making them a party to his superior position. He next explains that he strengthens his hold by telling jokes, directly confronting his hearers, and using such rapid speech and hand gestures that they are stunned. His intention is not to encourage penitence and to lead people to God, but to make certain that they will give generously. To this end he intimidates his hearers, through a kind of psychological blackmail and threat of humiliation, by avowing that those who are serious sinners will not have the grace to make an offering or buy a relic. Finally, he always preaches about greed, a topic especially designed to elicit contributions, so that he gains about a hundred marks (sixty-three pounds) a year, a large sum for the time. The Pardoner presents himself as a hypocrite, for he unabashedly admits his only intention is gain, yet he does not acknowledge that he himself is most guilty of the greed against which he preaches. The manner of preaching is much of the Pardoner's strong appeal; nevertheless, he acknowledges that his greatest effect comes from telling stories that ignorant people enjoy. As a preacher, he recognizes that abstract theology and moralizing are less appealing than illustrations of these through narrative adventures. He is, of course, also showing pride through manipulating others. The Pardoner's bravado seems to be strengthened by alcohol, for as previously noted there are references to his drinking "moyste* and corny† ale" (*new, †strong, 317 and 456, 322, 328). His clarity and brilliance in speaking do not indicate drunkenness and thus are a reminder of the limitations of literal dramatic readings.

The *Pardoner's Tale* demonstrates techniques of his preaching style that have been fully analyzed. The opening portion (463–660) is a powerful sermon on sins—swearing, lechery and drunkenness, gambling or dicing—well illustrated by examples. Some of these are obvious—Adam and Eve, Sampson, but Attila as a model of drunkenness is an unusual and vivid case. The assertion that dicing begets lies, perjury, blasphemy, manslaughter, and loss of property is sweeping, but not unusual in medieval thought. Since blasphemy is less noted today, emphasis upon swearing is especially notable.

Oaths that are lies are reprehensible, but taking the name of the Lord in vain is singled out, and the specific examples are all ones that recall the Crucifixion. As is characteristic in sermons, authorities are cited—the Old Testament, St. Paul, Matthew, Greek examples—but briefly. The general view of wretched mankind owes much to Pope Innocent III's *De miseria conditionis humane* that was also a source for the *Man of Law's Tale* and the *Monk's Tale.* Again the ideas are very familiar, but Chaucer gives them vitality through the Pardoner's evocative preaching. Immediate appeals punctuate the text: "But herkneth, lordynges, o word I yow preye" (573), "Namoore of this, for it may wel suffise. / And now that I have spoken . . . (588–89), "Looke eek that . . . (621). Attention is never allowed to wander; indeed the pace creates an eagerness for more.

The vitality of language and vividness of presentation make this initial part of the sermon memorable. However, the Pardoner's greatest strength is evident in the second portion, the exemplum, or illustration of his favorite text *Radix malorum est Cupiditas* (Greed is the root of evil. 1 Timothy 6:10). He tells the story of three rioters who seek and find Death, in 234 lines (661–895) of remarkably economical and swiftly paced narrative. The subject is a compelling one; there are analogues in old folktales of many lands, and several movies use the motif of would-be thieves who destroy each other, losing sought-after wealth and sometimes their lives. Chaucer's descriptive skill is never better than in the initial tavern setting, where the three rioters hear a bell clink before a corpse that proves to be a former companion. The scene is a *memento mori* (remember you must die) that vividly evokes the Black Death, a plague that came swiftly and without warning. Death is said to have slain a thousand in this "pestilence" (679). However, the rioters are not frightened; rather, they vow to slay "this false traytour Deeth" (699). This is a reversal of the motif of Death's coming to claim persons from all walks of life, as in the *danse macabre* or dance of death that decorated prayer books, charnel houses, and churches. Sins previously delineated by the Pardoner are practiced by the rioters, especially blasphemy. On the way they meet an Old Man, variously identified as Death himself or his messenger, the Wandering Jew, a hermit, even Christ, and ask to be directed to Death. Whether the Old Man is interpreted as good or evil, he sends the three to a tree, where they find gold, which they identify as a gift of Fortune (779). This reference, whose resonance is developed in the *Monk's Tale,* foretells a fall. One of the rioters describes their life as given to mirth and jollity, and there is an anticipation of "heigh felicitee" (787), although they had no expectation of "so fair a grace" (783). In fact, their greed is immediately evidenced. They first draw lots to decide who will go for provisions. The younger goes into town, where he buys poison to put into wine for the two older men, who at the same time have plotted his murder. They want a larger share of the gold, so that they can more freely play at dice. When the young man returns, he is killed, and the two are poisoned by drinking the wine, a form of gluttony, to celebrate. Each, then, is a deliberate sinner. The plotting young man is inspired by the "feend" (devil, 844); he not only wants to murder but also plans "nevere to repente" (850). The two murderers show no penitence; they sit, drink, and make merry after the deed.

This story is swiftly told. Its heavy reliance upon direct discourse, 154 or more than half of the lines, is well suited for oral presentation. The Pardoner's verbal skills in delivery are displayed in the voices of the rioters. The dialogue is interspersed with only five lines of description, twenty-three of narrative, and fifty-one of action. This simplicity yields to an elaborate apostrophe, a verse paragraph that summarizes—cursed sins, homicide, gluttony, lechery, dicing—and is punctuated with cries of "O." The address focuses upon "Thou blasphemer of Christ" (898), and "pride" is identified as a cause. There is lamentation, "Allas, mankynde," that is identified as "fals and so unkynde" to God, Creator and Redeemer. This intense rhetoric is followed by a direct appeal to the audience, as the Pardoner attempts to sell his pardons to those he has emotionally roused.

The daring of the Pardoner's conclusion is a subject of much debate. Proceeding from his usual plea for donations, purchase of his pardons and relics, and claim that the audience is honored to have a pardoner who can absolve sins (931), he first specifically calls upon the Host, as "most envolouped in synne" (942). The Host's refusal is sharp and brutal, a rebuff that is viciously personal and leaves the Pardoner speechless with anger. The obscenity of the reply is unparalleled, an indication that the Host was the most difficult pilgrim to attempt to con. Thus the motivation may have been a prideful wish to dominate. Perhaps the Pardoner's intent was always a planned great triumph over his hearers; having revealed his techniques, he then so dazzles that they can still be duped. Or he may simply have recognized that the pilgrims are moved by his tale, so that he decides to try his usual sell. Alternatively, the Pardoner, who is on a pilgrimage, might deliberately have sought humiliation, a penance to follow his confession. This interpretation mitigates the usual view of the Pardoner as evil, "the one lost soul" on the pilgrimage to Canterbury—a critical judgment that is too definitive.[2] The reconciliation achieved by the Knight's intervention when he has the Pardoner and Host kiss and make up indicates that the poem is not condemning any of the pilgrims. Chaucer again reminds his audience that severe judgment is not worthy.

The Pardoner introduced the killing of the three rioters and the swift conclusion of the tale with another of many addresses to his hearers: "What nedeth it to sermone of it moore?" (879). This might suggest such excellent preaching that there was no possibility of further sermons; however, Chaucer provided several alternative examples, and the first he assigned to Chaucer the pilgrim.

The Tale of Melibee

The religious and didactic purposes of the second tale told by Chaucer the pilgrim have never been questioned, but there have been varying critical judgments of its meaning and appropriateness. Often described as boring and dull, or as a joke to repay the Host's rude interruption, the tale is not usually included in selections of *The Canterbury Tales*. Nevertheless, its importance is increasingly being recognized. Its subject and attitude are to be found not only in other didactic works of the Middle Ages, but also in other works by Chaucer, so that it has been praised as central to an understanding of the poet's achievement. Ideas found here reappear as themes developed in other tales, so that the translation seems to have provided a rich resource for later imaginative writing as well as philosophical, moral, and religious commonplaces from classical and Christian thought. Chaucer's "moral tale vertuous" (VII.940) is a close prose translation of Renaud de Louens's *Livre de Melibée et de Dame Prudence* (after 1336). This French version of a Latin moral treatise *Liber consolationis et consili,* written by Albertanus of Brescia (c.1173–c.1270), was very popular in the fourteenth century. Chaucer seems not to have used the Latin original, but its title indicates the nature of the work, a book of consolation and counsel. The French title suggests a dialogue between a man and a woman, with an allegorical purpose. Indeed both titles are helpful introductions to "a litel thyng in prose" (VII.937). Chaucer's tale is the first use of prose in *The Canterbury Tales,* and it is not short; only the other prose piece, the *Parson's Tale* exceeds its length. It is also a bit longer than the *Knight's Tale,* and its Christian argument forms a balance to that romance, set in pagan antiquity and with serious philosophical content, directly indebted to Boethius.

The *Tale of Melibee* is a sustained argument, cast as an exchange between Melibeus and his wife Prudence. The occasion is a breaking into the young man's house, although it was carefully locked while he "for his desport* is went into the feeldes hym to pleye" (*amusement, 968). Three old enemies scale the walls with ladders, enter, beat his wife and give five mortal wounds to his daughter Sophie. Melibeus is "lyk a mad man" (974), overwhelmed by grief, and immediately summons counselors. Although their advice is varied (surgeons and physicians claim they will cure his daughter, the old warn about war and the young want action, friends and flatterers are not easily distinguished), he quickly decides to seek vengeance, to undertake a war against his enemies. Noting the confused circumstances for the advice, Prudence carefully reviews the situation and urges "pacience," forbearance rather than revenge. Her arguments are replete with citations from authorities, principally Seneca, Ovid, Cicero, Cato, Cassiodorus, Scripture (especially Solomon and Saints James and Paul), and many proverbs. A desire for revenge is the most primitive of responses, a form of retributive justice. Prudence argues against ire, covetousness, and hasty response. A wise advocate, citing the parable of the Woman Taken in Adultery (John 8:3–8), notes that Christ used "deliberacion" (1032), thus urging both leisure for decision and an attitude of mercy. Prudence favors caution and diligence. Anger, she tells Melibeus, can lead to error. Further, love is a greater protection against danger than strengthened physical fortifications, like towers that are symbolic of pride (1334). The response is that of Saint Francis's prayer "Lord make me an instrument of your peace," echoed in the setting out of opposites in the discourse (1287).

One dimension of Melibeus is his privileged situation. His name means "a man that drynketh hony" (1408), and Prudence chides her husband with too many "temporal riches and honors of this world." In a political interpretation of the poem this marks him as a man of property, a manorial baron perhaps, so that Melibeus's attackers are agents of social unrest, a notable element in the 1380s. Thus Prudence's advice becomes an attack on the misuse of riches, and an argument about how the privileged can preserve their possessions and authority. However, riches are also viewed as an occasion of sin. Prudence admits the necessity of temporal goods, but she counsels against the avarice that they often occasion. Indeed avarice is associated with death, as in the *Pardoner's Tale* (1610), and there is a minisermon on the folly of caring about things since all persons must die, however rich they may be.

Prudence's theological point is that riches are the occasion that led Melibeus to forget Jesus Christ. The three assailants are, then, equated with the three temptations: the world, the flesh, and the devil (1422) that have wounded his soul in five places, the deadly sins that have entered into his heart through his five senses. Recalled are the five physical wounds of his daughter and, more significantly, the five wounds of the crucified Christ. A perception of God within the human person is early affirmed by Prudence's insistence that Melibeus should rely not upon counsellors but upon "the heighe God" (1115); this modulates into her urging that he find counsel in himself with due deliberation (1137, 1365) and an admission that one is always alone. Prudence introduces this advice with the philosophical point that God is the "fer cause" and man the "neer cause" (1395), which prepares for the question of suffering and God's goodness. Prudence's assertion of faithful belief in God's "justice and rightwisenesse" is carefully anticipated. In the opening of the tale she had recognized suffering and acknowledged the rightness of expressing grief, citing as her authorities Ovid, Saint Paul, and Job. Feeling, then, is approved, but it must be tempered with careful thought. One mode of conveying this is the plethora of *sententiae* that punctuate Prudence's speech, and Melibeus is repeatedly convinced by what she says, gradually coming to a thoughtful and considered response rather than his initial vengefulness.

Another way of reading the *Tale of Melibee* is to emphasize its framework, the small fiction of a wife giving her husband advice. Again the text specifically raises the question when Prudence observes that her husband should not become distracted by concerns about male "maistrie." Thus the tale contributes to the Marriage Debate, initiated by the Wife of Bath. Prudence notes that a woman should give advice, and a man does not surrender to her, since he is always free to refuse the advice (1080). She cites examples of women from the Old Testament whose good advice advanced men and concludes that God called women the "help" not the "confusion of men" (1105). The last phrase is, of course, used assertively by Chaunticleer, an archetype of the proud male, one who is lost through flattery, in the *Nun's Priest's Tale*. In spite of a few antifeminine clichés, woman is seen as providing Wisdom; in fact, a clerk's proverb recognizes that woman is superior to Wisdom and nothing is above her. Later "perfection" is defined as "prudence," perhaps the clearest sign of an allegorical meaning in which the woman is given ideal expression.

Prudence's superiority is clear from the calm and thoughtful manner in which she responds to Melibeus's crisis. More notably, the two are set apart by her quiet acceptance of suffering, refusal to seek retribution, and specific arguing for an alternative response. Against his wanting revenge, Prudence urges mercy, a recognition of the grace of God and that "pacience is a greet vertu of perfeccioun" (1516). This quotation from the Epistle of Saint James (I:4) comes as the culmination of Prudence's argument, which includes Solomon, Seneca, and Cato as authorities. This central passage reiterates that "pacience" is the correct response (1480ff, for fourteen repetitions). Here is the wisdom of the New Testament: Christ was guiltless, and He suffered patiently; men should so bear their tribulations in this world, recognizing that the joy of God is eternal. Further, they should acknowledge their own sinfulness, to which present suffering may be attributed and which should also inhibit harsh judgment of others. At the end of the tale (1866) Prudence returns to Saint James's Epistle (2:13), quoting the statement that God will have mercy at the Last Judgment as the one judged has responded with mercy to others. Saint James's ideal of patience is acknowledged as a "perfection" to be sought, and Melibeus does not claim this holy condition. Prudence, then, offers a lesser alternative in the world, the exercise of law in righting injustice (1529). In fact, Melibeus achieves a reconciliation that comes from religious sentiment. He defers to Prudence, who speaks to the three adversaries, convincing them of their fault so that they respond with "greet contricioun and humylitee" (1735). Their penitence is expressed through confession of fault, a reconciliation in the community and a submission to God, Who is the fount of all goodness and virtue. Quite early in the tale the wise advocate spoke of "the grace of God" as a way of healing (1015, 1033); Prudence explains that only thus can the reconciliation between her husband and his enemies occur (1764). The final speech of the tale is Melibeus's summary of all that he, as the Christian struggling in this world, has learned. He affirms that he can respond with "grace and mercy" to their "pride and heigh presumpcioum and folie . . . necligence and unkonnynge" (1875) because this is part of the divine plan in which "God of his endelees mercy" will grant forgiveness for trespasses "in this wrecched world" to repentant sinners and "bryngen us to the blisse that nevere hath ende." With that "us" the sermon becomes universal. Chaucer the pilgrim concludes "Amen"; poet and man, audience and reader are also included, just as they are in the final Retraction to *The Canterbury Tales.*

Such "perfeccioun" is, of course, inhibited by the desires and actions of many in the world. Melibeus began as one among those especially committed to the riches of the world. He acknowledges that Fortune nourished him from childhood and helped him through many situations (1444). Part of Prudence's counsel was to "flee stryvynge," the fault of those whose stories are presented in the *Monk's Tale,* another sermon that chronicles the falls of ambitious men concerned with their own excellence and self-righteousness.

The Monk's Tale

Although they are part of the dramatic interplay, and thus more open to ironic interpretation, references to "pacience" (VII.1895, 1965) in the *Prologue to the Monk's Tale* provide continuity with the *Tale of Melibee.* Both tales address the situation of persons who are privileged and then experience a change of Fortune, but the circumstances and didactic points, as well as the styles, are very different. The *Monk's Tale* is a catalogue of "tragedies," stories of those who fell, and there is little evidence of hope or transforming grace. While Melibeus is given gentle and wise teaching by Prudence, allowed gradually to transform his vengefulness into a merciful attitude and experience God's grace, the figures in the *Monk's Tale* show little change and are only subjects of "tragedy." The best-remembered words of the Monk are those that define tragedy as the story of ones who were in high place and fell into misery and ended wretchedly (1973–82). This medieval definition is a far cry from more widely accepted views of classical and Renaissance tragedy as heroic, an expression of the grandeur and ennobling of the human spirit. The opening stanza states the exemplary intention of the tale: do not trust in "blynd prosperitee" but learn from these examples (1997–98). This heavily didactic purpose is reminiscent of one kind of sermon preaching. The effect is neither encouraging nor edifying, but intimidating.

The *Monk's Tale* is most directly indebted to Boccaccio, as the subtitle *De Casibus Virorum Illustrium* suggests. That work was presented as a kind of penitence by the Italian monk who is much better remembered as the author of *The Decameron.* Chaucer does not imitate Boccaccio's dramatic device of having each of the fallen recount his own story, a technique later elaborated in the English

Mirror for Magistrates (1554–1610), which was derived from John Lydgate's *Fall of Princes* (1431–38), an English version of Boccaccio via a French translation of Laurent de Premierfait. In short, the *de casibus* tradition is a long and popular one, going back to the Roman concept of Fortuna. Chaucer's interest in Boethius is again evident, but the attitudes found in the Monk's tragedies are less comprehensive. Here he follows Boccaccio's philosophical tenets. In this view Fortune came to power because of Adam and Eve's disobedience. Their fall introduced the possibility of the falls of princes and thus an origin for tragedy. Poverty defeated Fortune, and thus Misfortune was controlled, so that only men foolish enough to break its chains suffer. Human choice is thus crucial, but it is simplified; life in the world of daring is the cause of tragedy. This attitude is closely related to the idea that the only reason for failure is the choice of the active life. Frequently expressed, this theology is rooted in *contemptus mundi*, a contempt for the world, that was eloquently argued by Pope Innocent III in *De miseria condicionis humane*, as noted in the discussion of the *Man of Law's Tale*. Eschewing the world is an especially apt attitude for a Monk, albeit in sharp contrast to the outgoing character of the pilgrim figure presented in the *General Prologue*. A discrepancy between the two can be viewed as satiric, ironic, or simply as an example of the poet's constantly making his audience reconsider initial impressions and quick judgments. From the monastic tradition came both withdrawal from the world and knowledge derived from the study that was so crucial in monastic life during the centuries that are sometimes described as "Benedictine" because monasteries were the center of Western civilization. That era was over in the fourteenth century, but the *Monk's Tale* is a reminder both of former splendor and present inadequacy in an increasingly complex and secular society of renewed cities with power and wealth.

Written in verse, in a distinctive stanza that is an adaptation of rime royal, the *Monk's Tale* is mixed in its emphasis. The "tragedies" vary from one to sixteen stanzas in length and in attempts to explain the falls or to evoke discriminating responses. Of the seventeen figures of "tragedy" only Nabugodonosor is described as coming to accept God; the other sixteen finish in "adversitee," and the cumulative effect is to suggest a random fate that is not always explained, even as a consequence of human action. The capriciousness of Fortune is, then, dominant. This Roman view of the goddess, frequently represented in art with her wheel that inexorably takes people from high to low as it turns, is not modified by Christian faith, and there is only an implicit argument to set aside worldly ambition for contemplation.

This view of Fortune is at least in part attributable to the choices of persons as subjects of tragedy. Like the medieval cycle plays, the catalogue begins with Lucifer, who is the type of pride, an angel who could not be harmed by Fortune, but who fell from heaven. Then comes Adam, the type of fall on earth, one who was given paradise but lost his "heigh degree" because of "mysgovernaunce" (misconduct). A single stanza is devoted to each of these figures, both taken from the Old Testament. Other figures from the Old Testament are Sampson, Nebuchadnezzar, Belshazzar, Holofernes, and Antiochus. Against these seven are six from classical myth and history: Hercules, Zenobia (the only woman), Nero, Alexander, Julius Caesar, and Croesus. There are also four modern examples: Pedro of Castile, Pierre de Lusignan, and Bernabò of Lombardy, all of whom died in the late fourteenth century; and Ugolino of Pisa from the late thirteenth century, a figure memorably presented in Dante's *Divine Comedy* and generally regarded as the most successful of the Monk's tragedies because it powerfully evokes pity. The range of subjects, from Paradise to Italy in 1385, shows that falls from high place occur throughout history.

Among explanations offered are sexual temptation and betrayal by women, which destroyed the strength of Sampson and Hercules. Zenobia, a female warrior of strength, although long a successful conqueror, was finally seized by the Roman Aurelianus and led in his triumph before being reduced to bearing a distaff, emblem of female humbling for which the type is Eve. The arbitrariness of Fortune is most evident in the brief accounts of modern examples, perhaps a reflection of an unwillingness to make a judgment about anything so recent, especially since Chaucer knew Bernarbò personally and Pedro of Spain through John of Gaunt's marriage to his daughter Constance, and Pedro of Cyprus was renowned for his chivalry. Idolatry is the fault of Belshazzar and of Holofernes, while opulence and vice are pointed out in Nero. The most famous person included is Alexander, "The storie of Alisaundre is so commune" (2631) that all have heard of his fortune. Indeed in the Middle Ages his name was known second only to Jesus and Mary. A man of dual reputation, both revered for his greatness and reviled for his tyranny, Alexander is here described largely as a "flower of knighthood," "worthy," with leonine courage, one of "gentilesse," betrayed by "False Fortune." The Greek conqueror of the world was, of course, one of the Nine Worthies, as was Julius Caesar, whose success and fall are also attributed to Fortune. Here Roman historians—Lucan, Suetonius, Valerian—are cited for those who want to learn more. Pride as an explanation of falls from high place is made explicit in two accounts that frame these Worthies. Antiochus and Croesus, again one from the Old Testament and one from pagan antiquity, provide a summation. Antiochus is struck down, when "God daunted* al his pride and al his boost" (*conquered, 1609), and the fall is both spiritual and physical. The would-be conqueror is thrown from his chair, and his body becomes a *memento mori*, a reminder of death; suffering great pain, as worms creep through him and make him stink, he dies alone on a mountain.

Pride also explains the fall of Croesus, who is finally hanged from a tree in an enactment of his dream, correctly interpreted by his daughter as a warning but not heeded. This final tragedy concludes with a succinct statement that tragedies come when men trust in Fortune, who unexpectedly assails those who are proud. The didactic point is one of the great commonplaces of the Middle Ages. Accounts of the persons and the moral, philosophical, and theological principles are to be found in many of Chaucer's favorite sources. The *Monk's Tale* is, then, another expression of his interest in books, both classical and Christian authors, not only the Bible but also renderings like the *Bible Historiale* of Guyart Desmoulins and Vincent of Beauvais's *Speculum Historiale,* as well as Boccaccio, Dante, and Jean de Meun's *Roman de la Rose*. Thus, although the Knight cries out against more tragedies, stopping the flow of the Monk's seemingly endless stream, he objects not to the number but to the attitude so relentlessly reiterated: loss of prosperity rather than something "gladsom," and he asks to hear more of "joye and greet solas." As a sermon this has not been a success; indeed the Host specifically points out to the Monk that he has irritated and lost his audience. A more effective preaching than such "gloom and doom" follows immediately in the brilliant sermon of the Nun's Priest, which is both erudite and marvelously deft and amusing, yet also about a fall.

The Nun's Priest's Tale

In contrast to the Pardoner and the Monk, the Nun's Priest tells his tale without elaborate introduction. With no description from the *General Prologue* or previous interaction with pilgrims, he simply begins—and is immediately enthralling, witty, poised, and very learned. The only preparation is a brief request from the Host that the Nun's Priest tell something to gladden the hearts of his audience, whose attention has been lost by the Monk's disturbing catalogue, and that his own heart be "murie." With a gentle rejoinder that being only merry would be blameworthy, "This sweete preest, this goodly man sir John" (VII. 2817) tells a tale of the cock and the fox, a simple beast fable that frames an extraordinarily rich and clear demonstration of the learning of the Middle Ages. This combination of delight and edification concludes with an explicit didactic urging that the tale be understood for its "moralite," following the model of St. Paul's doctrine (Romans 15:4): "Takyth the fruyt, and lat the chaf be stille" (3443). Here is a sermon very different from all the other examples in *The Canterbury Tales.* To consider it as a sermon is to risk indignation from those who delight in its comic virtuosity, but there is no forced incompatibility. After all, medieval preachers often used beast fables in their sermons. What is necessary is a change in expectation: the Nun's Priest shows that erudition and morality can be presented with great wit and a light touch. His is the kind of sermon wished for, but rarely heard. Its compelling story telling is comparable to that of the *Pardoner's Tale,* but the speaker is self-effacing, or perhaps self-accusatory and admonitory through similarites between himself and Chauntecleer.

The *Nun's Priest's Tale* has long been recognized as a reply to the catalogue of tragedies that it follows. There are several reasons for this. Most obviously the story is of a fall from high place through pride; however, the Nun's Priest's hero is a cock, and he is saved in the end. In contrast to the *Monk's Tale* the view of mankind is a positive one; the Nun's Priest is described as a "good man," and he addresses his hearers as "goode men." The point of this sermon is, then, not to intimidate and overwhelm with a sense of sin, but gently to reassure by showing that sinners are not forever lost. An action of saving as well as fall comes because the fox, like the cock, makes a mistake. Since human fallibility is universal, man's only way is to accept his limitations, persevere, and seek salvation that comes through grace—which he must choose to accept. Chauntecleer is not caught a second time by the flattery of the fox. The Wheel of Fortune has, then, turned full circle. Moreover, something other than random change is evident. Chauntecleer has learned, and he will blame/curse himself if he is foolish enough to be beguiled again. The Nun's Priest thus articulates the Catholic medieval view of mankind under the providence of God, saved through grace, but also responsible to sin no more. The theological question is posed in a clear minidisputation about free will and predestination that follows the fox's seizure of the cock (3234–50). Recognizing the mass and complexity of scholastic debate of this question and disputation in the schools, the Nun's Priest here gives only the basic arguments of St. Augustine, Boethius, and Bradwardine, Archbishop of Canterbury (d.1349). A good preacher, he provides additional ideas for his intellectual hearers to pursue, but does not lose simpler members of his audience; the digression is brief, for he quickly resumes the beast fable.

Much longer is a consideration of dreams (2893–3156), a Chaucerian interest early manifested in *The House of Fame* and in *Troilus and Criseyde*. This is feasible because such ideas are easier to understand, and there are two stories of death and marvelous happenings, always popular in sermons, to enliven numerous references to authorities. Further, a clear distinction between dreams with natural causes, which have no significance, and prophetic dreams that are to be believed, is made but lightly, as when Pertelote tells Chauntecleer to take a laxative to purge himself of his anxiety (2943). This is both an exact comment on natural dreams and a reminder of the debate between authority (male) and experience (female) that the Wife of Bath so fully expounds. Such earthiness is blended with citations from Cato, Cicero, Macrobius, as well as references to heroes of the Old Testament and epics of Troy and Rome. Pertelote's herbal remedies are part of folk medicine, traditionally the province of women. They compare favorably with established medical authorities, like those named in the portrait of the Doctor of Physic or deadly poisons noted in the *Pardoner's Tale* and associated with Avicenna, an Arabic and thus pagan authority.

The juxtaposition of diverse elements in the *Nun's Priest's Tale* is perhaps its greatest distinction. Beast fables are a very ancient kind of story: Aesop is well known, and the medieval *Roman de Renart* is part of this literary tradition. By combining the beast fable with epic traditions Chaucer gives to the tale extraordinary humor, the clashing planes of the mock heroic that are favored by writers like Dryden, who translated Chaucer's tale and initiates the satiric tradition that dominated in eighteenth-century England. Recurrent precise details that remind the audience that Chauntecleer is a cock and Pertelote a hen illustrate the technique of mock heroic. In his hall Chauntecleer sits on a perch, which is too narrow for sexual encounters; there are two reminders that they will fly down from the beams; the cock's courtly praise of his lady's beauty is climaxed by the scarlet red about her eyes. Contrast between descriptions and evocations of human behavior is stronger than in many beast fables.

So encompassing and brilliant is Chaucer's treatment of rhetoric in the *Nun's Priest's Tale* that some have argued the real subject of the poem is language. The varied levels, from easy conversational to elaborate apostrophe, demonstrate a remarkable range and a respect for different modes of expression. Part of the tale's attraction for scholarly readers is a recognition of its witty handling of rhetorical theory, but as with the theological passages, much is accessible even without such knowledge. Typically, Chaucer uses extensive dialogue, which is well suited for oral presentation that allows different voices and direct appeal to an audience. Vigorous exclamations, like Pertelote's charge that Chauntecleer is a coward (2908), contrast with the cock's magisterial explanations of dreams and systematic advancing of evidence. (As any who have staged performances of the tale know, dramatizing is an easy task because there are fine speeches and many lines of narrative can simply be spoken by a character.) It is also helpful to remember that solitary readers often sound a text, a procedure especially favored when silent reading was not the norm. Much of the tale reads very simply, like a fable accessible to children, the place today for Aesop and stories of Reynard. There are many popular elements, for example the song, "My lief is faren in londe" (2879). Then there are passages of academic explanation, for example on dreams and predestination. Some lines are topical jokes; "Mordre wol out" (3053) playfully echoes the *Prioress's Tale*. Chauntecleer's Latin line "*In principio, / Mulier est hominis confusio*" is mistranslated as "Womman is mannes joye and al his blis" (3163–66), a satiric contrast to the expansive compliment to women in the *Tale of Melibee*. Obviously this is a statement against women, in fact a popular proverbial comic definition, reenforced by the meaning of Pertelote's name—"one who confuses someone's fate." It is also Chauntecleer's proud display of male knowledge of Latin, superior to female lack of education, and an example of the Pardoner's preaching technique of impressing an ignorant audience with a bit of Latin. In a tale about a fall because of vanity, explicitly triggered by the fox's insidious comparisons between Chauntecleer and his father (a nice bit of Oedipal psychology, 3295), a simple antifeminist reading is not cogent.

Similarly, rhetorical apostrophes in a high style function both as parodies and as illustrations of a style of writing that Chaucer employs to express moments of great emotion. Apostrophes occur throughout the tale and contrast with the dominant conversational style. However, the rhetorical, like the narrative, climax of the poem comes when the fox seizes the cock by the throat and carries him off. Three laments, replete with apostrophes—to Destiny, Venus, and Geoffrey of Vinsauf—fill a total of seventeen lines (3338–54). Again the Nun's Priest limits himself, so that the exuberance remains interesting, easily within bounds acceptable for high emotion in a sermon of this length. The manner of lamentation is derived from Geoffrey de Vinsauf's *Poetria Nova* (c.1210), the most influential medieval treatise of rhetoric. More specifically the model is a lament for King Richard I (Lion-Hearted) that enjoyed such popularity that it circulated as a separate literary gem. Thus Chaucer's imitation would have been quickly recognized, especially as it is signaled by an address to Venus, the choice of Friday for the day of action, as well as the naming of Richard and of "deere maister soverayn," Geoffrey de Vinsauf. Reliance upon rhetoric is often the mark of a young or unsophisticated writer who is learning his art. Chaucer wrote the *Nun's Priest's Tale* late in his career, and the tale's varied elements of style show mature virtuosity. The discrepancy between the death of a king and the seizure of a cock is great, and this creates a first response of laughter at a clever parody. However, although excessive grief over death is not appropriate, an acknowledgment of loss is acceptable, as noted early in the *Tale of Melibee*. After a series of comparisons between the woe of the hens and of noble ladies in classical stories of Troy, Carthage, and Rome, the Nun's Priest breaks from high style with the cry of the poor widow and her two daughters: "Out! Harrow and weylaway! / Ha, ha! the fox!" (2381–82). Further, the line continues "and after hym they ran." Thus rhetorical extravagance is replaced by pragmatic action: style is less important than behavior, the fruit is taken and the chaff is left. Moreover, the fantasy of beast fable recedes before a confrontation with the human predicament. Chaucer creates an unforgettable scene of frenzy in the barnyard, noisy and busy, at once farcical action and desperately serious because of the importance of the cock to the peasant family. A reference to Jack Straw, supposed leader of the Peasants' Revolt of 1381, seems to invite such awareness; it is one of the few explicit examples of direct political allusion in Chaucer's poetry. The comparison, of course, is only to the noises being made, shouts before killing, or earlier "yolleden* as feendes† doon in helle" (*yelled, †devils, 3389).

Chaucer's interest in birds, and his skill in using them to comment on social classes, was early manifested in *The Parliament of Fowls*.

The *Nun's Priest's Tale* is more fully developed; there are human persons as well as barnyard creatures who are given human attributes. The tale is framed by accounts of a poor widow, and this provides a different perspective, one that may be interpreted as fundamental to a reading of the tale as sermon. Widows often occur in Scripture, but two are especially notable. The starving widow whom Elijah asks for something to eat gives him a cake made with her last flour and oil; her faith and self-effacement are rewarded because jar and jug continually are filled so that she and her son are fed, and indeed her son is later restored to life by God (3 Kings 17:10). In the New Testament the poor widow at the temple who humbly gives her two mites, all that she has, is more highly praised by Jesus than the proud and rich that give more money (Mark 12:42). Widows are not subjects of tragedy, for they have not sought a high place from which to fall. The account of the barnyard confusion is followed by a reference to the sudden turning of Fortune, including allusions to pride. Chauntecleer flatters the fox to make him open his mouth so that he can fly away, but the cock's words are introduced by a prayer "as wys God helpe me" (3408), and there is no return to his former vanity, since he can now recognize that the fox is guileful. Thus the *Nun's Priest's Tale* accepts life in the world of daring, a reality for most people, and this does not necessarily end in loss, as was shown in the religious romances. Nevertheless, his final words, following poised advice about how to interpret his tale (sermon), are a prayer and affirmation of God's goodness and grace and a hope of union with God in eternity. The *Nun's Priest's Tale* does not lack high seriousness, however comic and diverting its surface. Its conclusion, already seen in the *Tale of Melibee,* recurs in the *Parson's Tale,* another long prose sermon that could not be more different in style.

The Parson's Tale

As a long prose piece the *Parson's Tale* suggests similarity to the *Tale of Melibee,* but it lacks even the modest story telling element of that argument for prudence and forbearance. When the subject is penance, levity is inappropriate; the penitent sinner feels remorse and experiences joy, not jollity. Laughter is a human way of managing the absurdity of the world, of mitigating human inadequacy and failure, but joy is a perception of the divine. As the pilgrimage ends, both to Canterbury and of life, a different response comes for Christians who believe that the temporal world is but a prelude to eternity. The beginning and end of the *Parson's Tale* establish this context. The first paragraph states that "Our sweete Lord God of heven" intends that all will come to Him for the "blisful lif that is perdurable*" (*eternal, X.74) and further notes that many "spiritual ways" can be followed to "Jerusalem celestial." The one that will not fail is penitence, and this is the Parson's subject. Then follow 1080 lines, nearly forty pages of double columns, that explain sin and penitence. At the end of the *Parson's Tale* is another statement: "Thanne shal men understonde what is the fruyt of penaunce; and after the word of Jhesu Crist, it is the endelees blisse of hevene" (1076). This is characterized by joy, a transcending of worldly limitations and ills; the statement indicates mystical union with God, the conclusion that is the beginning for those who believe. In addition to this framing there are also reminders of Doomsday, the Last Judgment when each must answer for sins committed. Early noted in the *Parson's Tale* is fear of the "day of doom and of the horrible peynes of helle" (157, also 117), and there is a final warning of the shame that will come to the impenitent at the "day of doom," when all that has been hidden in this world will be made known (1063). Medieval art abounds in visual images of Doomsday evoked by such references. Where the Monk recounted tragic falls without the prospect of salvation and the Nun's Priest wittily told of an eschewing of pride so that the cock could go on living in this world, the Parson gives a glimpse into heaven's bliss.

The structure of the *Parson's Tale* is an analogue of human existence, a minutely detailed concentration on life in this world with a brief but sustaining faith that there is eternal life for those who love and serve God. Systematic and unremitting analysis of sin is not very attractive to a modern audience; even fire-and-brimstone preaching is enlivened by bold showmanship and charismatic personalities. Contemporary theology, deeply influenced by twentieth-century psychology and social consciousness, does not favor this emphasis, but positively stresses life in this world. To cite one epitome: "We are so concerned with the Third World that we have forgotten about the next world." In today's context a formal manual about penance, the kind of handbook that a medieval parish priest would have studied, the *Parson's Tale* has not been a favorite. Usually described as dull, although it is acknowledged to be a rich storehouse of information, the tale has seemed to many an example of medieval tediousness. Like *Melibee,* it is not included in selections and is assigned only when absolutely the entire works are being read. Nevertheless, the view of the Parson as one of the "ideal" pilgrims has attracted attention, and the close linking of the *Parson's Tale* and *Prologue* with Chaucer's *Retraction* poses the most exacting critical question. Readers who delight in the exuberance and brilliance of *The Canterbury Tales* that celebrate the world and human life within it, are hard-pressed to accept Chaucer's final statement of remorse and denial of his worldly narratives.

A fuller sense of the nature of this tale is useful. Although it is crammed with information, the text is easy to outline; it is logical, divided into sections in which subdivisions are often numbered. A priest could find here material for many sermons, and the emphases indicate much about medieval belief. The practice of Confession was developed late in the Roman Catholic Church. For the first seven centuries at least penitence was public, and Celtic and monastic influences led to the use of private confession, though still infrequently. The significant change came with the decree *Omnis utriusque sexus* by the Fourth Lateran Council of 1215. This injunction of annual confession to the parish priest was an attempt to improve circumstances by placing a minimal obligation on all Christians. Thus the thirteenth and fourteenth centuries produced a religious literature that is pervaded by considerations of how the sacrament of penance is to be used. Confession meant an examination of conscience, and this is only possible when there is considerable religious knowledge. The Lateran legislation led inevitably to the production of manuals of instruction, the genre to which the *Parson's Tale* belongs. Ultimate sources for the tale are the work of two Dominicans, St. Raymund of Pennaforte, author of *Summa de poenitentia* or *Summa casuum poenitentiae* (1222/29), and William Peraldus, author of *Summa vitiorum* (1236). These discussions of penitence were the basis for many handbooks like the *Parson's Tale*. A source for the long passage about virtues, the remedies of the Seven Deadly Sins, is *Summa virtutem de remediis anime,* known as *Postquam* to avoid confusion. Possibly the work of a Franciscan author sometime in the middle of the thirteenth century, this source is particularly important; its use shows Chaucer as a thoughtful reader and adaptor, not just a slavish translator. Further, such a rich explanation of virtues alleviates the oppressiveness of sin and provides at the center of the tale another glimpse of eternal joy.

In most of the tale the Parson directly urges contrition and summarizes disciplines used in the Church. The text is divided into three main parts. In the first, Penitence is defined (1–315); a much briefer second part is devoted to Confession (316–85) with another long section presenting in great detail the Seven Deadly Sins and their Remedies (386–1027); a final brief part considers Satisfaction, the third part of Penitence that is usually expressed in alms giving and bodily pain (1028–55), and offers a final warning about ways in which Penance can be disturbed before concluding with a glimpse of eternity (1056–80). This monumental exposition is broken frequently by Latin titles, between parts and for the Seven Deadly Sins and Remedies.

Penitence, the Parson explains, comes from Contrition, which has six causes: (1) remembrance of sin, (2) "thralldom" or the slavery of sin, (3) fear of Doomsday, (4) a sorrowful remembrance of good works not accomplished, (5) recalling the Passion of Jesus Christ, and (6) a hope of forgiveness and the grace of God that come through Christ's Redemption of mankind in the Crucifixion. Contrition must be "universal and total," a sorrow for all sins. Further, it is argued that sins come first in thought and then in deeds. God is concerned with all and will forgive all and welcome the penitent into his grace. This is possible because "our sweete Lord Jhesu Crist hath spared us so debonairly* in our folies" (*graciously, 315). Without Christ's "pitee" we would "all sing a sorry song." The language effectively suggests the joy of devotion in a rather homely manner.

Contrition leads to Confession of sins, which is to a priest and must be complete. A brief account of sin's origin with Adam and Eve is followed by a distinction between venial and mortal or serious sin, with examples of how these differ. The conclusion, however, is more general: any sin, however slight, is grievous since it denies love of God. Again an alternative is provided with advice about how to restrain even venial sin: through the Eucharist, alms, saying the *Confiteor* (I confess) at Mass or compline (last evening prayers), good works, blessings of priests and bishops. This precedes an elaborate explanation of the Seven Deadly Sins, "their subdivisions, circumstances, and species." As a technique for preparation for Confession such manuals are similar to the pages of a modern missal, which contain questions about the Ten Commandments and laws of the Church to direct individual examination of conscience. Included in the account of the Seven Deadly Sins are many fascinating descriptions; for example, of clothing chosen by men and women who are guilty of Pride, which is also expressed in minstrelsy. These points are an enrichment of more predictable remarks about the foolishness of those who pride themselves for having good fortune. After Pride comes Envy, then Ire or Anger, Sloth, Avarice or Covetousness, Gluttony, and last Luxury or Lechery. Perhaps most interesting is the range of items included as sins of Ire. Anger can lead to homicide (here including not only bodily manslaughter but also contraception and abortion), or to desecration of the sacrament of the altar, swearing (even to the point of necromancy), lying, flattery, scorning of good works, idle talking, and mocking. Although last on the list, Lechery is richly illustrated. Adultery can occur through both desire and deed; differing attitudes of the Old and New Testaments toward adultery are cited. Lechery is a sin for all kinds of people; there is a section on those who have made religious vows of chastity. Parallel to the accounts of the seven sins are the remedies, respectively: humility and meekness, love of God and love of neighbor, patience and meekness with Christ as the model, strength and constancy, mercy and pity, abstinence, chastity and continence.

Although there is specific recognition of sin's origin in thought before consenting to the deed, the mental and spiritual act of Confession is not adequate in itself. The third part of Penitence is Satisfaction, the fruit of Confession, usually through alms and bodily pain; fasting and prayers are followed by good works. By these visible signs penance is known, and Satisfaction leads to "a seed of grace." This pragmatic approach is most useful for ordinary sinners, and its inclusion in *The Canterbury Tales* suggests Chaucer's interest in theology, an attitude common among the pious laity of the late fourteenth century.

As the last tale, the *Parson's Tale* summarizes, according to some readers, all that has gone before, for there are statements that can be used to evaluate the pilgrim tellers and characters in their tales, serving as a gloss for the metaphor of pilgrimage. However, in the end the *Parson's Tale* sets aside such earthly considerations, and only a hint of mysticism lingers. This is a reminder of the extraordinary spirituality of the age, best known through mystic writers like Richard Rolle, Walter Hilton, Dame Julian, and the author of *The Cloud of Unknowing,* who describe moments of awareness, the contemplation of God, or achievement of a vision when only God is seen. It is not accidental that the section just before the conclusion considers "wanhope in two maneres" (1069), the despair that comes from a belief that one's sin is too great and frequent to be forgiven and the efforts needed to persevere in goodness. Even those who achieve special contemplation of God sometimes find that this grace is withdrawn, but "joy" is always to be achieved again. This "meditacioun" (69) is the ending in "vertuous sentence" (essential meaning, 63) given by Chaucer to *The Canterbury Tales.*

8

Beginnings with Love and Fame

The portrait of the Squire in the *General Prologue* includes not only skills for fighting but also artistic accomplishments that suggest how a young man like Chaucer might have begun a poetic career at court. The Squire sings and plays the flute; "He koude songes make and wel endite*" (*write, I.95), and his principal concern is love. Chaucer's early poetry shows these interests, but also serious consideration of the role of a poet and expressions of piety. Survival and dating of poems is problematical, but it is generally accepted that before 1372 Chaucer had made some notable translations from French and written *The Book of the Duchess,* his earliest major poem. Among short poems "An ABC," or "La priere de Nostre Dame" as it is designated in manuscripts, shows devotion to the Virgin Mary, also honored in the *Second Nun's Tale,* perhaps written at this time. The lyric is a fluent translation from Guillaume de Deguilleville's *Pelerinaige de la vie* (Pilgrimage of human life , written 1331 and 1355), a popular allegory about an idea that is fundamental to *The Canterbury Tales.* Also attributed to Chaucer is a substantial translation from *Roman de la Rose,* the most influential secular poem of the Middle Ages, the work of Guillaume de Lorris, begun 1225 to 1230, and completed by Jean de Meun (le Clopinel), between 1269 and 1278. Chaucer's early work, then, is very much in the fashionable style of the English court that favored French culture. His additional indebtedness to French literature is evident in *The Book of the Duchess,* which draws deeply on Guillaume de Machaut, not least for its characteristics of dream vision. Before 1380 Chaucer had written other short poems, of which "Complaint unto Pity" is especially distinguished for its somberness, an attitude strongly evident in the *Monk's Tale,* also an early effort. The number of uncompleted works in this early period show Chaucer trying to find both subject and style, as well as considering his role as a *maker.* This term, which Chaucer uses rather than *poet,* nicely suggests a role of craftsman and the building materials are his reading. *Anelida and Arcite* shows experimentation, and stops with a greater sense of incompleteness than other poems that simply break off. Most intriguing is a work of 1378–80, *The House of Fame,* which contains a compelling self-portrait. Here Chaucer is both playfully comic about his personal appearance and habits, his work as a civil servant and inadequacy as a lover, and also impressively comprehensive in showing his compulsive reading, especially of classical authors and Dante, so that the strength of Italian influences rivals that of French authors. Most extraordinary are the excellence and mature achievement apparent at the start of Chaucer's career; none of these early works seems that of an apprentice learning his craft.

"An ABC" and "Complaint unto Pity"

These two short lyrics share formal intricacy and seriousness, as well as a heavy sprinkling of legal language that is appropriate to poems of pleading but also encourages an argument for Chaucer's early training. The poems are thematically linked by an idea of human vulnerability and need for intercession; the first is entirely devotional, a prayer for the Virgin Mary's help, while the second addresses allegorical Pity in a similar way. Yet the tones are sharply contrasted, one joyous and optimistic, rooted in faithful devotion, and the other gloomy and lacking in hope.

"An ABC" is an apt title for a poem whose stanzas begin with different letters of the alphabet, sequentially arranged. In manuscripts such alphabetical hymns are written with the initial letters large and often in red to provide a strong visual effect. Written in stanzas of eight decasyllabic lines, rhyming *a b a b b c b c,* this hymn is both a petition to Mary and a celebration of her "pitee," "merci" so needed by sinful man. The opening words of the beginning stanzas are *Almighty, Bountee, Comfort, Doute, Ever, Fleeinge, Glorious.* The first three proclaim Mary's strength, while the fourth affirms through counterargument, and the next two indicate a constant seeking of "mayde and mooder" who is glorious, one whose mercy is always forthcoming. This truth "Soth" (137) is constantly affirmed, and typological references to persons from the Old Testament—Moses, Isaac, Zachariah—offer "figures" for Mary and Christ, as well as fill out the alphabet. Immediacy is sustained through many forms of direct address—"Ladi," "Noble princess," "Queen of comfort," "mooder," "Temple devout," "Virgine"—both at the start and within stanzas. In addition, there are some skillful repetitions. The first three lines of one stanza (105ff) begin "O verrey light," followed by "O verrey lust of labour" and "O tresoreere" and provide rhetorical intensity. The syntax of lament—"Allas, I caityf, whider may I flee? / Who shal . . . / Who, but thiself"—heightens affirmation that Mary will save from "adversitee." Such exclamation and questions recall the Passion, which is explicitly referred to. There is one disclaimer, an inability to express Mary's grief at the cross (81–82), but in a later stanza Christ's Passion becomes central. Four repetitions of *And* introduce lines that describe the Crucifixion, its purpose of salvation, the sinner's failure and yet confidence that he will not be damned, and gratitude for Mary's succor. Chaucer effectively translates a lyric of traditional devotion to acknowledge sinfulness, reiterate a need for mercy, and promise penitence. These are commonplace, but no less sincere, sentiments, made fresh and personal through skillful handling of lyric form.

"The Complaint unto Pity" is also a very conventional poem, written in rime royal, a favorite stanza that Chaucer adopted for *Troilus and Criseyde*. Like "An ABC" this lyric conveys strong emotion, but the love is secular and unrequited so that sadness and despair pervade. Gloom is signaled almost immediately. The lover first says that he is as woeful as one can be without death; and when he seeks Pity, he finds her dead and buried in a hearse. Thus Chaucer creates a dramatic scene of mourning for one who has died, an allegorical figure vividly presented. The lover's first response is to swoon, and then he laments his loss. An initial insistence upon the singularity of the lover's grief for an unexpected death, one that came before he was able to approach Pity, evolves into a contrast between his feelings and those of others at the hearse. Beside Pity are "Bounte parfyt . . . / And fresshe Beaute, Lust, and Jolyte, Assured maner, Youthe, and Honeste, / Wisdom, Estaat, Drede, and Governaunce" (38–41). However, they stand happily, showing none of the woe of the grieving unrequited lover who has brought his "Complaint." This is a bill that he had addressed to Pity, hoping to secure a kind of legal redress against Cruelty, her opposite. However, recognizing that Cruelty is joined with all these virtues he withdraws and instead offers "The Bill of Complaint" to the reader/audience. The argument is that Pity's rival cruelty has deprived her of her place, "Beaute apertenant* to Grace" (*suitable, 70). Thus the plea is both for help to the lover but also a regaining of place, renown. Mercy is asked of the Queen of Furies, as Pity is designated. The lover's pain is absolute, and his devotion unmitigated. Nevertheless, his complaint is offered without hope of alteration. Pity is indeed dead, so that he can only "pleyne" futilely and continue in pain. Although the "Complaint unto Pity" is quite conventional, easily interpreted as a youthful exercise, for which no exact source has been found, it is a poem notable for its seriousness and use of a narrative frame to introduce the first-person complaint. This shows Chaucer already seeking the kind of detachment and distancing that are so characteristic of his poetry. Sentiments of love and allegorical figures are, of course, most familiar in *Roman de la Rose.*

The Romaunt of the Rose

Chaucer's Middle English translation of the most influential of all medieval romances is fragmentary, only about one third of a monumental total of almost twenty-two thousand lines. The *Roman de la Rose* is a work of the thirteenth century that was prodigiously successful; it survived in three hundred manuscripts, widely influenced many later poets, and was the center of a literary and social quarrel that included Christine de Pisan's *Dit de la Rose* (1402), perhaps the most deft defense of women against attacks in the earlier poem. Chaucer participates in the controversy in the *Prologue* to *The Legend of Good Women.* In an opening dream sequence, which provides a list of Chaucer's works, Alceste argues that a work celebrating women who have been true in love all their lives will compensate for what was "mysseyde / Or in the Rose or elles in Crisseyde" (F.440–41, G.430–31). These two poems are earlier identified as "translations," not done in malice but innocently (F.362–65, G.340–45). Severest charges of antifeminist attitudes are leveled against the author of the continuation, Jean de Meun, who writes explicitly and coarsely about sexuality without the courtly refinement of Guillaume de Lorris. The second part is also more loquacious, a kind of scholastic disputation rather than an allegory, which combines exquisite descriptions with psychological analysis of love.

The Middle English translation exists in three fragments, first printed as Chaucer's in Thynne's edition of 1532 from a manuscript that survives as Hunterian MS V.3.7, Glasgow. The portion known as Fragment A, the opening 1705 lines, is all that is generally accepted as Chaucer's on the basis of language and style. In addition, this part of Guillaume's poem is frequently echoed in Chaucer's early poetry. The subject of the *Romance of the Rose* is "al the art of love" (39–40), and the treatment is courtly. After a brief comment about whether dreams have significance, the "I" of the poem recounts an experience of his twentieth year, a dream whose events afterwards befell. His intention in rhyming is "To make your hertes gaye and lyght" according to the command of Love (31–34); "The mater fayre is of to make" (41), and the intent is to please she who is called Rose. Quickly, the dreamer begins a rich account of events that occurred five years earlier, and the reader is immediately in a world that sparkles like a manuscript illumination, a vivid and colorful picture of elegant beauty. There is much psychological exploration—through allegorical figures of the experience of love-longing, ideas already familiar in the romances of Chrétien de Troyes.

On a May morning, a time of love and jollity, the earth verdant after the harshness of winter and the air filled with the song of birds, the dreamer follows a stream until he comes to a walled garden. This is an impressive place; its walls are decorated with pictures of allegorical figures—Hate, Felony, Villainy, Covetousness, Avarice, Envy, Sorrow, Old Age, Hypocrisy, Poverty. The dreamer knocks at the gate, which is opened by a courteous maiden called Idleness, who is a friend of the owner Sir Mirth. Idleness, like the other allegorical figures is memorably (and conventionally) described: yellow hair, smooth white skin, gray eyes, well-proportioned, fashionably appareled, thinking only of her striking appearance and pleasure. The dreamer is admitted to the garden, a "paradys erthly" (648). Within the garden he meets other figures, as lovely as those outside were intimidating. He hears the singing of Gladness, a lady who is the love of Mirth. There is much singing and dancing; another lady, Courtesy, invites the dreamer to join the company. Most important is the God of Love, accompanied by a bachelor Sweet-Looking, who carries his two bows, one black and crooked and the other well proportioned and prettily decorated. Each has five arrows; respectively Pride, Villainy, Shame, Despair, New Thought, made of iron; Beauty, Simplicity, Fraunchise (generosity), Company, Fair-Seeming, made of gold. The female dancers, all attractive and appealing, are described: Beauty, Riches, Largesse, Fraunchise, Courtesy, Youthfulness. Similarly, the dreamer discovers exotic spices, fruits, trees, wells, and springs in the garden as he walks about until he comes to Narcissus's well. This permits a story within the dream, a warning to ladies, but the dreamer is heedless and looks into the water. There he sees two crystal stones on the bottom that reflect the sides of the garden. Into this mirror he looks and inevitably is ensnared in love, for he sees a mass of roses, desires to pluck one red bud but is deterred by the thorns.

Here Fragment A breaks off. In Fragment B the God of Love shoots his arrows; though the shafts are pulled out, the heads remain embedded, and the dreamer yields to the God of Love and must obey his commandments. There is much about lovesickness, changing states of being and the lack of a physician who can heal, all well-established conventions. In spite of Reason's warnings the lover persists, finally succeeding in flattering Danger (Power?), and with the help of Venus he is allowed to kiss the rose. Greater perils follow; Jealousy builds a tower surrounded by a moat. Here the roses are kept, guarded by an old woman, while Fair Welcome is imprisoned, and the lover is outside the walls. From this point, Jean de Meun's completion provides a very complicated set of arguments. Reason, for example, defines love negatively, including comments about women's objections to pregnancy and an account of prostitution. She further explains to the lover the superiority of friendship and how Fortune changes, citing Boethius's *Consolation of Philosophy* (5660ff). Fragment C, which resumes several thousand lines into *Roman de la Rose,* presents plans of Love's barons to attack the stronghold of Jealousy and a long discourse by False-Seeming about theological questions. The three fragments lack a substantial part of the poem, which culminates after the lover's violent entry into the castle—described in explicit sexual imagery—and plucking of the rose.

Something of the attractiveness of Chaucer's translation can be seen in a few illustrations from Fragment A. Almost immediately upon entering the garden the dreamer describes the bird's song as like "Song of mermaydens of the see" (680), and then explains that "mermaydens of the see" is an English term, while the French call them sirens. The account of Largesse is tied to chivalric heroes; she is first described as kin to Alexander the Great. Then her dancing partner is a "knyght of prys," newly come from tourneying and related to Arthur, widely praised by nobles and kings (1197–1210). Such courtliness is a strong appeal in Guillaume's *Roman*, and the leisurely movement and gentle if eager wooing suggest ideal social relations as yet unmarred by the harshness and aggression that Jean introduces.

The *Roman de la Rose* is far too complex and detailed to summarize effectively, but even a brief account indicates the poem's rich resources for Chaucer, who relied upon it extensively.[1] Jean has a long section about marriage; it describes women's debauchery and tricks, but also argues that a husband should not treat his wife as a possession, since love can only exist in a free and candid heart (*Roman de la Rose*, 9411–12), a passage that is echoed in the *Franklin's Tale*. However, Chaucer's indebtedness is most obvious in early poems that employ the dream vision with its advantages of detachment, vivid but stylized descriptions, and are concerned with love.

The Book of the Duchess

In his first major poem Chaucer established characteristics that persisted throughout his career. Particularly notable are: an interest in books, adaptation/translations of and references to wide reading, use of a dream vision, a detached and self-deprecating narrator, and the infusion of courtly aristocratic sentiments of fashionable French poetry with a style of English learned from popular romances. Amusingly the Man in Black, not the Dreamer, confesses, "Me lakketh both Englyssh and wit" (888), a modesty topos. The verse is a familiar type, octosyllabic (four stress) couplets, derived from Latin and widely used by medieval French writers and English metrical romancers. The lines are shorter than the pentameter (five stress) lines Chaucer favored, already noted in "An ABC" and "Complaint unto Pity," as well as the *General Prologue* and many *Canterbury Tales*. *The Book of the Duchess* is 1334 lines long, and direct parallels have been pointed out for 914 of these. The principal sources are French, all court favorites: the *Roman de la Rose,* Guillaume de Machaut's *Jugement dou Roy de Behaingne* and *Jugement dou Roy de Navarre,* and poems of Froissart. Indeed *The Book of the Duchess* is the first fully courtly poem in English. There is also an indebtedness to Ovid's *Metamorphoses*, probably through *Ovide moralisé*, to the book that the Dreamer is reading. Many attitudes in *The Book of the Duchess* that are regarded as Chaucerian have a counterpart in his sources, but the poem's emotion also suggests a specific occasion for composition.

The Duchess of the title is Blanche, daughter of Henry of Lancaster and first wife of John of Gaunt; she died September 12, 1368, of plague, as had so many during the Black Death of 1348–49. The poem may have been written soon after the beautiful young woman's untimely death, aged only twenty-eight years and mother of five children (including King Henry IV), or perhaps for a later commemoration service. A splendid alabaster tomb, the work of Chaucer's friend Henry Yevele, was placed in St. Paul's and there were chantry priests. Reading *The Book of the Duchess* would take about forty-five minutes. The subject of the poem has never been disputed; there are several references to "white" (905, 942) before "White" (Blanche, 948) is named; the last lines include other puns, "long castle" (Lancaster), "ryche hil" (Richmond), "saint Johan" (John of Gaunt) in the last lines (1318–19). A simple biographical interpretation is that Chaucer modestly uses the role of the Dreamer to console a mourning knight, the Man in Black (John of Gaunt), since it would have been presumptuous to offer such full consolation directly. The brilliance of his achievement is the gentle and slow soliciting of the Man in Black's expression of love and grief. The climax of the poem comes only at the end, when the knight identifies his loss by replying to the question "What may that be?":

> "She ys ded!" "Nay!" "Yis, be my trouthe!"
> "Is that youre los? Be God, hyt ys routhe!" (1309–10)

Earlier the Dreamer had asked "What los ys that?" (1139), only to hear more of the knight's love. There is, then, some suspense before this reply, one of Chaucer's most unforgettable couplets. After this, the poem ends quickly, since consolation, or therapy, has been achieved.

Dream poems in Western literature are familiar both in Scripture and classical writers.[2] Chaucer acknowledges these traditions at the start of the narrator's dream when he refers to Joseph (Genesis 4) and Macrobius, who expanded and wrote the commentary on Cicero's *Somnium Scipionis* (276–90), the most famous account of dreams in the Middle Ages. The Dreamer also says that he does not believe any will be able to interpret his dream, a very different attitude toward dreams from those expressed in the *Nun's Priest's Tale*. Declaring simply "This was my dream," he proceeds to recount it; however, he is more than a storyteller. The framework allows an imaginative exploration of feeling; persons in a dream, notably the Dreamer, can behave in ways not likely when awake. Thus the dream vision provides the poet with a public consolation and yet allows personal expression of feeling. Indeed there is much introductory material in *The Book of the Duchess*. The opening sixty-one lines establish the Dreamer's character; he is sleepless, lacks feeling, and for eight years has suffered from "a sickness" (unrequited love). He is also a reader. One of Chaucer's original touches is to introduce his dream visions through reading, the commonplace experience of dozing over a book. Here he specifies a "romaunce," a book of fables in which he finds a tale of kings and queens, actually Ovid's *Metamorphoses*. Then follow nearly two hundred lines (62–230) that recount the story of Seys and Alcyone. The choice is apt, for it is an account of a dream, the appearance of the drowned Seys to his grieving wife, who laments her loss and prays to Juno. Alcyone is sent to Morpheus, led by a messenger whose calls of "Awake!" are marvelously funny and delightfully evoke a sense of public performance. This comic interlude, built on the ordinariness of sluggish waking, precedes Morpheus's rising to take the body. Seys explains his fate, and his wife Alcyone sorrowfully cries, "Alas!" The Dreamer disclaims full retelling of the Ovidian tale and describes his insomnia, even though there is "a dedly slepynge soun" (162) in Morpheus's cave. He enters a first dream vision by saying that he would give the god of sleep a glorious featherbed if only he could get some rest. Morpheus answers, and the main dream vision begins.

Each phase is triggered by sound. In May the Dreamer is awakened by birdsong (294–97), and this singing fills his chamber so that he looks at its glass windows, which tell the story of Troy, and at the walls, painted "bothe text and glose" with the *Roman de la Rose,* Chaucer's explicit acknowledgment of influence (333–34). Another sound, a hunting horn (345, 354), leads him out of the chamber into the woods, where the Emperor Octavius hunts with a large party. A final blast (386) marks the end of initial entry into a dreamworld, and a dog provides the next guide until they come upon "a man in blak," sitting with his back against an oak tree (444–47) and complaining to himself. The central portion of *The Book of the Duchess* is an exchange between Dreamer and Man in Black, a gradual explanation of the young man's grief, solicited through a series of superficially obtuse questions that allow a slow revelation of a great love lost through Fortune. Here the fickle goddess is a player at chess, to whom the Man in Black loses his queen. The Dreamer not only counsels against suicide, which is damnable but, by encouraging full praise of the lady and recognition of a long mutual love, he also provides consolation. The dream vision ends as it began, with a sound, the tolling of a bell twelve times. Thus the narrator finds himself again in his bed with his book containing the tale of Seys and Alcyone, but also with a vivid memory of a curious dream that has just been recorded.

The Book of the Duchess is very closely modeled upon French aristocratic sources, but its freshness and vitality suggest originality and encourage an identification of the "I" of the poem as Chaucer. The role of the narrator, a persona that both participates and presents events, provides detachment that is familiar in French courtly poetry, and even the comic contrasts can be found in Machaut. It is, then, safe only to acknowledge that as a beginning poet Chaucer chose these characteristics, not simple melancholy lovesick dreamers. A case can be made that the "I" is all mourners; this views the poem as a public occasion when the death of a beautiful and loved lady is confronted and made bearable through memory of her virtues and the joy of the life now ended. This is a recognition and inevitable acceptance that "To lytel while oure blysse lasteth." A perception of transitory life underlies much of human endeavor, especially a dedication to fame, not least in the work of poets. Chaucer more fully explored the idea of fame, not love, in his second major work.

Anelida and Arcite

The name of the hero in *Anelida and Arcite* is familiar from the *Knight's Tale,* but his character is very different. In what seems to be an early attempt to use Boccaccio's *Teseida* Chaucer invented a false lover, the complete opposite of the devoted lover of Emily and companion of Palomon. "This fals Arcite" is governed by "his newfangleness" (desire for novelty, 141) and takes another lady, ignoring the "stidfastnesse" of Queen Anelida, who is devoted to him. The unfinished poem is only 357 lines, almost evenly divided between "The Story" and "The compleynt of Anelida the quene upon fals Arcite." An "Invocation" is to Mars, and Chaucer presents himself as translator, "in Englyssh to endyte / This olde storie, in Latyn which I fynde" (9–10). The authority cited is Statius, who provides an opening epigraph. From Boccaccio Chaucer took the Theban setting, beginning with the return of Theseus after his triumph over Scythia, when he brings his conquered wife Hyppolita and her sister Emily home to his "countre-houses." Most of the story is an analysis of Anelida's love and grief over Arcite's cruel betrayal. There are sharp statements and a contrast between the queen's doting devotion, which does not hold Arcite's love, and the "newe lady" who entraps and controls him through "daunger" (domination,186, 196). The story concludes with an exemplary statement: worthy women are urged to take example, and the analysis of male sexuality is simple—"For what he may not gete, that wolde he have" (203). There is, then, both male and female victimization in love, a preoccupation in many of Chaucer's early poems. In the *Knight's Tale,* where all the lovers are true, little attention is given to the young woman Emily, object of male devotion.

In *Anelida and Arcite* the greatest interest is the response of the betrayed woman, whose emotions are analyzed in a long Complaint, which is inspired by French courtly poetry. It is extraordinarily elaborate, with divisions into Proem, Strophe, Antistrophe, and Conclusion and using appropriate stanzaic forms. The sentiments are familiar ones, poignantly rendered. Remembrance is a sword of sorrow. Anelida contrasts her own love with Arcite's falseness, emphasizing her innocence and his cruelty and concluding the Strophe with concern about slander. The Antistrophe presents her grief and withdrawal, her questioning, and acceptance that her destiny is to die on the morrow. Anelida concludes that this is her swan song. Whether she dies or not is not known. Although the story continues when she rises from her swoon and goes toward the temple of Mars, the last phrase is "as ye shal after here." The Complaint, part of a long tradition of psychological analyses of passion, is compelling, for it shows changes of moods and a powerful voice. Such mastery in lyric is simpler and preceded the integration of emotion with narrative that comes in longer poems where a more complex treatment and story are required.

The House of Fame

Chaucer's *House of Fame* shows interests other than aristocratic love and chivalry, ideas derived from French literature and favored at court. The title indicates that fame is the subject; however, reputation can be good or bad, and its presence or absence is quite arbitrary. Fame can also mean rumor, and Chaucer combines these two basic meanings. Attitudes toward fame are, then, variable; few topics show a wider cleavage between classical and Christian ideals. This is especially true of views of poetry, a way of achieving fame for the poet and the community and also of glorifying God. Chaucer's poem is unfinished, breaking off abruptly at line 2158, after an exciting narrative that sweeps through space and seems to be reaching its climax with the entry of "A man of gret auctorite." Inconclusiveness has several facets. Written in octosyllabic couplets,

The House of Fame is technically more skillful than *The Book of the Duchess;* it is also much more difficult to interpret. Very learned, but introducing authorities lightly, witty and humorous but deeply serious, characteristically detached yet concerned—Chaucer is all of these. He never seems closer at hand and yet constantly elusive, demonstrating that elfish character that the Host saw in the pilgrim poet. There are several similarities with other early poems; again Chaucer uses a dream vision, and an animal serves as guide. The poet is passionately devoted to books, more interested in information than in love, at which he is not successful, and he receives much more attention than in *The Book of the Duchess*. As in the *Prologue to the Man of Law's Tale* Chaucer names himself; the eagle addresses the dreamer as "Geffrey" (729). In addition, there is an endearing and convincing self-portrait, as vivid as surviving pictures of Chaucer some details of which, like his plumpness, the eagle's struggles seem to confirm.

Book I begins with a *Proem,* "God turne us every drem to goode!" and a recognition of limits in human understanding. In a conclusion that disclaims opinion amid clerkly endeavors to explain, this is reiterated: "that the holy roode / Turne us every drem to goode!" (57–58). Prayers traditionally begin and conclude many medieval poems, so that they are often scarcely noted. Most of the *Proem* is a long sentence about kinds, causes, and effects of dreams; this *dubitatio* reinforces a sense of limitation that sets a context for an exploration of fame. The specific dream that is recounted is unusually dated as December 10 (63, 111), a day in winter, indicating that the spring delights typical of dream visions will be absent. The date is in the liturgical season of Advent, time of expectation and beginning with the coming of Christ in the flesh, but also of penitence since Christ will come again at the Last Judgment. *The Invocation* is first to the god of sleep, but the main prayer for telling a dream rightly is to "he that mover ys of al, / That is and was and ever shal," echoing the *Gloria patria* of the Mass. Concluding with a reference to the hanging of proud and materialist Croesus, who denied a dream foretelling his death, the poet also confesses a lack of charity (108).

This rather elaborate preparation for the *Story* is reinforced by an early reference to "pilgrymage" (116), and the vision of Book I finishes with a prayer to Christ to be saved from illusion (492–94). An immediate sense of fragility comes when the poet finds himself in a temple made of glass. In this place of Venus he views many golden images and decorated niches for statues with precious stones.

He beholds the opening words of Virgil's *Aeneid,* written on a brass tablet, and proceeds to scenes from the great epic of Augustan Rome, well known in the Middle Ages, not least as the starting point for Dante's *Divine Comedy*. The episodes show more deception than heroism: the destruction of Troy through Sinon's horse and Aeneas's subsequent flight toward Italy, interrupted by a storm that stops him at Carthage, where he becomes the lover of Queen Dido and then betrays her to pursue his fame. The most detailed description explores false appearances, the deceiving nature of men and wretchedness of women, complaints of Dido and her sister Anne, examples of other betrayed women. Uneasiness with these circumstances is scarcely offset by statements that "the book [*Aeneid*] us tellis" (426) that Aeneas was ordered to go on to Italy. Only the opening of Virgil's poem is featured; Aeneas's time in Italy is summarized in a single verse paragraph (451–65), though readers are referred to Virgil's book and other authors, Claudian or Dante. Book I of *The House of Fame* concludes with the poet's awe before rich images, but also his disorientation—he does not know where he is—and a resolve to get outside the Temple of Venus. This can be read as a rejection of the epic fame of classical antiquity. The poet reaches a large field, a desert place without habitation or vegetation; he prays to Christ, casting his eyes heavenward to behold a golden eagle that brightly dazzles.

Book II also begins with a *Proem* that prepares for what is to follow. The opening lines call upon all who understand English to listen and learn from his dream. This sounds a new voice, one that is not dependent upon other favored languages. Acknowledging a dual tradition, scriptural and classical, he concludes with an invitation to men to see whether what he writes has any virtue (523–28). The *Dream* proceeds with great energy and vividness, commencing with the eagle's swooping down and lifting the poet into flight. The effect is exhilarating but also frightening, a transfer from one element of nature to another, and with the eagle's speaking (in man's voice "Awak!" [556]) a crossing over into another creature's kingdom. Significantly, the poet's mind focuses when he hears human words, and the narrative takes on an ordinariness through lively conversational dialogue. The eagle, which is privy to its passenger's thoughts and feelings, chides him for nervousness and incompetence as a lover, but mostly considers him as a maker (Chaucer does not call himself a poet) of books, songs, rhymes, literary works, mostly about love. Sent by Jove, the eagle knows Chaucer's habits well; it describes his return from a hard day's work at his reckonings (he was controller of the wool trade) only to retire to his study to read, alone like "an heremyte" (659) until his look is dazed. The self-portrait is playful and certainly appealing; it also suggests a popular fourteenth-century religious order, the Carthusians, given to study each in his own study and cell. Chaucer's reward for his efforts is to be a visit to the House of Fame, where he will encounter "wonder thynges" and "tydynges" of lovers.

The eagle, whose explanations constitute most of Book II, can be interpreted in various ways: as a personification of philosophic thought, or thought that results in poetic interpretation, or contemplation. The information provided is diverse and often recondite. First there is a cosmology; the House of Fame is located between heaven, earth, and sea. Next comes a familiar scientific explanation of sound as a part of nature and its movement; all noises go upward to Fame's House. As a limiting of the power of words, no sharp distinction is made between speech and sound, since the fundamental effect is of wind. Finally, there is a philosophical and theological consideration; Geoffrey has a judgment to make "Take yt in ernest or in game" (822). Nevertheless, the eagle's words rush on, as it asserts an argument of simplicity—brief, free of terms of philosophy, poetic figures, rhetorical colors. And Geoffrey simply "answered and seyde, 'Yis' " (864). Having convinced with words, the eagle now proposes experiential learning and flies low enough for his passenger again to see the earth. The view from outer space makes the earth look quite insignificant—as it does to Troilus from the eighth sphere—and a view to the Milky Way expands a sense of the greatness of the universe and relative insignificance of the world. Such vision leads to a consideration of those who have flown. Flying, of course, is a sign of pride, an attempt to soar above normal circumstances, to look down on the terrestrial; such ambition is most famously illustrated by Alexander the Great's flight with the aid of griffins and also familiar in the fall of Icarus. Geoffrey's response is to praise God the Creator (970ff); he cites Boethius's recognition of the role of philosophy in giving wing to thought, but he cuts off Boethius's statement to end on the word *cloud,* which suggests the darkness that envelops even the wisest thinking, the mystic's *Cloud of Unknowing*. A late Roman, Boethius in *The Consolation of Philosophy* explores issues very pertinent to *The House of Fame;* he fell from a position of eminence and was executed on false charges, a victim of words and fame. The recollection of Boethius leads into a restatement of human limitation; as at the

Temple of Venus, Geoffrey does not know where he is, but now he goes further, proclaiming that God knows. The eagle seems to concur, noting that all of Geoffrey's reading of poetry does not give knowledge of the heavens. Thus they fly on until they come to the House of Fame, where Geoffrey is left with the eagle's parting wish that God send him the grace to learn some good in this place (1086–88).

Poetry and science are joined in the *Invocation* to Book III, which addresses Apollo, asking power to describe the House of Fame. Indeed the technique is to make the abstract accessible through precise description. The house is built on a rock, which Geoffrey immediately identifies as ice. From the outset, then, he realizes that the foundation is untrustworthy and that little glory is due the builder; these sentiments are framed by prayers to Saint Thomas Becket and to God (1131–35). Further, he perceives that the names of the famous are partially thawed and some letters imperfect. The point is succinctly made "What may ever last?" (1147). Nevertheless, Geoffrey is fascinated, and an imaginative and evocative account of castle, harpers, and magicians precedes his meeting with Lady Fame, who is besieged by many seeking largesse (gifts). Her hall, presented as in a chivalric romance, is crowded with petitioners—classical heroes, Jewish prophets, poets who wrote of Troy, Ovid, and other Latin poets, writers of old gestes—all contributing to the noise. These petitioners make their cases to Fame, and Geoffrey hears that there is no definite correlation between what is accomplished and reputation gained. Those who can offer good works, others who are deserving, some who eschew fame, including writers of works of contemplation, idle ones, traitors, shrews—with each, fame or its lack seems unrelated. Not surprisingly, Geoffrey, having been well prepared through the eagle's explanations and his own observations of futile petitions, seeks not fame, but the "newe tydynges . . . thinges" that the eagle promised (1885–95). Very simply, the maker needs not fame but material to sustain his work. Indeed the entire journey with the eagle is an expansion of experience, an attempt to understand in ways not restricted to the reading of books (878).

Thus Geoffrey proceeds to a House of Daedalus, builder of the Labyrinth that Theseus penetrated to slay the Minotaur. This House of Rumor is made of interwoven twigs of different colors, but its salient characteristic is the sounds that blow through it. Here Geoffrey is rejoined by his eagle that resumes the role of explaining and transporting, for it sweeps Geoffrey up and flies through a window.

He hears a quick set of exchanges—thus has he said, thus has he done, thus will it be, I wager, and so on—before the sounds are wafted off to Fame. After identifying among those present shipmen, pilgrims, pardoners, messengers, he hears a great noise and rushes toward the part of the hall where "love-tidings" are told to hear "What thing is that?" (2147). Eager anticipation is forever sustained, for the man of authority is seen but never heard.

The House of Fame is much more searching than Chaucer's earlier works, and its explicit self-identification warrants a reading as a poetic credo. More than any other work of Chaucer's it shows Dante's influence, and the three books have been equated with *Inferno, Purgatoria,* and *Paradiso* (albeit earthly). John Lydgate's fifteenth-century list of Chaucer's works omits *The House of Fame* but includes "Dante in Inglissh," an encouragement to equation. However, the poetic stances taken are very different; Chaucer shows great comic capacity that is quite absent in Dante, though a parody of the *Divine Comedy* seems unlikely. Where Dante judges relentlessly, Chaucer is timid and tentative, often reiterating his own inadequacy and uncertainty about everything except a belief in God's power and the limitations of human perception. Chaucer does not presume to show the light of salvation; his belief in God's grace is unwavering, as is his view of himself as a maker who is deeply indebted to authorities and enriching this knowledge with experiences, at least those of the imagination. The uneasiness of one who undertakes to be a "maker" is further evidenced in Chaucer's extended response to Boethius and further investigations of love and chattering birds.

9

The Consolation of Philosophy in Love and Politics

Claims for the significance of Boethius's *The Consolation of Philosophy* are very high indeed: there is no influence to compare with it throughout the Middle Ages, and because of it Chaucer became a philosophical poet rather than a courtly maker.[1] Among his early works are a full and careful translation, known as *Boece,* and a number of lyrics—"The Former Age," "Fortune," "Truth," "Gentilesse," and "Lak of Stedfastnesse"—which help to define Boethian thought that informs much of Chaucer's writing. Love remains a poetic preoccupation, but both the *Knight's Tale* and *Troilus and Criseyde* are distinguished by philosophical meditation that explicitly employs arguments and sentiments from *The Consolation of Philosophy. The Parliament of Fowls* is a detached observation about the limitations of earthly love; however, here the treatment is broadly comic, even though Nature is a descendant of Lady Philosophy. "Complaint of Mars" and "Complaint of Venus" continue the poet's lyric writing about love, mostly unrequited, but again there are unusual approaches to this most commonplace courtly theme. Finally, *The Legend of Good Women,* begun earlier and subsequently revised, was offered as an atonement for the showing of faithless women in *Troilus and Criseyde* and *Roman de la Rose.* The third longest of Chaucer's poems, a work written over a long period of time, it has until recently been less frequently read and interpreted. Like the other pieces considered in this chapter, *The Legend* is part of the crucial decade of the 1380s when Chaucer attained his full maturity, a maturity that would have been impossible without understanding Boethius.

Boece and Boethian Ballads

An attempt to assimilate the thought of pagan antiquity with Christian faith and experience is a recurring concern of the Middle Ages.

Chaucer's reading of classical literature inevitably led him to the work of Boethius (c. 480– 524). Probably the most renowned interpreter of the classical world, sometimes called "the last of the Romans; the first of the scholastics," Boethius was a favorite of poets and kings.[2] Dante places him among the twelve lights in the heaven of the Sun in *Paradise* (X.125), and *The Divine Comedy* can be read as an elaboration of Boethius's view of the soul's ascent to the contemplation of the mind of God and subsequent return to its place in the universe.[3] The deeply personal account of an honorable man who has fallen from high place and seeks answers to fundamental questions of providence and belief was cogent to public servants, especially in times of unrest.

Born to an ancient and aristocratic family, Boethius was appointed consul by the Ostrogothic king Theodoric in 510 and later given a position of public responsibility as head of the civil service and chief of palace officials. His decision to be a minister was not based on a desire for fame, but a commitment to public service, a sense of duty that he derived from Plato, whose ideal of government was by men who had studied wisely (1.p4.25). Boethius's personal preference would have been to devote himself more fully to study, so that his choice involved great self-sacrifice. Delight in learning and public service are characteristics he shared with Chaucer. In a time of oppositions, Boethius was more devoted to principles than to politics. On the side of the empire and its culture, he defended the rights of the Roman Senate against encroachments of the Germanic leader who effectually ruled, though there was an emperor in Constantinople. Theodoric was Christian, but an Arian, a heretical group who denied that the Father and Son were "one substance." Although he served Theodoric, Boethius took an orthodox theological position, siding with the East. This may have contributed to Theodoric's withdrawal of support, and Boethius's intervention on behalf of a senator accused without adequate evidence provided an occasion for charges against Boethius himself. He was exiled, imprisoned, cruelly tortured, and finally bludgeoned to death in Pavia.

While awaiting death, in prison, Boethius wrote *The Consolation of Philosophy*. Exact circumstances, and indeed the rightness of the case, are not known, but most accept Boethius's account. "I am without deffense dampyned to proscripcion and to the deth for the studie and bountes that I have doon to the senat" (1.p4.242). The philosophical issues, then, are evil and suffering, and the acceptance of these as part of God's providence. Chaucer's "pacience in adversitee," a solution in many of *The Canterbury Tales,* is an epitome of *The Consolation,* which looks beyond justice. Boethius chose the form of a Platonic dialogue, allegorized as his conversation with Lady Philosophy, and serving as a *consolatio,* a moral medication/remedy for illness. A skilled scholar of Greek, Boethius combined great knowledge of classical philosophy—he had set himself the task of translating Aristotle and Plato and reconciling the two—and his Christian belief in God the Creator and eternal bliss.

The circumstances of awaiting death and probably writing without the resources of a library though with a fine memory of his reading, suggest why the work is so accessible. It is neither a philosophical nor theological treatise and thus free of the difficult vocabulary and complex arguments usually found in such works. Instead the situation is intensely emotional: Philosophy not only argues a way to become reconciled with circumstances that seem impossible to accept; she also soothes Boethius's sobbing and wipes away his tears. The solution is to focus on permanent values, recognizing the transitory nature of this world, especially the fickleness of fortune and fame, and seeing the earth in a transcendent universe where the limits of man's knowledge and perception of time are contrasted to God's knowing (5.pr5). Boethius's lack of specific references to Christ suggests a view of the universality of belief in reason and an omnipotent God still deeply rooted in classical philosophy and education. Nevertheless, he was unquestionably a Christian who believed in a very personal God; the conclusion of *The Consolation* urges prayer to God, an expression of piety at the end of a philosophical justification that relies upon the individual's ascent through meditation.

During the eight centuries that separate Boethius from Chaucer many responses to *The Consolation* were developed. Chaucer worked not only from the Latin text but also from a French prose translation of Jean de Meun, upon which he relied more heavily, and several commentaries, principally that of Nicholas Trivet. Chaucer's translation is a close and careful one, enriched and made more precise by the commentaries. Boethius has five Books, each containing several chapters that combine a metrical poem and a prose statement. Chaucer's *Boece* renders everything in prose, a typical way of translating more literally. This choice may also be a response to Boethius's argument against poetry as a way of consolation: Philosophy rejects the poetical muses, the "mermaydenes," whose comfort will not provide the medicine needed to cure Boethius of his common sickness.

His illness is a deceived heart, eyes darkened "by the cloude of mortel thynges" (1.pr2.19–26). Philosophy shows the inconsistency between deeds and the condition of the doer; the good do not necessarily have prosperity, nor the wicked adversity (Gloss, 1.pr4. 288–94). Book 2, which owes much to Aristotle's *Nichomachean Ethics,* emphasizes practical circumstances. Fortune is identified as constantly changing, and Boethius introduces the image of a turning Wheel, an ever-changing from highest to lowest. A gloss defines tragedy as a literary work that describes prosperity for a time that turns into wretchedness (2.pr2.7), as had the *Monk's Tale*. Boethius's honors and reputation, all worldly glory, are thus viewed as things outside himself and not amenable to control; dependent upon Fortune, they lack stability and cannot offer "tranquillitie of soule" that is to be found in the self (2.pr5.135). Ill-fortune can be more profitable than good, for it teaches rather than deceives (2.pr8). Philosophy continues to argue the falseness and uncertainty of worldly riches, whose increase only leads to further human wants (3.pr3).

Book 3, which is central, builds an affirmation of God's bliss that reaches a climax in a hymn to God the Father and Creator (m9), which avows God's governance by eternal reason and the beauty of His all-embracing creation. In Chaucer's translation the last line is "thow thiself art bygynnynge, berere, ledere, path, and term; to looke on the, that is our ende." This poem had its own commentaries in the Middle Ages; it was seen as a Platonic hymn, an epitome of the opening of the *Timaeus,* but the conclusion echoes St. John's Gospel. Subsequent sections elaborate on God's goodness and urge that worldly affections, as well as earthly things, be set aside to come to God. Life in the world is fragmentary, and thus men should always seek the divine. Philosophy's case is a strong one, but the concluding example of Orpheus is a harbinger of further difficulty. Book 4 sustains an argument that good is strong and bad is weak, even urging that the wicked be pitied (4.pr3). Nevertheless, Boethius still questions, notably about the difference between what God does and the chance of fortune, the relation between Providence and Fate (4.pr5). Philosophy, "a litelwhat smylinge," acknowledges that they are now moving into "gretteste of alle thinges that mowe been axed" (pr6). The solution offered is that increasingly as the soul detaches itself from tangible things it approaches nearer to God/Providence—a still and simple center. Thus consolation comes with detachment from the world (pr7), a wisdom that denies the significance of second causes, the merely Necessary as distinct from the Divine. The question of evil in the world is, then, answered by divine peace. God/ Providence is not dependent upon temporal events; lacking past and future, God is a timeless present, eternal, while the world has many moments. God's knowledge is thus not incompatible with man's exercise of free will. "Eternite, thanne, is parfit possessioun and al togidre of lif interminable; and that shewethe more cleerly by the comparysoun or collacioun of temporel thinges" (5.pr6.13–17). Several sections point out the difference between man's knowing and divine intelligence (5.pr5), one evocatively contrasting "whanne the soule byholdeth and seeth the hye thought (that is to seyn, God)" and "now, while the soule is hidd in the cloude and in the derknesse of the membres of the body" (5. m3.43).[4] Chaucer's frequent explorations of destiny, providence, free will show how significant Boethius was to the development of his understanding. In addition to long passages in the narrative poems, several shorter lyrics present Boethian ideas.

"The Former Age," which survives in only two manuscripts, may be a commentary rather than an independent lyric. Closely tied to *Boece,* it is a rendering of Book 2, metrum 5, which describes a "Golden Age," a familiar idea in classical literature from the time of Hesiod's *Works and Days*[5] that recurs in some of Chaucer's favorite books—Virgil, Ovid, *Roman de la Rose*. Today in popular language the idea is expressed as "the good old days." Chaucer's treatment of the commonplace idea is fresh and technically skillful; for example, in the powerful reiteration of "No" to begin all lines of stanza three that establishes the loss that is lamented by reiterated "Allas, allas" in the concluding stanza. An earlier time of simplicity and peace, "A blisful lyf," (1) of "parfit quiete" (40) contrasts with the present, "oure dayes" of "covetyse, / Doublenessse, and tresoun, and envye, / Poyson, manslawhtre, and mordre" (61–63). Boethius's metrum 5 is one comment on changes wrought by fickle Fortune, and Chaucer reiterates the idea of loss and decline in good fortune. His most distinctive rendering is a subtle introduction of several images from scripture: the fruits of the earth come without the wounding of the plow (9), a reference to Adam's work after the Fall; the people of the former age were "lambish" (50), free of vices, a loving community that is the ideal of Christ the Lamb. Boethius's praise of God the Creator seems to be particularized by an example of mining, the sweaty work of taking metals from the earth (28–29), a reminder of ecological destruction, already serious in the fourteenth century. The lyric goes beyond description by naming sins like pride and avarice (53), a familiar part of medieval didactic art. Covetousness is given as a first explanation (32) and begins the longest list of evils (61); similarly, envy appears more than once (53, 62). Intensity of sentiment may indicate a comment on circumstances at the end of King Richard II's reign.

Chaucer's political concern is specified in another lyric, commonly called "Lak of Stedfastnesse." This "Balade" begins with the same idea as "The Former Age"—"Somtyme the world was so stedfast and stable." This line, whose use of alliteration and unusual word order (an emphatic opening with an adverb *somtyme*) sets a style that shows Chaucer's artistry, a lyric skill that recurs in early poems of Tudor poet Sir Thomas Wyatt and is fully developed by John Donne. The second stanza repeats interrogatory "What maketh/ What causeth" (8, 13) that sustains the energy of reaction against changes in a world aptly described as "turned up-so-doun" (5). Stanza 3 defines those changes, and a bold use of caesura in the opening line "Trouthe is put doun, resoun is holden *fable" (*deceit, 15) forces deliberation that is confirmed by a more explicit reiteration in a description of the changes "Fro right to wrong, fro trouthe to fickelnesse" (20). The refrain of three stanzas gives the reason for what has happened: "That al is lost for lak of stedfastnesse," and again "covetyse" is the sin that precipitates the change. The poem concludes with "Lenvoy to King Richard," an exhortation to honor, concern for the people as well as self and maintaining of kingly estate, a return to law. Chaucer, like many of his contemporaries, hopes for a restoration of what had been a fine beginning for a young king; "And wed thy folk againe to stedfastnesse," as the final refrain urges.

King Richard II, of course, was one who fell from high place. Chaucer's *balade* "Fortune" presents both a familiar idea, including the image of the wheel (46), and another note of politics in the concluding "Lenvoy de Fortune," which is addressed to "Princes," sometimes identified as Dukes (Lancaster, York, Gloucester), so crucial early in Richard II's reign. "Fortune" is divided into three parts, a dialogue between Fortune and Plaintiff that recalls Boethius's dialogue with Lady Philosophy. Plaintiff, as the refrain states, begins by defying Fortune. She replies that man makes himself wretched by his striving, she insists that all men are subject to her variableness, and enigmatically refers to a best friend. The final *balade* combines responses of Plaintiff and Fortune: the former decries Fortune as a blind goddess who brings "adversitee" (49), but the latter insists that her condition is "mutabilitee" (57), inevitable in a world of "resteles travayle" (70). Both speak the refrain: "In general, this reule may nat fayle," and the concluding dedication to Princes reintroduces an unidentified "beste frend" (78) for Plaintiff and reaffirms that better estate may come.

Two other Boethian lyrics indicate alternatives to the randomness of Fortune's Wheel by expressing contemporary views of morality that urge worthy attitudes and behavior. "Gentilesse" and "Truth" are both modern titles, but the former is identified in manuscript as "Moral Balade of Chaucier" and the latter labeled as "Balade de Bon Conseyl." The idea of "gentilesse" appears in *Boece* (3.pr6), after an explanation that tragedy comes from seeking glory; though "gentilesse" should encourage men to emulate their worthy ancestors, all comes from God. The "Moral Balade" reiterates Boethius's point by urging "Vertu to love and vyces for to flee" (4) and attributing all "to the firste fader in magestee" (19). However, another point is made; not only is "gentilesse" dependent upon virtue rather than riches, but also it comes from the individual not an inheritance. Chaucer's richest use of the concept is in *The Wife of Bath's Tale,* where Dante is cited as source of an idea that was commonplace.

If the gentle person is to flee vice, those who seek "Truth" must "Flee fro the prees and dwelle with sothfastnesse." The number of surviving manuscripts (twenty-two) and early printings, indicate that this was Chaucer's most popular lyric. Like others here discussed, this "Balade de Bon Conseyl" is the work of a polished poet. The use of strong imperatives conveys a conviction that can compel conversion to the poet's good advice. However, it seems likely that the appeal of "Balade de Bon Conseyl" was based more upon meaning than style. Here Chaucer affirms Boethian detachment from the world by reiterating the ills of the present so powerfully evoked in "Former Age." He warns against the ambition that makes one prey to "Fortune"—"The wrastling for this world axeth a fal" (16)—and urges self knowledge and devotion to God. The command "Forth, pilgrim, forth!" (18), which reminds that life is a spiritual pilgrimage, rests upon the promise of the Gospels, explicitly echoed in the refrain "And trouthe thee shal delivere, it is no drede" (John 8:32). Appropriately, the poem appears in one manuscript next to the portrait of the Parson in the *General Prologue of The Canterbury Tales*. The "Envoy" to Vache is found in only one manuscript, but it is generally agreed that the person addressed is Sir Philip (de) la Vache, who was in disfavor at court. The interest in an individual as well as a general articulation of worthy behavior particularizes the meaning of "Truth." Like the addresses to "Princes" in "Fortune" and to "King Richard" in "Lak of Stedfastnesse," it provides a glimpse of the world of the court with which Chaucer was associated. Thus he, like Boethius, acknowledges his living in a world of changing Fortune where individuals were at risk and goodness and vice did not necessarily determine outcomes.

The Parliament of Fowls

Chaucer probably completed *The Parliament of Fowls* before he finished the translation of *Boece,* but the Roman philosopher contributes to an underlying seriousness in one of Chaucer's most delightful and joyous poems. As in other earlier narratives, most notably *The Book of the Duchess* and *The House of Fame,* Chaucer employs a dream vision. Again the narrator is distinguished first by his love and understanding of books and second by his interest but inexperience in love; the relation of the two is established in opening stanzas. The first line "The lyf so short, the craft so long to lerne," a familiar proverbial phrase, is here specific to love, but it is traceable to Hippocrates (c. 460–c. 370 B.C.), Greek father of medicine who applied it to his own attempts as a physician. Chaucer as poet, makes analogous attempts, describing how he seeks to learn from "olde bokes."

The Parliament of Fowls identifies his latest reading, "Tullyus of the Drem of Scipioun" (31). This conclusion of *de Republica* by Marcus Tullius Cicero (106–43 B.C.) contained much more than an account of dreams, and Chaucer referred to it in other works. An ongoing reading is explicitly stated later, when he explains that he "hadde red of Affrican byforn" and thus could identify personages in his dream. The narrator also indicates that the text was transmitted when he names "Macrobye" (111). "The Dream of Scipio" was preserved for the Middle Ages by Macrobius (c. 400), who added extensive commentaries about both Neoplatonic philosophy and general education. These, of course, are interests of Boethius. More specifically, Macrobius interprets Scipio's dream as a warning to live virtuously and a reminder of eternal life, Heaven, and the Day of Judgment. This moral element explains the work's popularity and influence in the Middle Ages, and Chaucer introduces his systematic summary by identifying his purpose as giving the "greete" (substance) of Scipio's "sentence" (meaning, 35). Hence he marks—with "Thanne," followed by some variant of told, asked, showed, prayed—each phase of the younger Scipio's dream meeting with Scipio Africanus, his grandfather, a famous general who imparts not worldly but spiritual wisdom. Although the emphasis is upon an afterlife and the limitations of "the lytel erthe that here is" (57) cast against the heavens, Africanus begins with an argument that dedication to the good of others is the way to "a blysful place" where joy is without end (48–49). Thus along with a warning against the delights of the world, there is also an acknowledgment that good deeds on earth are a means to heavenly bliss and that evil deeds result in pain and suffering after death until their doers are forgiven and God through his grace welcomes them to bliss. Boethius's *Consolation of Philosophy* was, of course, an attempt to survive an experience of great suffering in spite of living a good life of public service, so that there is a total eschewing of the world, a case for survival only by expecting nothing. Macrobius, albeit principally devoted to a discourse about immortality, still seems hopeful about life in the world. He is, then, a helpful guide, rewarding the dreamer for reading him with such devotion ("That sumdel of thy labour wolde I quyte" 112).

Africanus leads the dreamer to a walled park or garden that has a gate bearing two Dantesque inscriptions: one in gold promises "good aventure" in a perpetual Maytime, and the other in black offers Disdain and Danger, which mean lack of fruitfulness. Understandably such "gret difference" immobilizes the narrator, whose quide pushes him inside, with a reassurance that he is not at risk because he is not Love's servant. This echoes a Boethian case for the irrelevance of ambitious seeking, and it also is the occasion for broad comedy. Again, as in *The Book of the Duchess* and *The House of Fame,* Chaucer creates a narrator that can be seen as self-characterization, whether interpreted as playful or humble. Africanus's role effectively concludes with a stanza about the dreamer's dullness and a final reassurance: he may not be an active participant, but he can observe and with cunning will be able to write (162–68). Chaucer quickly demonstrates his capacity, for the entry into the garden is a transformation like a film cut from black and white to color, as in *The Wizard of Oz.*

Gardens figure both in classical poetry and in Scripture,[6] and Chaucer shows himself writing more from books than physical observation. A rather conventional list of trees is followed by an exquisite stanza describing a blossomy garden beside a river where fish flash through the clear water of springs. As in other dream visions, however, the aural seems more crucial than the visual, for the initial impression is climaxed by the song of birds, "With voys of aungel in *here armonye" (*their harmony, 191), sounds so ravishing that God never heard better. Then the narrator provides a list of inhabitants with allegorical names, noted as he moves toward the spot where Venus disports herself with Riches. The goddess is half-clothed, a reminder perhaps of contrasting lust and natural love. In the description of the garden Chaucer closely follows an unacknowledged literary influence, Boccaccio's *Teseide,* and the familiar world of sighs evolves into yet another list, this time of unhappy lovers from classical literature. Nevertheless, Chaucer does more than re-create the *Roman de la Rose.*

Not Venus, but Nature presides over the action, and she is a descendant of Boethius's Lady Philosophy, though Chaucer's immediate bibliographical acknowledgment is to "Aleyn, in the Pleynt of Kynde" (316). Alanus de Insulis (1125/30–1203) wrote *De planctu naturae,* another popular allegorical dream vision that complains of man's moral failures and includes lists of birds as part of the description of her robe, a rather more substantial garment than Venus's attire. Dame Nature's halls and bowers are made of boughs, and on this occasion of St. Valentine's Day she arbitrates among birds who are seeking mates. Nature, who is identified as "the vicaire of the almyghty Lord" (379) serves as Speaker at a lively Parliament of Fowls, where debate is varied and heated over a *demande d'amour,* and often uses legal and scholastic terminology.

The assembly is widely representative, including birds of prey, waterbirds, seedbirds and wormbirds that vaguely parallel human social hierarchy. Proprieties are observed, since the initial case is a royal one. Three tercel eagles plead for the love of a "formel" (female) eagle, respectively arguing greatest love and promise of service, longest love, and truest love. These aristocratic cases are made in courtly language, bespeaking a high idealism, which irritates lesser creatures that cry out, "Have don, and lat us wende! . . . Com of! . . . Kek kek! kokkow! quek! quek!" (492, 494, 499). The juxtaposition of styles, a contrast of vigorous colloquial diction and rhythm with stately and elegant utterance, is extraordinary. Chaucer's effective combination of social levels is never more compelling, especially since *The Parliament of Fowls* is relatively brief, just short of 700 lines, so that the switches occur with dazzling rapidity. The tercels, which are the only wooers competing for the same mate, persist with suggestions for reasoned decisions, while the lower fowls regard everything less seriously and put a case that love seldom is characterized by reason, and high idealism yields to practical self-interest. Only the turtledove argues for an everlasting love, a dedication unchanged by circumstances "til that the deth me take" (589). The duck thinks this attitude a joke, an obvious lack of reason; and the cuckoo is even more pragmatic, caring only that he get his own mate immediately. All such opinions are inconclusive, and the quandary is resolved through Nature's authority. Although Reason would award the "formel" eagle to the royal tercel, Nature leaves the choice to her, an unusual situation for a lady in the courtly world of aristocratic arranged marriages, as Chaucer shows with Emily in the *Knight's Tale*. Personal autonomy is the more notable if, as many believe, *The Parliament of Fowls* is an occasional poem, perhaps written during negotiations for the marriage of Richard II and Anne of Bohemia. The formel's choice is for a year's respite, the same conclusion that occurs in Shakespeare's *Love's Labour's Lost,* where aristocratic young men also woo without proving anything except verbal skills. Denial of sexual gratification provides further opportunity "For to do wel" (663), a return to Africanus's view that good deeds influence rewards. In contrast, all birds of lower orders immediately secure mates.

Many interpretations of Dame Nature's decisions are defensible. Chaucer gives to Nature the role of assuring that love will not always be constrained, and sometimes choice is given to the female. The delay suggests faulting of the sophistication of courtly wooing, but the colloquial urgings of lesser fowls occasion greatest laughter, so that perhaps another alternative is being urged, something between artificial words and simple physical impulses. Some possibility of harmony is demonstrated by the poem's concluding roundel, a favorite French form of lyric, sung by the birds. Its repeated refrain welcomes summer, a time of brightness after winter's darkness. The shouting wakes the narrator, whose immediate action is to read other books yet more intensely, hoping to improve. Song, Nature explained, is the traditional way of celebrating St. Valentine's Day, and Chaucer made another contribution in the "Complaint of Mars."

"Complaint of Mars" and "Complaint of Venus"

The love affair of Mars and Venus is one of the more notorious in classical literature, known in the Middle Ages especially from Chaucer's favorite poet Ovid (*Metamorphoses,* IV.171–89). The relationship was adulterous because Venus was wed to Vulcan; all were subjects of ridicule to their fellow gods after the jealous husband captured the lovers in a net while they were amorously together. This seems a somewhat unlikely, or at least unconventional, love to celebrate for St. Valentine's Day as does Chaucer in the "Complaint of Mars." Similarly, the "Complaint of Venus" is unusual in having a woman as speaker. These two lyrics thus provide a further comment upon Chaucer's interests during the 1380s, a time when he was deeply influenced by Boethius and also writing extensively about love, exquisitely celebrating its beauty and power but also chronicling human inadequacy in sustaining high idealism. Boethius offers a response to discrepancies between human expectation and real disillusionment, and his influence is discernible in both "Complaints." In addition, they illustrate Chaucer's working from a traditional form of French lyric into narrative; his characteristically creative translations are of both thought and form.

One explanation of the complaints is as a comment upon a court scandal. This has been argued since the scribe John Shirley (?1366–1456) followed his copy (Trinity College, Cambridge, MS R.3.20) with a note that "some men sayne" the "Complaint of Mars" was written with specific individuals in mind, Isabel of York and John Holland.[7] Shirley identifies Chaucer's source as the French poet Sir Oton de Graunson, knight of Savoy, who wrote the "balade for Venus" with Isabel in mind. Further, a prefatory note states that the poem was written at the command of John of Gaunt, whose daughter Elizabeth was the object in another of Holland's scandalous liaisons. These historical associations lend immediacy and provide a picture of court life, but are also contestable. Such reading is encouraged by the line "This is no feyned mater that I telle" (173), but the sentiment also appropriately characterizes Mars, speaker of the Complaint. It is known that Graunson, internationally renowned for his chivalry, stayed for long periods in London; he served John of Gaunt, Richard II, and Henry IV. On two occasions his name and Chaucer's appear together in Gaunt's accounts. More importantly, Chaucer identifies

Graunson as his source in the "Complaint of Venus," calling him "flour of hem that make in Fraunce" and noting how difficult it is to render exactly French intricacies into English that has fewer rhymes (80–82). This last point shows Chaucer at work as a careful translator, aware of his own language and identifying his literary indebtedness.

Whatever the historical allusions, Chaucer deflects such human identifications by presenting Mars and Venus as planets and meticulously describing astronomical movements. Most notably Phoebus, the sun god, replaces Vulcan as the interrupter of the lovers. This shift of emphasis to heavenly influences provides a contrast with earthly love. The spontaneity of passion is thus set against some higher force that determines outcomes. An opening exuberance, then, modulates into a somber statement. The "Complaint of Mars" begins like an echo of *The Parliament of Fowls* with an energetic call, "Gladeth, ye foules," but the opening stanza also carries a warning that daylight can expose lovers when wicked tongues and jealousy do their work. Then the poet explains that these are the words of a bird, and he himself promises a song for St. Valentine's Day (22–28). After these initial 28 lines, "A Story" describes (in 126 lines) the love of Mars and Venus: they meet, are attracted to each other, become lovers, are parted when Phoebus burns them with his heat. Mars responds by arming himself, while Venus withdraws into a dark cave, where Mars follows but not before she has met Mercury, so that Mars can but make his "Complaint." This longest (133 lines) part fills the remainder of the poem.

The Story is one of courtly love, replete with the lady's demands and the man's subjection before achieving a mutual love and joy, and it is told in familiar language for an "aventure" and "mysaventure" of lovers. Mars and Venus, pagan gods but also planets, thus are also typical courtly lovers. Their world is of knighthood, and their chamber and palace, could be in *Troilus and Criseyde*. Yet movements are recounted in an astronomical language of heavenly revolutions, planetary influences, compass, sphere, courses, and positions precise enough to describe the skies for 1385, when there was a notable conjunction of Venus and Mars in Taurus. As in "The Complaint unto Pity" Chaucer provides a very elaborate framing for the Complaint itself, which is the most interesting part of the poem.

An opening stanza recognizes rules for such compositions, principally that there must be right cause, and this is the lament's subject.

However, of five sections, each with three stanzas, only the first praises the lady to justify the lover's service. The remainder are given to questioning that evolves from a rhetorical "To whom shal I than pleyne of my distresse?" (191) to a questioning of God as the maker of the universe. Just as *Boece* challenges changes from good to bad fortune, so Mars asks why love alters: "What meneth this? What is this *mystihed?" (*mysteriousness, 224). Section 3 concludes with a popular image of catching lovers, in which God is a skillful fisher and lovers the fish. In a famous treatise of love, Andreas Capellanus derives *amor* from *hamus* (fishhook), but Chaucer here speaks of God, a Christian deity among the pagans, so that another likely allusion is to Christ's calling the disciples, as fishers of men (Matthew 4:18–22). To take this bait would not cause death or a severe wound, but not all respond. The appeal of earthly love is reiterated in section 4, which offers the Brooch of Thebes as example of beauty that attracts, a treasure whose subsequent loss occasions great woe. Here the argument becomes more Boethian; while the lover first blames God as the creator of beauty he later acknowledges his own responsibility in responding, admitting his "*unwit that ever I clamb so hye" (*foolishness, 271). The three stanzas of section 5 are addressed to hardy knights of renown, to ladies, and to all lovers; however, the point is the same—have compassion and lament all. In a transient world, where love is precarious, there is still "honour" and "gentilesse," and he urges "sum kyndenesse" be shown. Compassion is, of course, the response enjoined by Christian teaching that recognizes all as sinners who are redeemed through the Crucifixion.

A similar high sentiment appears in the "Complaint of Venus," a rather free translation of three of Graunson's *balades* here put together and made the expression of a woman's sentiments. In 1 she remembers the man she loved, extolling his worthiness, especially his humility. *Balade* 2 presents the uneasiness that comes with Jealousy, and 3 argues for Constancy, averring that to love the worthiest is itself sufficient. This conclusion is another iteration of a response that does not demand good fortune but accepts what love brings. A lyric statement like the "Complaint of Venus" does not have to stand the trial of narrative exposition. Chaucer in his longest works of this period, *Troilus and Criseyde* and *The Legend of Good Women,* meets that challenge. He began first with a collection of short narratives about noble and constant women who might have uttered the sentiments of "Complaint of Venus."

The Legend of Good Women

Medieval collections of stories that reiterate the same theme are not among the narratives most favored by modern readers of Chaucer.[8] Because *The Legend of Good Women* comes late, after *Troilus and Criseyde* and at least partially concurrent with *The Canterbury Tales*, there is no excuse of an early effort, and many critics have evoked a mature poet's boredom to dismiss the stories. Just as the many tragedies of the *Monk's Tale* are neglected, though the definition of tragedy in the *Prologue* is often cited, so generally the *Prologue to the Legend of Good Women* is read but the stories of women's fates slighted, even though they are interesting for the choice of subjects, attitudes toward the good women, and passages of poetic beauty. The *Prologue* is more fascinating because it includes Chaucer's continuing comments about his work, what he has read and what he has written and some responses of his readers. In decasyllabic couplets, the verse form here perfected, Chaucer returns to the dream vision of his earliest poems. He re-creates the beauty of a May morning, the song of birds for a St. Valentine's Day celebration, familiar allegorical figures, and languor before falling asleep and entering the dream. An innovation is his gazing at and charmingly worshiping the daisy. Here the beseeching wife is Alceste; since the Dreamer is identified as Chaucer, the subject is his role as poet, not lover. There are two versions of the *Prologue*, with substantial differences, indicating that one is definitely a revision of the other; thus evidence of Chaucer's concern and ongoing work on the *Legend* is clear.

The work was perhaps a response to a royal command from Queen Anne and King Richard II; at least it shows Chaucer's interest in the courtly. The G version, usually taken as the revision, deletes reference (F.496) to the royal manors of Eltham and Sheene and to the Queen. She died in 1394, and in his extreme grief Richard ordered Shene House torn down. In the *Confessio Amantis*, a fellow poet John Gower refers to Chaucer's "testament of love" as yet unfinished, and Venus commands that it be completed. Chaucer includes *The Legend of Good Women* in two major lists of his writing: as "the book of the XXV. Ladies" in the *Retraction* of *The Canterbury Tales* (X.1085) and as "The Seintes Legende of Cupide" in the *Man of Law's Prologue* (II.61), where he describes it as a "large volume" and lists the subjects. The usual title comes from the *Prologue of the Legend*, when Alceste, who intervened with the God of Love on behalf of the poet, defines his "penance." Chaucer must spend his time in making "a glorious legende / Of goode wemmen, maydenes and wyves" (F.483–84, G.473–74) to offset what he said against women in the translation of the *Roman de la Rose* and in *Troilus and Criseyde* (F.440–41, G.430–31).

This collection of stories, second only to *The Canterbury Tales*, is thus introduced by a frame story. The terms *penance* and *legend* indicate seriousness, whether for sacred or earthly love, and most of the Latin *Incipits* and *Explicits* (Here begins and Here ends) include the word *martiris* (martyr), which suggests that the legends are like lives of saints, and Lucrece is identified as a "seynt" with a holy day in Rome (F.1871). Nevertheless, the women are all taken from classical literature, and usually quite different from Christian martyrs. Again Ovid is a major source, especially *Heroides*, a collection of imaginative love letters that describe a range of human passions and create a voice for women's experience, as well as offer romantic Greek tales in a new way.[9] *The Legend of Good Women* provides a series of brief episodes that recount deaths with some exploration of causes. Related to collections about falls of women from Fortune, like Boccaccio's *De claris mulieribus, The Legend* is also a significant part of Chaucer's retelling of classical literature. For example, his is the first English account of Cleopatra. As in his other explorations of pagan antiquity, Chaucer ranges through episodes that both provide examples of nobility and problems of response, since the ends of many are violent and suicidal. Suffering, as Boethius recounts in *The Consolation of Philosophy*, is hard to accept, especially when the injuries seem undeserved. Indeed *The Legend* provides a parallel equivalent of woman's experience, replacing loss of position with loss of a man's love.

The subject matter poses some difficulties for a male audience; it focuses upon women, whose lives are quite different from those of men, being more exclusively defined in personal relationships. More specifically their suffering, typically a consequence of loving and self-sacrifice, is usually caused by male betrayal. Thus *The Legend* has invited the interest of feminist critics. It has been described as a parody and as an example of the influence of patriarchy in creating the text, both as a way of controlling and evading difficult issues.[10] Whether or not they were written at royal bequest, are a genuine atonement for negative presentations of women, or are a further expression of male dominance, these stories offer some alternatives simply because they are nominally about women and their experience of suffering. The opening of the *Prologue* suggests a modest and tentative approach and a larger context than gender.

Chaucer begins with a brief statement about limitation. Men attempt to define hell and heaven, but no one has seen either or can prove their assumptions. Nevertheless, "sooth" (truth) is acknowledged beyond human perception, and this is twice attributed to God. The first authority cited is "Bernard the monk" (16), probably St. Bernard of Clairvaux (?1090–1153), an extraordinarily influential churchman, whose mysticism was an alternative to the relentless intellectualism of scholastic thought. His devotion to the Virgin Mary fostered a strong spirituality and exaltation of the feminine. Mary's principal role, as the mother of Christ, is first to accept the will of God and then to intercede with God to save the innocent and to ease the sufferings of others. In the dream portion Alceste's asking mercy after appropriate penance is a Christian response to human failing. This model for living the Gospel is an alternative, albeit little evident in the world of male ambition and pride with expectations that Boethius rejects and chides against. Chaucer's delight in "olde bokes," so strong that no game can take him away, and his declaration that books are the key of remembrance are thus set in a context of limitation and humility.[11]

There are nine legends (one centers on two women) that provide both examples of crisp and concise story telling and a Boethian argument about adversity. By beginning with history, Chaucer establishes immediacy. Cleopatra's legend is "storyal soth, it is no fable" (F.702). She is a queen in her own right, and although there is much about Antony, Chaucer's account—like Shakespeare's—notes that both sacrifice political power for love. However, their situations are not the same. Antony abandons Rome for Cleopatra, but he kills himself after being defeated at Actium, a sea battle that Chaucer vividly evokes, relying upon a heavy use of alliteration that sets this most memorable passage apart. Antony' s lament is for loss of honor, not of love, and he does not mention Cleopatra. In contrast, she prefaces her suicide with a statement that she can keep their "covenant" (F. 688, 693). In her long declaration of being faithful to her knight, she uses the language of wifehood, but her last words are a claim that in love there never was "a trewer quene" (F.695). Their modes of dying are very different, not simply because Antony stabs himself and Cleopatra leaps into a pit of adders, the second distinctive scene in this legend. He "sterte" (F.660, cf. 697) out of his wits for despair, while she receives her death "with good cheere / For love of Antony" (F.701). The contrast establishes a distinction between male and female responses; one is self-centered and angry, while the other is focused on others and resigned, an acceptance of Fortune. This persists when Chaucer stops the story ("Herkneth") to introduce Cleopatra's death with an address to men who swear that they will die if their loves be angry (F.665–666). Thus a commonplace courtly exaggeration, a poetic or rhetorical statement, is set against a specific act from history to show woman's "trouth." The episode from Roman history contains correspondences to fourteenth-century England. Antony, senator of Rome and worthy warrior, is described as a knight of chivalry, while Cleopatra is "fayr as is the rose in May" (F.613), but physical description of her is minimal, so that interest focuses on her behavior rather than appearance. With characteristic detachment Chaucer notes that Cleopatra "coude of Cesar have no grace" (F.663). Like Antony, she is compelled toward an action by political power, but she controls response to the condition; she chooses a celebration of devotion not a regret for what has been lost.

While Cleopatra is a queen, broader applicability of her situation is indicated in the second legend, when Thisbe also emulates male behavior. Pyramus turns courtly avowal into reality; he kills himself, when he thinks his lady has been slain by the lioness. Thisbe repeats his act, even using his sword to stab herself. Her declarations indicate that she will be Pyramus's fellow in death, and her final thought is that she must demonstrate that a woman can be as true as a man in loving. The poem concludes with a statement that he is one of the few examples of a man who is true and kind. However, this must be read in the context of several earlier passages that stress the peril of life in a world of daring. The lovers are separated by a wall, sign of the way in which maids are strictly kept and protected. Death occurs because Pyramus and Thisbe, who have cursed such separation, defy society's constraints in a hope of controlling their fates. She forsakes friends, putting all trust in a man, to elope. The danger of such action is most eloquently argued by Pyramus, when he blames himself first for putting her at risk and then for arriving late (F.833–841). Indeed fear made Thisbe flee the appointed spot when the lioness came to drink at the well (F.860–861). Even as she prepares to stab herself and chides fathers who would keep lovers apart, Thisbe thus warns gentle women that they should not be overconfident and put themselves "in swich an *aventure" (*chance, fortune, F.909).

After these two legends that show mutuality in passion, *The Legend* proceeds to women who are victims of a man's ambition or sexual violence. An initial passion provides some motivation, but the lovers of Dido, Hypsipyle and Medea, and Ariadne are men renowned for great deeds, which are achieved through the exploitation and subsequent abandonment of the women who love them. For Aeneas, Jason, and Theseus seeking fame takes precedence over love and truth. This is reiterated in the penultimate legend; Phyllis's lover Demophon imitates the behavior of his father Theseus. Even these cases are a far cry from the most notorious examples, Lucrece and Philomela; wife and maiden, both are innocent and both are raped.

Dido is the character whose literary tradition is richest, as Chaucer's opening reference to "authors" makes clear (F.924, 928), and this is the longest legend (434 lines). Both Virgil and Ovid are cited, but Chaucer favors Ovid's exaltation of Dido and does not spare the Trojan hero, denying him the divine mission of founding Rome, which Virgil uses to exonerate his betrayal of Dido. Here Aeneas is not a hero, but a "traytor" (F.1328), an opportunistic lover who simply enjoys himself and then moves on. Suddenly changing Fortune (F.1044) aptly describes Aeneas's circumstances, and he is without moral awareness. After the destruction of Troy he is in despair, but passes easily from this hell to a paradise of love (F.1098–1105), only to grow quickly weary of Dido's devotion. Aeneas's appearance as knight (F.1066–74) is false, and Dido's plight is pitiful when he refuses to marry her, even though she has given him great riches and is carrying his child. Very telling is her question "Is that in ernest?" (F.1303); she does not know when he is serious or playing. Several complaints involve the audience in Dido's emotional distress, but she is not an innocent victim. She has acted from passion, inspired by pity over the man's lost good fortune, the novelty of someone who comes from another land, and enraptured by the stories that he tells of his adventures, as is Shakespeare's Desdemona. In short, Dido initially torments herself like any smitten lover (F.1165–67) and finishes pathetically, groveling at his feet (F.1311–15) and no longer recognizable as a queen. The scene is one of humiliation, and Chaucer does not show Aeneas reacting. Not surprisingly, this legend has the strongest warning to women against trusting men who are fickle in their loves (F.1254–64). The placement of this warning before Dido's hysterical pleading, emphasizes woman's vulnerability. The emotional level in Dido's legend is very high, and the poet concludes by referring readers to Ovid for the letters of Dido to her sister Anna and to Aeneas.

The legend of Hypsipyle and Medea is another tale of betrayal, and the combination of two women in one legend suggests lack of individuation. Indeed interest is more on Jason, winner of the Golden Fleece, than on either of the women that he first uses to secure his fame and then casts aside. The opening lines are a complaint against Jason, and the familiar story—Chaucer draws upon Guido delle Colonne's *Historia destructionis Troiae* as well as Ovid—is attenuated. Medea's killing of her children would have been impossible to turn to account for a record of good women. What remains is a somewhat uneven account of male deception, though Jason is exposed as a smooth talker, a calculating deceiver. Chaucer includes a number of explicit statements that he is steadily cutting his sources (F.1552, 1557–59, 1563, 1634, 1678–79), and sometimes provides only a plodding recitation of events (F.1559–79). Nevertheless, Medea's final plaint provides a turn, for she questions how her sexual impulses led her to forget "honestye."

Ariadne, in contrast, was calculating, wanting the position that comes with alliance to a man like Theseus. The lure of royal connections and of the title "Duchess of Athens" (F.2122–35) is more powerful than the man himself. At age twenty-three, Theseus is a youthful knight whose declarations of love echo the conventions of medieval courtly love, but are really improvisations to further his quest against the Minotaur. In this legend Chaucer creates a doting romantic heroine, most grotesquely in the conclusion when she kisses the steps on which the departed Theseus walked and speaks a complaint to the bed in which they slept, but also when she accepts as "stedefastnesse" Theseus's fervent declaration that he has loved her for seven years without ever seeing her (F.2114–23). Even among the extravagant exaggerations of troubadour lyrics this is an extreme claim, and this legend exposes excesses in many late medieval romances. The insidiousness of such attitudes is reiterated in the legend of Phyllis, where the next generation makes the same choices, and the poet confesses his own disenchantment with the subject: "But, for I am *agroted herebyforn / To wryte of hem that ben in love forsworn" (*fed up, F.2454–55). Phyllis's repeating of Ariadne's experience is explicitly noted (F.2544–49); she provides proof and authority that wicked fruit comes from a wicked tree.

The legends of Lucrece and Philomena go yet further in showing the evil of men; not abandonment, but rape is the fate of these women, both of whom are innocent and noble. Lucrece's "storye" is told by Ovid, Livy, and St. Augustine (pagan poet, Roman historian, Christian philosopher), and Chaucer's powerful narrative synthesizes much that occurs in *The Legend of Good Women.* Vanity, male competitiveness about women's virtue and men's possessive control, is the occasion. This is set against female fear and vulnerability. The concentration of attention is upon the rape. Chaucer builds anxiety and suspense as he describes Tarquin's increasing lust and self-torment that culminate in his decision to return to the house of Collatinus. A king's son and a knight who knows chivalry, he sneaks in at night like a thief, and his villainous attack is quick and unambiguous. Through a series of rhetorical questions Chaucer makes clear that women cannot defend themselves in these circumstances because they lack physical strength. At first, with a sword at her heart, "No word she spak" (F.1796), but then "She axeth grace, and seyth al that she can" (F.1804). However, Lucrece is a lamb alone with the wolf, and Tarquin claims the power of words as well, threatening to slander her as an adulteress with her boy. The reputation of a Roman wife is crucial, and Lucrece first swoons. Then she summons husband, friends, and family and puts aside her sense of shame to tell of the rape. All judge her innocent, but she kills herself. Subsequently, the story, "The horryble dede of hir oppressyoun" (F.1868), is widely known. Chaucer here follows his source, the historian Livy. However, he concludes Lucrece's legend with Christ's recognition of female strength: the greatest faith in Israel was that of a woman (F.1879–82, Matthew 15: 28).

The greatest test of faith is, of course, confrontation with evil. Chaucer most directly poses the question in the legend of Philomena, which begins with an address to the "yevere of formes" (F.2229). God, having it eternally in mind, made the fair world but suffers grizzly deeds and men like Tereus who rapes and mutilates his wife's virgin sister. The scene is again one of horror, with mounting terror and isolation. Philomena is described as both lamb (Christ) and dove (Holy Spirit). She suffers, but she survives and, deprived of speech, weaves letters in a tapestry (truth is known through the Word). The final scene is of the two sisters together in their grief, united in love, which is all that sustains them against the evil of the world, the cruelty of men that is not intelligible but can be endured.

The sense of triumph through suffering, the paradox of the Crucifixion, governs the two remaining legends. Phyllis does not die, nor does Hypermnestra. Indeed the final legend tells of a woman's refusal to obey the dictates of male violence but also a willingness to sustain a man's life. Of all Aegyptus's daughters only Hypermnestra disobeys her father's order that she slay her husband Lynceus.

Mercy and fear culminate in love; she embraces and warns him to flee, and he goes quickly. The narrator questions why he did not take her, but she simply accepts: she sits down (F. 2721). This is the wisdom of resignation counseled by Lady Philosophy in *Boece*, and Chaucer goes no farther. *The Legend of Good Women* breaks off with the line "This tale is seyd for this conclusioun—." In *The Canterbury Tales* there are more stories, all part of the Christian pilgrimage. *Troilus and Criseyde*, firmly rooted in pagan antiquity, was his only example of closure in a long work.

10

A Romance of Love and War "ful blisfully" Completed—*Troilus and Criseyde*

Modern readers of Chaucer are more devoted to *The Canterbury Tales* than to *Troilus and Criseyde,* or at least the audience is larger and more varied. This is perhaps inevitable because *The Tales* are unmatched in complexity, and no other work provides such rich resources for exploring fourteenth-century England and indeed the Middle Ages more generally. In addition, *Troilus and Criseyde* is less easily read in the human terms typical in mimetic criticism of the early twentieth century. Nevertheless, Kittredge's description of the poem as "the first novel, in the modern sense, that ever was written in the world" long held sway.[1] The attitude persists in many midcentury readings of Chaucer's most substantial completed work, for emphasis is often upon the appeal of Criseyde and the role of Pandarus—though Chaucer's Retraction to *The Canterbury Tales* calls the poem, which is the first named work, "the book of Troilus" (X.1085). Often readers are skeptical about Troilus as a lover: his being tossed into bed with Criseyde by Pandarus provokes incredulity among late-twentieth-century readers who are accustomed to a different kind of sexuality. Many argue about the conclusion, which seems to reverse all that the poem has established by leaving the delights and excellence of human earthly love for dedication to divine eternal Love.[2] Although there are strong arguments for an Augustinian interpretation, the significance of Boethius to Chaucer's poem, both for concepts of tragedy and detachment from the world, remains crucial.[3] Chaucerians have devoted themselves to reevaluating the role of courtly love, to medieval views of pagan antiquity, and more recently to attitudes toward gender, identifying narrative voices and language, and defining Chaucer's audience. In short, *Troilus and Criseyde* offers "God's plenty," albeit not to the widest and most diverse readership, since its polish, elegance, and aristocratic subject matter somewhat set it apart.

An intended sophistication is evident in Chaucer's choice of verse form for *Troilus and Criseyde.* Rime royal, a seven-line iambic pentameter stanza rhyming *a b a b b c c,* was associated with ceremonial literature; the name is derived from its use by the Scottish king, James I. Chaucer, whose technical virtuosity reestablished English as a language for literature, had already perfected rime royal in *The Parliament of Fowls,* with its many voices, sprightly narration, and fine descriptions.[4] The use of a stanza form, rather than couplets, gives greater shape to the poem, providing formal sections in a narrative that is built up through distinct episodes. *Troilus and Criseyde* contains fifty scenes: thirty-two dialogues, nine soliloquies or monologues, two trios, and seven larger groups. Much of the poem, then, is discourse. This allows lively presentation to an audience, a social context beautifully illustrated in the frontispiece to MS 61 Corpus Christi College, Cambridge, where a poet stands at a pulpit before a royal audience with a scene of travelers and castle in the background. Chaucer's concern with excellence, evident in the polished subtlety of the verse, is clearer in *Troilus and Criseyde* than in any other work, and in the centuries after his death it was his most esteemed poem.

This most refined effort is gracefully designed with a carefully balanced structure and, moreover, finished; it has an ending. Divided into five books, *Troilus and Criseyde* is elegantly patterned. The main events of the story are the awakening of sexual love, its realization, and its diminishing. Book III, recording the achievement and celebration of the love of Troilus and Criseyde, is central and self-contained, a time set apart from other events and concerns. It contains Chaucer's most sustained praise of sexual love, an evocation of ecstasy not found in his other works and seldom rivaled. On either side of this center are two books quite different in tone and experience. In Book I (1092 lines) Troilus, a prince of Troy, first sees Criseyde, a beautiful and diffident widow, and falls immediately and desperately in love, so that he accepts the assistance of his eager friend Pandarus, who is also Criseyde's uncle, in presenting his lovesuit. Book II (1757 lines) recounts the evolution of the love: Pandarus serves as go-between, and Criseyde deliberates but responds favorably. Troilus is ennobled by his love, fighting more valorously against the Greeks. After an unspecified time, an initial meeting is arranged at Deiphebus's home, where many are gathered to offer help to a fearful Criseyde, left alone in Troy after her father Calkas's defection to the Greeks. Book III (1820 lines) begins when Criseyde finally meets Troilus, who is bedridden because ill from lovelonging; her kindness restores his health, and his valiant deeds and nobility increase. After very complicated arrangements Criseyde, on a rainy night, joins Troilus at Pandarus's home, and the love is consummated. Almost immediately news comes that Criseyde must go to the Greeks, in exchange for Trojan Antenor, recently taken prisoner. Book IV (1701 lines) details Trojan deliberations in parliament, the grief and quandary of Troilus and Criseyde about secrecy and separation, and a decision that she will leave Troy as ordered. In Book V (1869 lines) Criseyde is exchanged and immediately attracts the attention of Diomede. With the lovers separated there is a counterpoint of scenes, a shifting from Troy to the Greek camp. Criseyde has promised to return to Troilus in ten days' time, and there is much grief and anxiety about her coming. Gradually a still-fearful Criseyde becomes committed to Diomede, who offers protection, while Troilus recognizes that she is not coming back to him. He gives all his energy to fighting the Greeks, until he is killed by Achilles. From the eighth sphere, outside human time, Troilus looks down on this little earth and laughs.

This short summary of events is a far cry from the complexity of Chaucer's poem. Compared to other Middle English narratives of its length, *Troilus and Criseyde* presents few events and concentrates upon a small number of characters. Chaucer memorably evokes a world that shows the best of pagan antiquity in circumstances of medieval chivalry. Trojan society is rendered extraordinarily attractive and vivid; the city is a highly civilized community where the delights of life on earth are experienced, but also inevitably sorrows. Boethius's *Consolation* warns of changing Fortune and reiterates that any expectations are ill-advised. In *Troilus and Criseyde* Chaucer first conveys the experience of good Fortune, especially ennobling human love and a close community, and then the suffering when all seems lost, before he concludes with a point of view that is outside of time. Remarkably, both perceptions are sustained, each having its place in human comprehension and anticipation of eternity; the initial celebration is not dimmed by the final knowing that what seemed all-encompassing was but a limited moment.

The title of this chapter indicates a choice to read *Troilus and Criseyde* as a "romance."[5] This seems in some ways arbitrary; the opening line echoes the style of epic, "The double sorwe of Troilus to tellen" (I.1), but the sorrows are in "lovynge" and then losing his lady, not martial and public actions. Further, Chaucer suggests an interest in *de casibus* or fall literature, earlier explored in the *Monk's Tale,* for he identifies the narrative action as "how his aventures fellen / Fro wo to wele, and after out of joie" (I.3–4), and change of fortune is emphasized when Troilus is left alone (III.1625–28). Nevertheless, the conclusion is "Go, litel bok, go, litel myn tragedye" (V.1786). Here Chaucer follows Ovid and Boccaccio in addressing his "book" and thus evading genre; however, he then indicates "tragedy," which is immediately balanced by a prayer for "som comedye" (V.1788). In contrast, "romance" is both named and evoked. Criseyde and her attendant ladies at the palace read "the geste / Of the siege of Thebes" (II.84–84), later identified as a "romaunce" (100). On the night that the lovers meet at his house, Pandarus withdraws to the fire and appears "to looke upon an old romaunce" (III.980). These two scenes indicate ways of reading romance: aloud to a group (of ladies) and alone. Remembrance of romance is shown when Criseyde recalls Tristan and Iseult by asking herself, "Who yaf me drynke?" (II.651). A tension between love and war, as was noted in the *Knight's Tale,* is traceable throughout the development of romance. Chaucer seems to reserve the designation "romance" for those of "prys" (excellence, *Canterbury Tales,* VII. 897), and he names several in *Sir Thopas.* [6] These very popular romances contain many chivalric adventures and much physical action, but also usually have a strong moral purpose, generally the knight's self-discovery. As is typical in medieval romance the young knight Troilus is the center of the story; his interests drive the action, and it is he who gains understanding through the events that transpire. His physical combats are limited and little attention is given to fighting techniques. Successes of Troilus, who is identified as a second Hector (II.158; V.1804), are stated, not described as exciting encounters. Attention centers in Troilus's discovering truth about himself and consequently changing his values. Other characters do not. Thus "the book of Troilus" is an accurate title, for it places the poem with other romances that bear only the male hero's name and tell the story of knightly development. Most cogent is *Guy of Warwick,* well known to Chaucer; there are two distinct parts: Guy's first pursuing a lady and then serving God.

The term *geste* indicates adventurous story, but love provokes questioning and analysis as warfare does not for a medieval audience. However, such story telling is only the first level made explicit by Chaucer. His "book" is sent to kiss the steps where walk Virgil,

Ovid, Homer, Lucan, Statius (V.1791–92); this suggests a seeking of fame, a place among the great writers of pagan antiquity, but Chaucer wants to be subject to all poetry, not to be competitive. He also dedicated his work to "moral Gower" and "philosophical Strode," whose epithets indicate another level. Like many Middle English romances *Troilus and Criseyde,* even though it is set in the pagan context of the Trojan War, concludes with a prayer to Christ and an affirmation of faith (V.1856–69). In a world of ignorance and unpredictability and seemingly arbitrary changes of fortune, pessimism is an obvious reaction. This conclusion is inherent in the Trojan myth of loss and destruction, but Christian philosophy, as in Boethius and Dante, makes possible an alternative response. By setting worldly achievement against God's eternity, "tragedye" is subsumed. As with God, in the medieval romance everything is possible; neither human causality nor merely random circumstances suffices.

Seeking to win a lady's favor through prowess in fighting usually comes early in a knight's career, as with Chaucer's Squire. Typically he leaves a single court or baron's castle to fight in tournaments and wars in order to gain fame, often traveling great distances. Troilus, in contrast, is tied to Troy, a city under siege. Fighting the Greeks to establish prowess is part of his wooing, but Chaucer's emphasis is upon personal relationships not martial action. Troy is a city of many rich households and resembles London, which in the fourteenth century was sometimes called "New Troy." Chaucer's Trojan princes live in a social ambience that evokes the world of English barons like John of Gaunt. Hospitable gatherings take place in five distinct households, the homes of Troilus, Criseyde, Pandarus, Deiphebus, and Sarpedon. In Troy people enjoy their gardens, read books, sing and dance, laugh, gossip, and tease; they are solicitous of each other and loyal, enjoy friendship, participate in parliamentary debate, have philosophical thoughts, grieve over the death of great Hector. Trojans are highly civilized; theirs is a very attractive society that values honor. Greeks do not enjoy such amenities and ideals; their interests are self-serving; they are wary, more pragmatic and calculating.

There are significant differences in the Trojan story read by medieval and modern audiences, since only a primitive Latin redaction of Homer was known and classical dramatists were unknown. This lack was offset by two purportedly eyewitness accounts, Dares Phrygius's *De Excidio Troiae Historia* and Dictys Cretensis's *Ephemeris de Historia Belli Troiani*, conveniently pro-Trojan and pro-Greek, brief, reassuringly historical, with emphasis upon battles and character portraits and free of the machinery of the gods. Both were probably written during the first century A.D., but they were accepted as authentic. Chaucer cites them in opening and closing books (I.146 and V.1771). The Trojan War entered the world of medieval romance through the monumental efforts of Benoît de Sainte-Maure, who about 1160 wrote *Roman de Troie*. His 30,300 lines remedy the deficiencies of the early histories of Dares and Dictys, for love and marvels abound, enriching their bare realistic details. Nevertheless, the Trojan War was largely perceived as history rather than romance because in 1287 Benoît's French verse was translated into Latin prose by Guido delle Colone, whose *Historia Destructionis Troiae* restored the emphasis upon history by reducing the interest in love stories and marvels; it was thus accepted as genuine, rather like a contemporary chronicle.[7] A freer use of Troy has strong artistic appeal, and interest in Troy was partially inspired by Chaucer.[8]

Although Chaucer knew Benoît and Guido, as well as other versions, his own immediate source was Giovanni Boccaccio's *Il Filostrato,* written in the1330s and indebted to Benoît and Guido but very much a personal statement of frustrated passion. Chaucer's *Troilus and Criseyde,* like the *Knight's Tale,* most clearly shows an inspiration from Italian literature, though again mediated through much other reading, so that his poem is not just a rendering of Boccaccio's "The One Prostrated by Love."[9] Chaucer's Troilus, of the three principal characters, seems closest to Boccaccio's hero, but *Troilus and Criseyde* is almost twice as long as *Il Filostrato*. Philosophical reflection, particularly about destiny and necessity, is an obvious addition from Boethius, and Petrarchan lyric heightens sentiments of love. Greater use is made of Troy: the story is present in history, both society and the war loom larger than in Boccaccio, and the role of community is set against private considerations.

The English Troilus is not a simple lover, nor is his story one of facile intrigue. To many modern readers he seems boring and ineffectual, a courtly lover who lacks incisiveness. His character is the closest to an ideal, showing the nobility of pagan antiquity and the ennoblement of a medieval lover, debts but also limitations distinguished and qualified by Christian Chaucer. Chaucer's Criseyde and Pandarus are reassuringly flawed, "human" and more readily judged, and they are among his most memorable creations.

Pandarus, who is utterly consistent in behavior—always eager, busy, leaping into rooms (II.939, 1107) and sweating (II.943), joking, not successful in love but loving vicariously and even pruriently, repeating proverbs—is memorable because of his distinctive voice. He speaks with vigor in a noncourtly idiom, and the colloquial rhythm is one of Chaucer's finest achievements. Yet his role is that of messenger, a go-between that is a stock character in romance and *fabliau,* and conventionally not pleasant. He seems to initiate action because of his aggressive manner, but is constantly responding, always adapting to immediate needs and ultimately not compelling because he is neither effectual nor altered by anything that happens. His involvement in the love affair becomes absurd when he tosses Troilus into bed and pulls off his shirt (III.1096–99); and when he teases Criseyde the next morning (III.1555–75), humor degenerates into meanness and sexual aggression. He is a useful reminder that not everyone in Troy is noble; his insistent voice is markedly different from the refined speech of his noble friend. Troilus, the second Hector, seems to need a better friend. Yet Troy would be a duller place without Pandarus; he fills time in the linear succession of events. More importantly, he shows a lower form of eroticism that intensifies the beauty of the love of Troilus and Criseyde, which all his interference and crudeness cannot dim. He calls attention to himself and raises questions about the aristocratic values of courtly love and society.[10]

Criseyde is a bewitching heroine, one who early provoked male readers; Robert Henryson (fl. 1480) branded her a leper in *Testament of Cresseid,* and Shakespeare made her a type of the wanton in *Troilus and Cressida* (1601–2). This view of Criseyde was challenged by later readers of the poem, who emphasized Chaucer's ennobling of Boccaccio's heroine and creation of ambiguity, and sometimes sustained her condemnation, even while pitying her.[11] Early harsh judgement has been replaced by consistent recognition of the elusiveness of the character who is, nonetheless, an object of enchantment and love.[12] More recently, sympathetic readers who emphasize social conditions and feminist awareness urge the constrictions of Criseyde's position.[13] Many readers discern Chaucer's unwillingness to admit a fault, to acknowledge love betrayed. Extenuation begins with a building up of Criseyde's fear, establishment of her political vulnerability, her dependence upon the wishes of men (father, uncle, lovers). Not surprisingly, she is cautious and skeptical rather than trusting like Troilus or opportunistic like Pandarus. Further, the night of consummation is facilitated by rain and planetary influences, which mitigates personal choice. The Narrator's habit of muting simple judgments, through comments that usually undercut what might appear obvious, is especially clear in his treatment of Criseyde, as a few instances will show. Book IV begins with a qualification of her forsaking "Or at the leeste, how that she was *unkynde—" (*unnatural/ cruel, 16), and the Narrator eschews judgment again in Book V: "Men seyn—I not—that she *yaf him hire herte" (*gave, 1050), where he also evades whether Troilus understood (1639–45). Repeatedly the Narrator does not presume to represent their emotions, joy (III.1191–97 and 1310–16) or grief (III.442–48; IV.799–805; V.799–806). This suspends judgment.

The formal portrait of Criseyde is an especially notable example of discretion and moderation, describing beauty but not perfection, and wittily denying knowledge of the lady's age. Much has been made of the phrase "slydynge of corage" (V.825). It is worth recognizing that in *Boece* Chaucer uses *slydyng* to describe both Fortune (1.m5) and hope (4.m2), where the meaning "changing" is truer than "wavering." A word like *corage* suggests determination, but also means "mood," which alters in humans and characters in *Troilus and Criseyde* . The attention given to Criseyde—her awareness of self (strengths and weaknesses), analytical skills, role-playing, making choices—distinguishes her from most heroines of romance, who tend to be somewhat flat characters. Through her actions and the Narrator's comments, the audience is involved; Criseyde seems a woman, not a goddess; her feelings are communicated, felt, not simply stated.

Chaucer alerts the audience to the problems he is confronting through prologues to Books II, III, and IV. Respectively, he considers language (what is he to say?), love's universal nature, and Fortune. Book II's prologue of seven stanzas is an appeal to Clio, muse of history, for assistance with the rhyme of the book. Specifically, the concern is with language; there is recognition of change, with once valued words now become "*nyce and †straunge" (*affected, †unknown II, 24). Further acknowledged is diversity in customs of love, those in one land not behaving like those of another. The image is of a journey to Rome—suggesting both classical literature and pilgrimage—with different paths taken. This declaration of detachment is reinforced by a reiteration "Myn auctour shal I folwen, if I knonne" (II.49). As in the *apologia* of *The Canterbury Tales,* there is formal distancing of the Narrator, and a recognition of limitation. His role is to comment, usually briefly and less emotionally, but he becomes as significant as any of those making the action. Typically the Narrator distances the reader from what has been said, or at least provokes an alternate response or suspension of easy judgment. Unlike Dreamers in earlier poems this Narrator is concerned about what is occurring rather than merely witnessing and recording. Like a historian he presents events with a commentary, leading responses to what has happened, and his approach is a Boethian one of acceptance, a remarkable detachment from the events recounted.

A reiteration of the universality of love provides the substance of the prologue to Book III. Again seven stanzas long, this address is to Venus, goddess of love, but it also invokes Calliope, muse of epic poetry and one esteemed for a fine voice. These two prologues are linked, as is the action at Deiphebus's house which spans Books II and III. The final prologue to Book IV is briefer. In only four stanzas, Fortune and her wheel are vividly evoked: Fortune's beguiling is observed, and the replacing of Troilus by Diomede is calmly noted, a suggestion of Boethian response to changes. Those who make complaints are asked to help in this account of Criseyde's forsaking of Troilus, and thus there is a return to the poet's need for proper language to express his story fully. Books I and V lack prologues, and this calls attention to differences in emphasis upon private and public experience.

Book I begins with a brief background of the Trojan War, which has gone on for ten years and involves vast numbers, ten-thousand Greek ships having been sent to rescue Helen, wife of Menelaus, stolen by Paris, who is a brother of Hector and Troilus. Recently the Trojan seer Calkas has defected to the Greek camp, leaving his widowed daughter Criseyde in the besieged city. The Narrator explains that his story is not of Troy's destruction, well-known in the *gestes*, but of one episode that begins immediately and with a formula from romance: "And so bifel, whan comen was the tyme / Of Aperil" (155–56). Nevertheless, this initial framing is reiterated through recurrent brief reminders of Troy. In the opening scene Troilus, who has believed himself immune to love's snares, first beholds a modest Criseyde. However, their meeting occurs at an important community function, in a temple that holds the Palladium, an image of Pallas Athena, goddess of wisdom and war, and patron of Troy. An immediate consequence of Troilus's love is a loss of confidence, intense isolation, and oppression. A philosophic note is sounded, "O blynde world, O blynde entencioun!" (211), and the confident young man is quickly made subject to love, or as he describes his state in the language of commerce, "Youre hire is quyt ayeyn, ye, God woot how!" (334). Alone in his chamber,

Troilus experiences passionate longing, which is deliberated in his song "If no love is, God, what fele I so?" (400–420), and hopes that the lady will pity him. A proper courtly lover, Troilus is moved to ever more valiant deeds against the Greeks; however, he is no longer influenced by loyalty to Troy and family but by his own self-interest in attracting the lady (470–83). His valor increases when Pandarus agrees to help his suit. Inspired by love of Criseyde, Troilus serves Troy well: he is superlatively friendly, noble, generous, admirable, and an inspired warrior (1071–85). Devotion to personal love and community can, then, be mutually reinforcing.

Indeed the two fuse in Book II, in a street scene, an opening out of the narrative from the privacy of households where all the dialogues, schemes, and songs about love have occurred. Pandarus, in response to Criseyde's need of reassurance, has told her of Troilus's love, deploying an artistic flashback (505–88), an evocative recreation of the young man's love longing. A first sight of Troilus reinforces her initial deliberations: Troilus rides by, "a knyghtly sighte trewely" (628), as all shout his praises. The moment, rather like one in the *Chanson de Roland,* evokes the essence of the chivalric ideal: a man of prowess bravely riding forth, richly armed but with his head bare; he seems invincible, but the bleeding wound of his horse is a reminder of uncertain fate, an image of dependence for even the boldest fighter. Similarly, Criseyde does not remain totally apart. Although an attraction is already acknowledged (651), Criseyde proceeds to a long debate with herself, considering issues of honor, estate, her independence as a widow, her fear, the falsity of men and reputation. But the scene shifts again, as Criseyde moves through the palace, going to the garden, where her three nieces play. One, Antigone, sings a song of love in which all the qualities of a lover are reiterated. The song, Criseyde is told, was made by queen Helen, who appears later as a guest at the home of Deiphebus, where Criseyde first meets Troilus. Indeed Helen affectionately encourages the suffering Troilus and specifically urges him "To ben good lord and frend, right hertely / Unto Criseyde" (II.1677–78). Such details initiate a comparison of love affairs. The fortunes of Troy and Troilus are, of course, analogous and parallel. But Chaucer's reminders of the origin of the Trojan War, Paris's abduction of Helen, are strategically placed; they come when choice is still open to the new lovers, who can exercise free will in responding to passion. But the history of Troy is one of extremes, where individual sexual unions—as in the Arthurian legend—ultimately destroy a noble community. Chaucer also repeats the street scene, not in Boccaccio, after Pandarus delivers Troilus's first letter. Troilus rides past a second time (II, 1247–52), and on this occasion looks are exchanged. The Narrator establishes distance by denying description; he defers to Criseyde's response, affirming that she is struck by love (II.1261–74).

Troy is almost forgotten in Book III while Troilus and Criseyde enjoy their brief time together, safely enclosed in Pandarus's house. The bliss of the lovers is transcendent, but exclusive, and there are soon warnings. Pandarus, after all his advocacy and facilitating, now urges temperance, arguing remembrance of fortune's adversity, the loss of prosperity (1625–38). Troilus sings of Love, but his song is derived from Boethius (2.m8) rather than Boccaccio, and already there is a sense of an alternative. Following this song, the larger story of Troy is reasserted. Troilus's role as knight is at a high point: "In alle nedes for the townes werre / He was, and ay, the first in armes dyght" (1771–73); his reputation is second only to great Hector's. Nevertheless, Troilus remains besotted; he thinks that anyone not in the service of love is lost (1793–94). The Narrator summarizes in a final stanza that reiterates "Th'effect and joie of Troilus servise, / Al be that ther was som *disese among" (*distress,1815–16), again balancing extreme feeling.

In Book IV interests of community are most relentlessly and fully inserted. The public world impinges upon a private personal relationship. During a siege there is military action: "on a day, wel armed, brighte and shene / Ector and many a worthi *wight out wente" (*person, 38–39). In this Trojan foray against the Greeks, Antenor is taken captive. A truce ensues and an exchange is sought. Calkas, with a full account of his actions, claims delivery of Criseyde as reward for his service to the Greeks. Just as scenes shifted between Troilus and Criseyde, so now those of nations alternate. A Trojan parliament debates the terms. To preserve secrecy Troilus remains silent, but chivalric Hector argues against selling a woman. However, such chivalric idealism, an underlying force in the Paris-Helen story, does not prevail. Now male interest (Antenor) and the strength of the community are preferred. The combination of chivalric prowess and romantic love that characterize the Trojans is repeated. Troilus more readily would have sacrificed lives of his family or his own than his love. His energy and thoughts are all of grief and desperation, and wishes for death dominate. He rejects Pandarus's pragmatic suggestion that there are other loves, and then refuses a proposal that he abduct Criseyde. Here Troilus reveals a thorough understanding of Troy's situation and its relation to personal and communal honor. The city is at war because of ravishing women, only blame can result if he interferes in an exchange that was "for the townes goode" (553), and his father King Priam ratified the decision in parliament. These explanations put community before personal interest, and Troilus decides not to repeat Paris's act in taking Helen. A fear of slander—though Troilus identifies it as his strongest feeling—comes only afterwards. He rightly sees the two opposed interests as "desir and reson" and acknowledges that they are pulling him apart (572–75). Although Troilus's emotional outpouring parallels his complaints as an unsatisfied lover, his situation is quite different. He is alone but goes to a temple—a place of community, not private isolation—to pray; in a long discourse (958–1082), based on Boethius (5.pr.3) he considers questions of predestination, free choice, necessity, concluding with a plea for either pity or death. Still overwrought, believing Criseyde dead when she swoons, Troilus prepares to kill himself. "But as God Wolde" (1212), Criseyde revives. The pagan remedy for despair and disgrace is not for Troilus, even though his commitment to honor falters when he asks her to flee with him. To refute this plea, Criseyde proposes that she will return in ten days. She too appeals to public circumstance, arguing that there is talk of peace, with the restoration of Helen an expected condition (1345–51). At this point Criseyde's strength and loyalty to community seem to equal Troilus's; she notes that all her kin, except her father, are in Troy. The Narrator expresses an inability to discern her motives (1415–21), but Troilus is relentless in his analysis of Calkas's likely decision to marry Criseyde to a Greek and in his belief that the Greeks will not agree to peace. Nevertheless, he acquiesces and parts ruefully. The Narrator confesses inadequacy to tell "The cruele peynes of this sorowful man" (1697).

In the final book scenes shift between Troy and the Greek camp, and again a few details remind the audience of community in the midst of the difficult narrative of Criseyde's betrayal and Troilus's response. First there is the exchange, and through Diomede a manner of behaving that contrasts sharply with the Trojan community. Totally lacking in subtlety, his overtures ignore any possibility of a loyalty to Troy, and he is confident that self-interest will prevail, though he believes Criseyde has left a lover behind. Troy is recalled when Troilus revisits places in the city that are dear to their love, and from a distance "Ful rewfully she [Criseyde] loked upon Troie, / Biheld the toures heigh and ek the halles" (V.729–30). This is one of the poem's most powerful images, a vast distance between lovers and joy now supplanted by grief. Similar is the scene of curfew, a closing of the gates and recalling of those outside the walls, as night falls and Troilus rides "homeward" to Troy (1177–83). Separation is complete. At the end of Book V Troilus is once again a fearless fighter, showing his greatness and knighthood in many cruel battles against the Greeks. He has been disillusioned by knowledge of Criseyde's betrayal, but like Boethius he knows his innocence: "That ye thus doon, I have it nat deserved" (1722).

As a good pagan, he might again be tempted to suicide; death, rather than Christian hope, is emphasized. However, as a knight of romance Troilus chooses instead to fight. Revenge, an obligation for pre-Christian warriors, is a motive, but he is also fighting Troy's enemies. The Narrator reminds the audience that he is writing of love, not "The armes of this ilke worthi man" (V.1766), so that the battles are not detailed. Nevertheless, the last point of the story is Troilus's being slain by Achilles. Death warrants but a line (1807), a simple statement that contrasts with earlier rhetorical emotional outbursts when death was sought. Before giving this information, Chaucer bade his story farewell, "Go litel bok, go, litel myn tragedye."

The Palinode, last twelve stanzas, is a culmination of philosophical awareness already established. For Christian believers death is only the beginning; this wisdom is gained by Troilus after his death, when from the eighth sphere he looks down on "This litel spot of erthe" (1815) and laughs. "Swych fyn" hath all that was recounted; even blissful love is trivial before the Love that is God. The prayers that conclude *Troilus and Criseyde* consider the nature of the divine: not just the inadequacy of "payens corsed olde rites" (1849), but a distinction between God the creator of man in His own image (1839) and "that sothfast Crist . . . hym the which that right for love / Upon a crois, oure soules for to beye, / First *starf, and roos" (*died, 1860, 1842–43). Christ entered the world, human time, formed a community, and died for all mankind. This suffering is triumph, a denying of the self in order truly to become. On earth the way is through community. Trojans try to live this ideal, even though some betray it through personal love that violates community. Early in the poem Chaucer refers to Troilus's "fyre of love" (I.436). The reference is to his desire for Criseyde, but by the end of the poem signifies purification, as in the mystic writing *Incendium Amoris* of Richard Rolle (d.1349). However, the final emphasis is upon "mercy" (1861, 1867, 1862). Troilus in the ecstasy of his love recognized that "mercy passeth right" (III.1282), that he did not deserve Criseyde's love. Such awareness of unworthiness contradicts his initial assumptions that he can win Criseyde because of skilled wooing, by his achievements as a warrior, nobility gained through love. Similarly, when Troilus realizes at the Trojan parliament that Criseyde will be given over, he asks, "Is ther no grace, and shal I thus be spilt?" (IV.262). The answer, of course, is yes and no. No one act, not even a beautiful and fulfilling love, is the whole of a life. Thus Troilus is not a hero of *de casibus* tragedy. Faced with the loss of Criseyde, he experiences genuine suffering that goes beyond courtly conventions. The *ubi sunt* ("Where is" V.218ff, 1673ff) of his final complaints is addressed to Criseyde, but also recalls those who lived before and lost cities like Troy. Ultimately, human existence is only a stage, and a larger community brings one closer to God than a private love.

As noted in chapter 9, time is crucial in Boethian thought, and indeed in Christian belief. Through a recognition of temporal and eternal comes understanding of the distinction between destiny and providence. The one is observable in a linear series of events in human time (like the love affair) that are influenced by individual human choices, while the other is a unity of all events in time and perceivable only from beyond this world. In Christian terms faith means belief in the vision; without this, despair is likely, as is shown by a pagan like Troilus. Just as Boethius faced a death that appeared unwarrantable, so Troilus faces an undeserved loss of his love. Both grow beyond self-pity, but pagan Troilus's realization comes only when he is beyond the world's time. This elasticity is apparent also in Chaucer's treatment of time within the story. A reference to April (I.155–56) is followed by the specific May 3 (II.56), presumably within a month after Troilus first saw Criseyde. Exact linear time is not specified. The period of union includes "many a nyght . . . thus Fortune a tyme ledde in joie" (III.1713–14). The Narrator does not know how long the time was between a decision to attack and the foray in which Antenor was captured (IV.36–37). References to time (nine days, two months, uncertain) and the Narrator's comments in Book V obscure the sequence of Criseyde's betrayal and Troilus's recognition (1086–92). A scene of Troilus's anxiously waiting follows indications that months have passed and the information that Criseyde has given a bay steed and Troilus's brooch to Diomede.

At any given moment only some appearances are available, and often identified as a working of Fortune, defined as an arbitrary force. Events in *Troilus and Criseyde* are seen more complexly; they are mutable, ever changing, as Lady Philosophy explained to Boethius. Stemming from both external circumstances and the inner workings of a character's mind, events are neither absolute nor controllable, as Troilus and Criseyde fondly refuse to perceive. One example illustrates this. When Pandarus first tells Criseyde of Troilus's love in Book II, he urges that Troilus will die unless she responds to his love (316ff), and he thinks he is manipulating her. But Chaucer shows Criseyde catch Pandarus by his clothing and then explains her fear. He also includes what she "thoughte," including both a recognition "It nedeth me ful sleighly for to pleie" and the "sorowful sik" that prefaces her reply to her uncle (456–63). There is, then, deliberate role-playing, a choice. This is obvious in the shifts in her rhythm of speech to echo the man with whom she is speaking, but goes beyond verbal play. Criseyde, who anticipates Shakespeare's Cleopatra, role-plays when she promises to return; since this is unlikely, she seems to be trying to comfort her distraught lover. Even when she is alone, Criseyde casts herself: as Isolde, with the line "Who yaf me drynke?" when she first sees Troilus after learning he loves her. Troilus's behavior suggests a parallel. His exaggeration and fantasy suggest he has been playing at courtly love with his sighs and illness. Even in Book III Troilus describes his circumstances as "this game" (1084), and in Book V (267–73) he returns to role-playing, suffering as the courtly lover when he needs distraction. (Significantly, the Narrator disclaims reporting this correctly.) Andreas Capellanus formally codified *The Art of Love*, and Troilus seems to know the rules as well as Pandarus. Although Troilus is a suffering lover, he is healthy enough to triumph over the Greeks and ride into the city. Men in the street, casual observers, explain that he is going this way because it is the only open route from the gate. That he goes past Criseyde's house is "happy" (lucky), but "necessitee" is twice qualified, "sooth to seyn" and "men seyn" (II.615–23).

The love of Troilus and Criseyde is necessary in Chaucer's scheme, part of the experience of this world's best and finest, a perception that contributes to but is superseded by Troilus's view from the eighth sphere. A true and loyal hero of romance, Trojan Troilus through reason and suffering, and Chaucer's admiration, gains transcendence; his new understanding is that of faith in something more than even the most compelling love on earth.

11

The Comic Vision of Geoffrey Chaucer

Many of Chaucer's poems break off, apparently stop without an ending; however, a "litel bok" that is intended as an introduction seems to need some mark of completion. Although lack of conclusiveness and variety of interpretation from readers of Chaucer's poetry are salient, a simple "comic" vision may perhaps be discerned. Three short lyrics—"Lenvoy de Chaucer a Scogan," "Lenvoy de Chaucer a Bukton," "The Complaint of Chaucer to His Purse"—are associated with the last three or four years of Chaucer's life. The persons most likely identified as Scogan and Bukton were part of the Chaucer circle, those with an affinity to the king, essentially self-made men.[1] These lyrics, along with the Retraction to *The Canterbury Tales,* seem to be personal statements, but they also provide occasions for various interpretations. Thus along with some lines marked "Proverbe of Chaucer" in the manuscript and the address "To Adam Scryven," probably written earlier, they afford a means to an ending. On the one hand, the lyrics are occasional poems, written to friends and acquaintances about specific circumstances. But they also suggest Chaucer's view of himself as maker of poetry and man in this world and a believer in eternal time.

"Lenvoy" is a letter, and Chaucer's light epistolary verse is used to consider once again matters of love. "Lenvoy a Scogan," written in rime royal but as playful bantering instead of the traditional, more ceremonial tone, considers an unsuccessful love. Beginning with a jest about disturbance in heaven, the poet moves to talk of love, referring to the fifth circle of Venus and commenting on Scogan's renunciation of a lady who did not reciprocate his feelings. Poet and friend are then allied by their being ignored by Cupid, and this modulates into Chaucer's protest that he will write no more. Finally the point of view again shifts, when Chaucer implores Scogan to include him in a plea for favor at "the stremes hed / Of grace" (Thames, 43–44), glossed as Windsor Castle in the manuscripts. The tone is quite mixed, both playful and serious. Perhaps most interesting is the contradiction in vowing to desist from writing while writing a poem. Interest in the poet's making of "prose or ryme" (41) seems no less sincere than strong feelings of friendship. Chaucer's reference to himself as "olde Grisel" (gray-haired, 35) recalls earlier self-portraits in *The Canterbury Tales* and *The House of Fame* when he ruefully accepted his physical appearance. Here Chaucer attributes to Scogan the comment and expectation that he "lyst to ryme and playe!" (35). The sixth stanza is most challenging, for it is a denial of further writing ("for I m'excuse—/ God helpe me so!") clearly explained: "But al shal passe that men prose or ryme; / Take every man hys turn, as for his tyme" (36–42). This is a recognition, analogous to the Retraction, that the maker of poetry is thus occupied only for a time and that the work will pass. Nevertheless, the concluding stanza perseveres with a request that his friend intercede for him and finally reasserts that Scogan should not defy Love. There is, then, rapid shifting, an explicit awareness of poetic accomplishment but also of its limitations.

In "Lenvoy a Bukton" Chaucer again considers love, here whether his friend should remarry, an occasion for a return to familiar themes of "The sorwe and wo that is in mariage" (6) and a citing of the Wife of Bath as authority (29). Chaucer's characteristically teasing self-denigration comes across in a concern that he himself might have to remarry; he notes St. Paul's point that it is better to wed than to burn, but seems to advise Bukton against a giving up of freedom. However, the shifts are so quick and contradictory, and the tone playful, so that only a sense of verbal and mental facility and good will seem clear. The opening lines alert the audience that Chaucer is not going to be absolute:

> My maister Bukton, whan of Crist our kyng
> Was axed what is trouthe or sothfastnesse,
> He nat a word answerde to that axing,
> As who saith, "No man is al trewe," I gesse. (1–4).

Like any friend, Chaucer comments about his friend's possible marriage, but does not offer a simple judgment. He heeds the Gospel warning against judging others, and even when citing Scripture he qualifies with "I gesse."

The two letters to Scogan and Bukton address serious personal relations; about human behavior Chaucer preserves a distance, being sure only of change in situations. In "The Complaint of Chaucer to his Purse" the point is very clear: he is in need of money and is appealing to Henry IV. Again employing the effects of a love *balade,* in three stanzas he presents his purse as a lady and longs to have her heavy again. The wordplay is clever, references to yellow and sun applying equally to a lady's hair and to coin, and the refrain is urgent "Beth hevy ageyn, or elles moot I dye." The tone is witty, so that Chaucer makes his case without being unpleasant. In the last stanza he turns serious and compliments the king, who has the resources to answer a supplication and to resolve his difficult lack of funds.

The "Complaint to his Purse" recalls "Chaucers Wordes unto Adam, His Owne Scriveyn." A single stanza of rime royal urges care in writing and expresses the poet's dismay at having to make corrections, "to rubbe and scrape," because of the copyist's negligence and haste. The works referred to are "Boece or Troylus," which may indicate earlier composition. The poem evokes memorably both the medieval means of writing on parchment and the author's vulnerability to a scribe who could misrepresent his text.

These interests would seem to indicate a poet much concerned with his reputation and unlikely to conclude *The Canterbury Tales* with a Retraction that foreswears so much of the poetry that has delighted audiences for centuries. Yet repeatedly Chaucer simultaneously creates and disavows, constantly showing a Boethian view of linear time in the world and of eternal Time. This is one way of explaining the unusual number of unfinished poems, those that break off: *The House of Fame, The Legend of Good Women, Anelida and Arcite,* not to mention a number of individual tales and *The Canterbury Tales* itself—if one expects a work like that proposed by Harry Bailly—and the changed perspective at the end of *Troilus and Criseyde.* "Proverbe of Chaucer" begins with a question about casting away clothes on a hot day, and cautions that cold (change) will recur. Then there is a statement about man's incapacity to embrace the largeness of the world and a reminder that attempting too much will result in retaining little. This homely statement is another version of the Retraction.

The Retraction is an epitome of Chaucer both maker and man. He begins with the courtesy of courtly poetry, allowing choice and modestly introducing his efforts. But almost immediately the intent changes, when he declares that all he has written was possible only through the grace of "oure Lord Jhesu Crist, of whom procedeth al wit and al goodnesse" (X.1081), and confesses that he would have done better if he had been able. This introduces a modest prayer for mercy and forgiveness of faults. Such repentance is commonplace, but Chaucer next becomes very personal by listing his own works, most of which he disclaims. Only for "the translacion of Boece de Consolacione, and othere bookes of legendes of seintes, and omelies, and moralitee, and devocioun" is he thankful. These, of course, are works that lead one away from the world. Thus he beseeches Christ and His mother Mary, and the saints, to send him the grace for "penitence, confessioun and satisfaccioun." Since these are the subject of the *Parson's Tale,* some have argued that the Retraction, which follows it, really is part of that argument rather than Chaucer's own statement. In fact, the two are part of a oneness, the Christian belief that defines the fourteenth century. Chaucer shares with the Parson a belief in "the benigne grace of hym that ys kyng of kynges . . . that boghte us with the precious blood of his herte" and thus hopes that he "may be oon of hem at the day of doom that shulle be saved" (X.1090). Through this faith all may transcend worldly distinctions as well as the inconclusiveness and uncertainties so richly explored through the poems that Chaucer revokes. In the twentieth century even theologians are often more devoted to psychological ease and social resolutions than to a transcendent God; Chaucer's vision, a Christian's faith in a stable and universal reality, is not thus temporally rooted. A consequence of this vision, shown in Troilus's laughter after his death, is a freeing from the grimness of much of life. Perhaps more important is a realization that the intensity of involvement in human fortunes, as Boethius learns from Lady Philosophy, is misguided, a taking seriously what is not really important. With such understanding a Retraction is neither problematical nor exacting.

The great Victorian poet-critic-educator Matthew Arnold (1822–88) faulted Chaucer for a lack of "high seriousness," by which he intended a grand style and sense of gravity. G. K. Chesterton (1874–1936), an Edwardian, saw much Chaucer criticism as a curse, noting that "while the poet is always large and humorous, the critics are often small and serious."[2] Geoffrey Chaucer is the first major literary figure in English; his remarkable body of work has attracted readers for six-hundred years and inspired massive and varied commentary, particularly since the nineteenth century and almost overwhelmingly since the 1950s. Interpretations are as numerous as critics, and a recent bibliography notes that the number of items translates as one appearing every day for the last ten years.[3] Chaucer is the most accessible of medieval authors because his work combines an extraordinary knowledge of traditions—the range of his reading is astonishing—and richly diversified experiences as a public man with a style and attitude that allow many interpretations across the ages. Even a cursory reading of the critical heritage shows how much a reader's response determines interpretation. Although countless others had written about Chaucer, John Dryden, the first great English critic, evaluating *The Canterbury Tales* at the end of the seventeenth century, provides perhaps the surest note: "There is such a variety of Game springing up before me, that I am distracted in my Choice, and know not which to follow. 'Tis sufficient to say according to the Proverb, that here is God's plenty." Today's reader and student of Chaucer must thus respond to both the original texts and to interpretations of them. Like Shakespeare, Chaucer has a universal quality that appeals and has been accessible from his own time to the present. The brilliance of his story telling assures a good read and an increased thoughtfulness as well as laughter. However, Chaucer is very much a man of his age, so that some knowledge of the contexts in which he wrote prevents easy assumptions that he can be read simply as a contemporary. An initial response of recognition that the worlds of the fourteenth and twentieth centuries share tension, violence, corruption, disintegration, and instability, must be tempered with an awareness that these circumstances do not elicit the same responses. There are also experiences of faith, personal nobility, loyalty, and compassion. Neither an entirely individual nor some monolithic "spirit of the age" is, then, a felicitous reaction, for as Dryden notes: "Mankind is ever the same, and nothing lost out of Nature, though every thing is alter'd." Dryden's view offers many possibilities. A recognition not only of Variety but also of Game (play, joke) and the difficulty of Choice encourage "Chaucer's irony," favored by many to resolve that difficulty; however, the citing of a Proverb seeks a tradition, a precedent that is both generous and an acknowledgment of the divine. A conclusion, then, must reaffirm Chaucer's own frequent statements of the limitations in the human condition, "My wit is short, ye may wel understonde" (*Canterbury Tales*, I.746). Further, his own modest admission and his further reassurance that the reader can always "Turne over the leef and chese another tale" (*Canterbury Tales*, I.3177) provide a gentle and inviting way to conclude.

Notes

Chapter 1: A Man of the Fourteenth Century

1. There is also a conjecture that Chaucer had a daughter, or perhaps a sister. An Elizabeth Chausier (Chaucy) was admitted as a nun in the Priory of St. Helen, London, in 1377, and received gifts from John of Gaunt upon being made a nun at Barking Abbey in 1381.

2. All citations are from *The Riverside Chaucer*, general ed. Larry D. Benson (Boston: Houghton Mifflin, 1987). Citations from *The Canterbury Tales* include only references to Fragments, numbered I–X. For an explanation of order and parallel listings for Groups A–I, see p. 40.

3. Chaucer's associations with Merton are his strongest university connection. He also knew a Ralph Strode in London, a lawyer who was common sergeant and standing counsel for the city, and who lived in Aldersgate and had a wife and son. Although so drastic a change in career and personal style was unusual, the Oxford and London Strodes were likely the same person.

4. See Paul Strohm, *Social Chaucer* (Cambridge, MA: Harvard University Press, 1989).

5. Another early version is in the Houghton Library, Harvard University, and a similar painting is at UCLA.

6. Editions of Chaucer by Benson and Fisher, cited in the bibliography, contain very useful introductions to the language, which becomes more understandable after listening to recordings in Middle English, also cited.

7. A standard introduction to the period is May McKisack, *The Fourteenth Century 1307–1399* (Oxford: Clarendon Press, 1959). See also Maurice Keen, *A History of Medieval Europe* (London: Routledge and Kegan Paul, 1968; pub. by Penguin Books, 1969); M. M. Postan, *The Medieval Economy and Society* (London: Weidenfeld and Nicolson, 1972). Other useful social histories, not specifically about Chaucer, include: Christopher N. L. Brooke, *London 800–1216: The Shaping of a City* (Berkeley and Los Angeles: University of California Press, 1975); A. R. Myers, *London in the Age of Chaucer* (Norman: University of Oklahoma Press, 1972);

Sylvia L. Thrupp, *The Merchant Class of Medieval London [1300–1500]* (Ann Arbor: University of Michigan Press, 1948). See also Margaret Wood, *The English Medieval House* (1965; London: Bracken Books,1983); Colin Platt, *The English Medieval Town* (London: Martin Secker & Warburg, 1976; Paladin Books, 1979); David Herlihy, *Medieval Households* (Cambridge, MA: Harvard University Press, 1985); Joseph Strutt, *Sports and Pastimes of the People of England*, enlarged and corrected ed. J. Charles Cox (1903); Lilian M. C. Randall, *Images in the Margins of Gothic Manuscripts* (Berkeley and Los Angeles: University of California Press, 1966).

8. Among many helpful introductions are: W. A. Pantin, *The English Church in the Fourteenth Century* (Cambridge, UK: Cambridge University Press,1955; rpt. Toronto: Medieval Academy Reprints for Teaching 5); Robert W. Ackerman, *Backgrounds to Medieval English Literature* (New York: Random House, 1966); K. B. McFarlane, *Lancastrian Kings and Lollard Knights* (Oxford: Clarendon Press, 1972); Anne Hudson, *The Premature Reformation: Wycliffite Texts and Lollard History* (Oxford: Clarendon Press, 1988); Janet Coleman, *English Literature in History 1350–1400* (London: Hutchinson, 1981); Stephen Medcalf, ed., *The Later Middle Ages* (London: Methuen,1981).

9. Speght's edition of Chaucer in 1598 confirms this impression by referring to a record at the Inner Temple noting that "Chaucer was fined two shillings for beating a Franciscan Fryer in flete streate." Current scholarship argues Chaucer's general objection to mendicant orders, shared by many in the fourteenth century.

Chapter 2: "God's Plenty"—*The Canterbury Tales*

1. A brief list of summaries of critical interpretation is in the bibliography.

2. A handy list of manuscripts and principal editions is in Pearsall, 321–26. The fullest account is in *The Riverside Chaucer,* ed. Larry L. Benson.

3. It was the basis of the late nineteenth-century edition of Walter W. Skeat (1894) and of the standard text of F. N. Robinson (1933), recently revised for a third edition by Larry L. Benson (1987), as well as John H. Fisher's edition of all of Chaucer's works (2nd ed., 1989).

4. An alternate designation is by groups (A-I) to indicate an ordering devised first by Henry Bradshaw to order the geographical references and supported by later scholars, notably Baugh and Pratt.

5. R. W. Southern, *The Making of the Middle Ages* (New Haven, CT: Yale University Press, 1953), 222. Early argument for a significant shift in European experience is Charles Homer Haskins, *The Renaissance of the Twelfth Century* (Cambridge, MA: Harvard University Press, 1927).

6. Linda Georgianna, "Love So Dearly Bought: The Terms of Redemption in *The Canterbury Tales,*" *Studies in the Age of Chaucer* 12 (1990): 85–116, for a review of attitudes toward commercial values.

7. Peter Brown, *The Cult of the Saints* (Chicago: University of Chicago Press,1981) and Benedicta Ward, *Miracles and the Medieval Mind* (Philadelphia: University of Pennsylvania Press, 1982) provide rich explanations of medieval views of saints and miracles.

8. Becket was the archetype of church authority against the state, and Henry VIII's own Archbishop of Canterbury, William Warham, before the House of Lords, in 1530, declared himself in support of the principles for which his predecessor had died.

9. The cover of *The Riverside Chaucer* is an illumination showing these three representatives of medieval society.

10. Jill Mann, *Chaucer and Medieval Estates Satire* (Cambridge, UK: Cambridge University Press, 1973).

11. Most notable are George Lyman Kittredge, *Chaucer and His Poetry* (Cambridge, MA: Harvard University Press, 1915); John Livingstone Lowes, *Geoffrey Chaucer and the Development of His Genius* (Boston: Houghton Mifflin, 1934); John Speirs, *Chaucer the Maker* (London: Faber & Faber, 1951); Robert M. Lumiansky, *Of Sondry Folk: The Dramatic Principle in the Canterbury Tales* (Austin: University of Texas Press, 1955); Robert B. Burlin, *Chaucerian Fiction* (Princeton: Princeton University Press, 1977).

12. Kemp Malone, *Chapters on Chaucer* (Baltimore: Johns Hopkins Press, 1951); Bertrand Bronson, *In Search of Chaucer* (Toronto: University of Toronto Press, 1960); Robert M. Jordan, *Chaucer and the Shape of Creation* (Cambridge, MA: Harvard University Press, 1967); Helen Cooper, *The Structure of the Canterbury Tales* (London: Gerald Duckworth, 1983), Derek Pearsall, *The Canterbury Tales* (London: George Allen & Unwin, 1985); C. David Benson, *Chaucer's Drama of Style* (Chapel Hill: University of North Carolina, 1986).

13. The *Epilogue* seems to have been written early in the composition of *The Canterbury Tales*, when the *Tale of Melibee* was probably assigned to the Man of Law. The tale assigned to the Shipman also was changed, since originally it was for a female teller.

14. Kittredge, 211.

15. Kittredge initiated the idea of a "Marriage Group." See Benson, 863–64, for a summary of later revisions. My own view is in "Pacience in Adversitee: Chaucer's Presentation of Marriage," *Viator* 10 (1979): 323–54.

16. J. A. Burrow, *The Ages of Man* (Oxford: Oxford University Press, 1986), 60–64. Division into five ages was less used by classical and later authorities, as indicated by Shakespeare's "seven ages of man" in *As You Like It* (II.7.139–66).

Chapter 3: Secular Romances

1. For a survey of attitudes toward romance, see the opening chapter of my *The Popularity of Middle English Romance* (Bowling Green, OH: Bowling Green University Popular Press, 1976).

2. Laura Hibbard Loomis, "Chaucer and the Auchinleck Manuscript: Thopas and Guy of Warwick," *Essays and Studies in Honor of Carleton Brown* (New York: New York University Press, 1940) and "The Auchinleck Manuscript and a Possible London Bookshop of 1330–1340," *PMLA* 57 (1942): 595–627. This is reviewed in the Introduction to the facsimile edition *The Auchinleck Manuscript* by Derek Pearsall and I. C. Cunningham (London: The Scolar Press, 1977).

3. A threefold division was defined in a late *chanson de geste* about Charlemagne's wars, the *Chanson des Saisnes* : the matter of France (Charlemagne and his paladins), the matter of Britain (Arthur and Knights of the Round Table), and the matter of Rome the Great (Alexander, Caesar, stories of Thebes and Troy).

4. The list of supreme heroes is introduced by Jacques de Longuyon in a poem *Voeux du Paon*, which was an early fourteenth-century continuation (c.1310) of the *Romance of Alexander*. Listing noble persons was not new, but Longuyon provided a clear formulation. This classification is an elaboration of the division of romances into three matters. The Nine Worthies were extremely popular; for example, they are represented gloriously in medieval tapestries now at the Cloisters in New York and the Historical Museum in Basle, and in illuminations of Thomas of Saluzzo's *Chevalier Errant* (where also are shown Nine Heroines). The Nine Worthies are the rustic entertainment in Shakespeare's *Love's Labour's Lost,* only one illustration of their popularity in the Renaissance. Maurice Keen, *Chivalry* (New Haven, CT: Yale University Press, 1984), see esp. 121–24, provides a context of "Historical Mythology."

5. Chaucer uses the form "listeth" only in this tale, see also line 833, and in *The House of Fame*, 511, when he specifically addresses an audience that understands English. This linguistic detail indicates his care in matching the style.

6. *Guy of Warwick* is the capstone of my study of *The Popularity of Middle English Romance.*

Chapter 4: *Fabliaux*

1. Vagabond scholars of the twelfth and thirteenth centuries wrote Latin verses on a variety of subjects, especially sex, waywardness, spring, pleasures of the tavern, clerical abuses. The lyrics are typically mocking or satirical, irreverent social commentary. The term *goliard* may come from *gula* (gluttony), and Golias is associated with Goliath, the giant slain by David. Goliard poets often adapted verse forms of Church hymns and offices in burlesque and parody. The modern composer Carl Orff used these poems in his cantata *Carmina Burana*.

Chapter 5: Religious Romances and Saints' Legends

1. Margaret Schlauch, *Chaucer's Constance and Accused Queens* (New York, 1927; AMS reprint, 1973).

2. V. A. Kolve, *Chaucer and the Imagery of Narrative* (London: Edward Arnold, 1984), 297–358.

3. See my article "Pacience in adversitee," *Viator* , 10 (1979), 323–54.

4. Cited in *The Riverside Chaucer*, 883.

Chapter 6: Tales with Satiric Warnings

1. The Harrowing of Hell is an episode derived from an apocryphal Gospel of Nicodemus. Christ after his death descended into Hell to bring out the souls of the righteous. The subject appears frequently in art.

Chapter 7: Sermons

1. Susan Gallick, "A Look at Chaucer and His Preachers," *Speculum* 50 (1975); 456–76, is a useful introduction.

2. John Livingston Lowes, *Geoffrey Chaucer* (1934; Bloomington: University of Indiana Press, 1958), 186, citing Kittredge.

Chapter 8: Beginnings with Love and Fame

1. The entire text is readily available in Charles W. Dunn, ed. and trans., *The Romance of the Rose* (New York: E. P. Dutton, 1962). For a variety of interpretations, see C. S. Lewis, *The Allegory of Love* (Oxford: Clarendon Press, 1936); Alan M. F. Gunn, *The Mirror of Love* (Lubbock, TX: Texas Tech Press, 1952); D. W. Robertson, Jr., *A Preface to Chaucer* (Princeton: Princeton University Press, 1962).

2. A. C. Spearing, *Medieval Dream-Poetry* (Cambridge, UK: Cambridge

University Press, 1976) is a comprehensive study, including critical analyses of Chaucer's dream poems.

Chapter 9: *The Consolation of Philosophy* in Love and Politics

1. W. P. Ker, *The Dark Ages* (1923; New York: New American Library, 1958), 72–81, and Ralph Hanna III and Traugott Lawlor, Introduction in *Riverside Chaucer*, 396.

2. The phrase is explained in H. R. Patch, *The Tradition of Boethius* (New York: Oxford University Press, 1935), 127. Boethius spans centuries of English literary tradition; King Alfred made an Old English prose translation of *The Consolation*, and Queen Elizabeth I her own Renaissance version.

3. V. E. Watts, Introduction, Boethius, *The Consolation of Philosophy* (Harmondsworth, England: Penguin, 1969), 8. This edition provides useful background information and a modern translation.

4. The fourteenth-century mystical treatise *The Cloud of Unknowing* describes the experience.

5. A Greek poet, Hesiod probably flourished in the eighth century B.C. *Works and Days* combines an account of daily life with allegory, fable, personal history. In addition to presenting an ethical argument against idleness and strife and for honest labor, Hesiod offers advice to his brother, who apparently sought to deprive him of his inheritance by bribing corrupt judges. This is analogous to Boethius's situation of being falsely accused.

6. Most frequent is Paradise in Genesis (2:8–10). Also important is the enclosed garden ("hortus conclusus") of the Song of Songs that provides a parallel to architecture (Canticles 4:12) and powerful erotic imagery that the Catholic Church allegorizes as the union of God with His Church.

7. Haldeen Braddy, *Chaucer and the French Poet Graunson* (1947; rpt. Port Washington, NY: Kennikat Press, 1968) is the fullest treatment. Another view of the poem is as an aristocratic entertainment, a "disguising" or "mumming." There were public celebrations by social organizations of St. Valentine's Day by 1400.

8. Robert W. Frank, Jr., *Chaucer and "The Legend of Good Women"* (Cambridge: Harvard University Press, 1972) initiated greater attention and praise through an emphasis upon *The Legend* as a way into *The Canterbury Tales,* arguing that it was a significant step in Chaucer's freeing himself from the limits of the courtly literature that influenced his early poetry and judging it a major step in Chaucer's development of skill in writing short narratives.

9. Letters I-XV are from women to men, and XVI–XXI are three paired

exchanges with both male and female writing letters. A number of Chaucer's examples appear among the first type: Dido, Hypsipyle and Medea, Ariadne, Phyllis, Hypermnestra. Other women, like Thisbe and Philomena, for example, owe more to Ovid's *Metamorphoses*.

10. Elaine Hansen, "Irony and the Antifeminist Narrator in Chaucer's Legend of Good Women," *JEGP* 82 (1983): 11–31, and Carolyn Dinshaw, *Chaucer's Sexual Poetics* (Madison: University of Wisconsin Press, 1989), 65–87. An alternative application of literary theory is Donald W. Rowe, *Through Nature to Eternity: Chaucer's "Legend of Good Women"* (Lincoln: University of Nebraska Press, 1988), which stresses the role of the narrator in a drama of cyclical readings (prevision-vision-revision) shared with the audience, a complex intertextuality in which remembrance comes through old books, and *The Legend* is viewed as sacramental poetry fully achieved in the mind of the reader.

11. There is interesting revision in this passage: "though that I konne but lyte" in F becomes "that my wit be lite" in G (29), and "Farewel my bok and my devocioun!" (F) becomes "Farewel my stodye, as lastynge that sesoun!" (G 39). The lines in G, generally presumed to be the revision, indicate increasingly modest claims for understanding and a recognition of alteration.

Chapter 10: A Romance of Love and War "ful blisfully" Completed—*Troilus and Criseyde*

1. Kittredge, *Chaucer and His Poetry*, 109.

2. John M. Steadman, *Disembodied Laughter: "Troilus" and the Apotheosis Tradition* (Berkeley, Los Angeles, London: University of California Press, 1972).

3. Monica E. McAlpine, *The Genre of "Troilus and Criseyde"* (Ithaca and London: Cornell University Press, 1978).

4. Chaucer also employed the stanza in the *Second Nun's Tale, Prioress's Tale, Man of Law's Tale,* and *Clerk's Tale.* These tales I have identified as Religious Romances, noting an emphasis on high sentiment and spiritual values, and the crucial roles of women.

5. A. J. Minnis, *Chaucer and Pagan Antiquity* (Cambridge, UK: D. S. Brewer, 1982) is a richly detailed study of various medieval attitudes toward ancient culture and a reading of *Troilus* as a "romance of antiquity" that both admires and recognizes the limits of pagan society.

6. VIII. 897 and 849. The Dreamer in *The Book of the Duchess* reads a "romaunce" to help himself go to sleep; in fact the tale comes from Ovid's *Metamorphoses*. Most frequent reference is to "the Romaunce of the Rose," a different kind of poem.

7. See Mary Elizabeth Meek, trans., *Historia Destructionis Troiae* (Bloomington: Indiana University Press, 1974) for Guido delle Colonne; R. K. Gordon, *The Story of Troilus* (1934; Toronto: Mediaeval Academy Reprints for Teaching, 1978) translates relevant parts of Benoît's *Roman de Troie* and all of Boccaccio's *Il Filostrato*. For an overview, see also C. David Benson, *The History of Troy in Middle English Literature* (Woodbridge, Suffolk: D. S. Brewer, 1980).

8. There are three translations of Guido into Middle English, *The Gest Hystoriale of the Destruction of Troy, The Laud Troy Book,* and John Lydgate's *Troy Book,* all dating from the start of the fifteenth century and using characteristics of romance.

9. C. S. Lewis, "What Chaucer Really Did to *Il Filostrato*," *E and S* 17 (1932): 56–75; Sanford B. Meech, *Design in Chaucer's Troilus* (Syracuse: Syracuse University Press, 1959).

10. Thomas A. Kirby, *Chaucer's Troilus: A Study in Courtly Love* (Baton Rouge: Louisiana State University Press, 1940). Charles Muscatine, *Chaucer and the French Tradition* (Berkeley and Los Angeles: University of California Press, 1957),124–65, distinguishes bourgeois and courtly styles.

11. Robert K. Root, *The Poetry of Chaucer* (Boston: Houghton Mifflin, 1906), 105–15, suggests turn-of-the-century attitudes.

12. E. Talbot Donaldson, *Speaking of Chaucer* (London: Athlone Press University of London, 1970), 65–83, 53–59, most eloquently confesses how she has "enchanted."

13. See, for example, Margaret Schlauch, *English Medieval Literature and Its Social Foundations* (1956; New York: Cooper Square Publishers, 1971), 240–46; Maureen Fries, "'Slydynge of Corage": Chaucer's Criseyde as Feminist and Victim," in *The Authority of Experience: Essays in Feminist Criticism*, ed. Arlyn Diamond and Lee R. Edwards (Amherst: University of Massachusetts Press, 1977), 45–59; David Aers, *Chaucer, Langland, and the Creative Imagination* (London: Routledge and Kegan Paul, 1980), chapter 5.

Chapter 11: The Comic Vision of Geoffrey Chaucer

1. Paul Strohm, *Social Chaucer* (Cambridge, MA: Harvard University Press, 1989), 41–46. Henry Scogan (?1361–1407) was a squire in the king's household and later became tutor to the sons of King Henry IV. He

quoted Chaucer's "Gentilesse" lyric in his own "A Moral Balade." Peter Bukton, the most likely identification, was a steward to the earl of Derby, who became King Henry IV, and then to his son Thomas of Lancaster.

2. *Chaucer* (London: Faber and Faber, 1932), 18.

3. Lorrayne Y. Baird-Lange and Hildegard Schnuttgen, *A Bibliography of Chaucer, 1974–1985* (Woodbridge: Brewer, 1989).

Select Bibliography

Texts

The Riverside Chaucer. General ed. Larry D. Benson. Boston: Houghton Mifflin, 1987.

The Complete Poetry and Prose of Geoffrey Chaucer. Ed. John H. Fisher. New York: Holt, Rinehart, Winston, 2nd ed., 1989.

Language

Burnley, David. *A Guide to Chaucer's Language*. Norman: University of Oklahoma Press, 1984.

Davis, Norman et al. *A Chaucer Glossary*. Oxford: Clarendon Press, 1979.

Kökeritz, Helge. *A Guide to Chaucer's Pronunciation*. New York: Holt, Rinehart and Winston, 1961.

Ross, Thomas W. *Chaucer's Bawdy*. New York: Dutton, 1972.

Biography

Brewer, Derek. *Chaucer and His World*. London: Eyre Methuen, 1978.

Brusendorff, Aage. *The Chaucer Tradition*. Oxford: Clarendon Press, 1925; rpt. 1967.

Crow, Martin M. and Clair C. Olson. *Chaucer Life Records*. Austin: University of Texas Press, 1966.

Gardner, John. *The Life and Times of Chaucer*. New York: Knopf, 1976.

Howard, Donald R. *Chaucer: His Life, His World, His Works*. New York: Dutton, 1987.

Hussey, Maurice. *Chaucer's World. A Pictorial Companion*. Cambridge, UK: Cambridge University Press, 1967.

Rickert, Edith. *Chaucer's World*. Eds. C. C. Olson and M. C. Crow. New York: Columbia University, 1948.

Contexts

Ackerman, Robert W. *Backgrounds to Medieval English Literature*. New York: Random House, 1966.

Bennett, J. A. W. *Chaucer at Oxford and at Cambridge.* Toronto: University of Toronto Press, 1974.

Brewer, Derek. *English Gothic Literature.* New York: Schocken, 1983.

Coleman, Janet. *English Literature in History, 1350–1400: Medieval Readers and Writers.* London: Hutchinson, 1981.

Heffernan, Thomas J., ed. *The Popular Literature of Medieval England.* Knoxville: University of Tennessee, 1985. Studies in Literature 28.

Kelly, Henry Ansgar. *Love and Marriage in the Age of Chaucer.* Ithaca and London: Cornell University Press, 1975.

Medcalf, Stephen, ed. *The Later Middle Ages.* London: Methuen, 1981.

Patterson, Lee. *Negotiating the Past: The Historical Understanding of Medieval Literature.* Madison: University of Wisconsin Press, 1987.

Pearsall, Derek. *Old English and Middle English Poetry.* London: Routledge & Kegan Paul, 1977.

Criticism

Baldwin, Ralph. *The Unity of the Canterbury Tales.* Anglistica, V. Copenhagen, 1955.

Blamires, Alcuin. *The Canterbury Tales. The Critics Debate.* London: Macmillan, 1987.

Boitani, Piero, ed. *Chaucer and the Italian Trecento.* Cambridge, UK: Cambridge University Press, 1983.

Boitani, Piero and Jill Mann, eds. *The Cambridge Chaucer Companion.* Cambridge, UK: Cambridge University Press, 1986.

Bowden, Muriel. *A Commentary on the General Prologue of "The Canterbury Tales."* New York: Ferrar, 1945.

Brewer, Derek. *An Introduction to Chaucer.* London: Longman, 1984.

———. *Chaucer the Poet as Storyteller.* London: Macmillan, 1984.

———, ed. *Chaucer the Critical Heritage.* 2 vols. London: Routledge & Kegan Paul, 1978.

———, ed. *Writers and Their Background: Geoffrey Chaucer.* London: G. Bell & Sons, 1975.

Bronson, Bertrand H. *In Search of Chaucer.* Toronto: University of Toronto Press, 1960.

Bryan, W., and G. Dempster, eds. *Sources and Analogues of Chaucer's Canterbury Tales.* Chicago: University of Chicago Press, 1941.

The Chaucer Library. Athens: University of Georgia Press, 1978 *The Chaucer Review,* 1966–

Chesterton, G. K. *Chaucer.* Faber and Faber, 1932.

Clemen, W. H. *Chaucer's Early Poetry.* London: Methuen, 1963.

Cooper, Helen. *The Structure of "The Canterbury Tales."* London: Duckworth, 1983.

Curry, Walter C. *Chaucer and the Medieval Sciences.* 1926. New York: Barnes & Noble, 2nd ed., 1960.

David, Alfred. *The Strumpet Muse: Art and Morals in Chaucer's Poetry.* Bloomington: Indiana University Press, 1976.

Delany, Sheila. *Chaucer's House of Fame: The Poetics of Skeptical Fideism.* Chicago and London: University of Chicago Press, 1972.

Dempster, Germaine. *Dramatic Irony in Chaucer.* Stanford Publications in Language & Literature, IV, 3: Stanford University Press, 1932.

Donaldson, E. Talbert. *Speaking of Chaucer.* London: Athlone Press University of London, 1972.

Economou, George M., ed. *Geoffrey Chaucer: A Collection of Original Essays.* New York: McGraw Hill, 1976.

Frank, Robert Worth Jr. *Chaucer and "The Legend of Good Women."* Cambridge, MA: Harvard University Press, 1972.

Howard, Donald R. *The Idea of "The Canterbury Tales."* Berkeley and Los Angeles: University of California Press, 1976.

Huppé, Bernard F. *A Reading of "The Canterbury Tales."* Albany: State University of New York, 1964.

Jordan, Robert M. *Chaucer's Poetics and the Modern Reader.* Berkeley, Los Angeles, London: University of California Press, 1987.

Kane, George. *Chaucer.* New York: Oxford University Press, 1984.

Kean, Patricia M. *Chaucer and the Making of English Poetry.* 2 vols. London: Routledge & Kegan Paul, 1972.

Kittredge, George Lyman. *Chaucer and His Poetry.* Cambridge, MA: Harvard University Press, 1915; rpt. 1970.

Kolve, V. A. *Chaucer and the Imagery of Narrative.* Stanford: Stanford University Press, 1984.

Koonce, B. G. *Chaucer and the Tradition of Fame: Symbolism in "The House of Fame."* Princeton: Princeton University Press, 1966.

Lowes, John Livingston. *Geoffrey Chaucer.* Bloomington, IN: University of Indiana Press, 1934; rpt. 1962.

Lumiansky, Robert M. *Of Sondry Folk: The Dramatic Principle in "The Canterbury Tales."* Austin: University of Texas Press, 1955.

Manly, John M. *Some New Light on Chaucer.* London: Bell, 1926.

Mann, Jill. *Chaucer and Medieval Estates Satire.* Cambridge, UK: Cambridge University Press, 1973.

Miller, Robert, ed. *Chaucer Sources and Backgrounds.* New York: Oxford University Press, 1977.

Minnis, A. J. *Chaucer and Pagan Antiquity.* Cambridge, UK: Brewer, 1982.

Muscatine, Charles. *Chaucer and the French Tradition.* Berkeley and Los Angeles: University of California Press, 1955.

Pearsall, Derek. *The Canterbury Tales.* London: George Allen & Unwin, 1985.

Robertson, D. W., Jr. *A Preface to Chaucer: Studies in Medieval Perspective.* Princeton: Princeton University Press, 1962.

Root, Robert K. *The Poetry of Chaucer.* Boston: Houghton Mifflin, 1906.

Rose, Donald M. *New Perspectives in Chaucer Criticism.* Norman, OK: Pilgrim Books, 1981.

Rowland, Beryl, ed. *Companion to Chaucer Studies*. New York: Oxford University Press, 2nd ed., 1979.
Ruggiers, Paul G. *The Art of the Canterbury Tales*. Madison, Milwaukee, and London: University of Wisconsin Press, 1967.
Schoeck, Richard, and Jerome Taylor, eds. *Chaucer Criticism*. 2 vols. Notre Dame, IN: University of Notre Dame Press, 1960.
Strohm, Paul. *Social Chaucer*. Cambridge, MA: Harvard University Press, 1989.
Studies in the Age of Chaucer, 1979–

Recordings

Bessinger, J. B., Jr. *Geoffrey Chaucer: "The Canterbury Tales" General Prologue in Middle English*. Caedmon, TC 1223, 1967.
Coghill, Nevill, Norman Davis, and John Burrow. *Geoffrey Chaucer: Prologue to the Canterbury Tales*. Argo, PLP 1001, 1964.
———Lena Davis, and John Burrow. *Geoffrey Chaucer: The Nun's Priest's Tale*. Argo, PLP 1002, 1966.
Kökeritz, Helge. *"Beowulf" and Chaucer Readings*. Lexington, LE 5505, 1957.

Films

Gallagher, Joe. *Chaucer Reads Chaucer: The Miller's Tale*. Caritas Productions, 1988. Videotape. Films for the Humanities.
Pasolini, Pier Paolo. *The Canterbury Tales*.
Richmond, Velma Bourgeois. *A Prologue to Chaucer*. University of California, Berkeley, Office of Television and Radio Production. Funded by the National Endowment for the Humanities. Videotape. Distributed by Films for the Humanities, 1987.

Index